Pocket Rough Guide

NEW YORK CITY

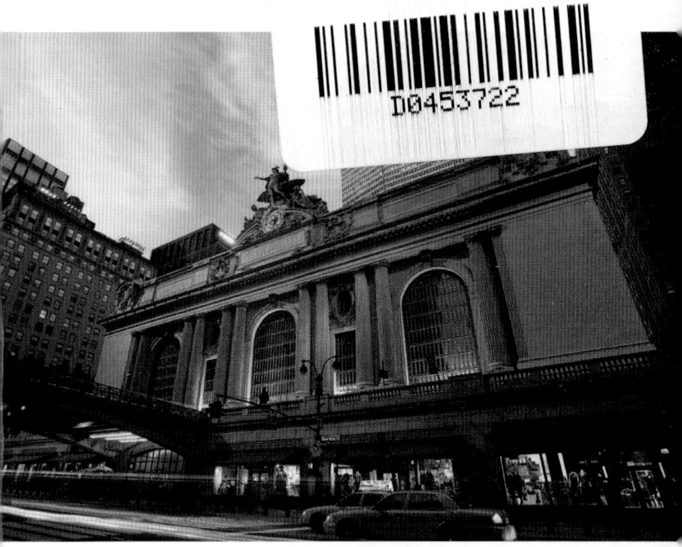

written and researched by

MARTIN DUNFORD, STEPHEN KEELING
AND ANDREW ROSENBERG

Contents

<< GRAND CENTRAL TERMINAL
< THE CHRYSLER

INTRODUCTION TO

NEW YORK CITY

No superlative, no cliché does New York City justice. It may not serve as the official capital of the US or even of New York State, but it's the undisputed capital of the world in many regards. High finance, media, art, architecture, food, fashion, popular culture, urban style, street life... it's all here, in plenitude and peak form. Best of all for visitors (and residents), you don't have to look too hard for any of it. Often the sights, both big and small, are just staring you right in the face: the money fortresses of Wall Street; the raised torch of the Statue of Liberty; the iconic Empire State Building; the hype and hustle of Times Square; Fifth Avenue's foot traffic; the proud lions of the Public Library. For energy and dynamism, cultural impact and sheer diversity, New York cannot be beaten.

MANHATTAN BRIDGE

GRAFFITI

You could spend weeks here and still barely scratch the surface, but there are some key attractions and pleasures you won't want to miss. The city is packed with vibrant ethnic neighbourhoods, like Chinatown and Harlem, and boasts the artsy enclaves of Chelsea, Tribeca and Greenwich Village. Of course, you will find the celebrated modern architecture of corporate Manhattan in Midtown and the Financial District, complemented by row upon row of elegant brownstones in landmarked areas like Brooklyn Heights. Then there are the city's renowned museums, not just the Metropolitan Museum of Art or the Museum of Modern Art, but countless smaller collections – the Old Masters at the Frick, the prints and manuscripts of the Morgan Library – that afford days of happy wandering.

In between sights, you can (and should) eat just about anything, cooked in any style: silky Korean pork buns to pressed sea urchin sandwiches, Jewish deli to Jamaican food cart. You can drink in virtually any company at any time in any type of watering hole imaginable: unmarked cocktail dens that mix up the latest artisanal concoctions or joints where folks will look at you sideways if you order anything but a bottle of beer. You can see comedy or cabaret, hear jazz combos or jug bands, and attend obscure movies. The more established arts – dance, theatre, opera and classical music – are superbly catered for; and New York's clubs are varied and exciting.

Best places for bagels and lox

A bagel with cream cheese and lox is the city's classic bite, found all over at cafés, delis, bagelries and speciality food shops – though best sampled from a Jewish "appetizing" store (basically, a place that sells fish and dairy products) such as hundred-year-old, family-owned Russ and Daughter's (p.65). **THESE ARE OUR OTHER FAVOURITES:** > **Absolute Bagels p.151** > **Barney Greengrass p.151** > **Zabar's p.151**

WINDOW-SHOPPING IN SOHO

For the avid consumer, the choice of shops is vast, almost numbingly exhaustive, in this heartland of the great capitalist dream. You can spend your dollars at big names like Bloomingdale's or contemporary designers like Marc Jacobs, and visit boutiques full of vintage garments or thrift stores with clothes priced by the pound.

New York City comprises the central island of Manhattan along with four outer boroughs – Brooklyn, Queens, the Bronx and Staten Island. To many, Manhattan is New York, and whatever your interest in the city it's here that you'll spend most time and, unless you have friends elsewhere, where you are likely to stay. That's not to overlook the virtues of the other boroughs: the ragged glory of Coney Island, the stunning botanical gardens of the Bronx and Brooklyn, the uplifting Noguchi Museum in Long Island City, these are just a few of the sights that make worthy detours, and you'll find great neighbourhood restaurants and bars along the way. The subway and bus system can take you everywhere, but New York is underrated as a walking city, and you'll want to spend plenty of time wearing out your shoes while taking it all in.

When to visit

Pretty much any time is a good time to visit New York. Winter can be bitingly cold but the city can be delightful during the run-up to Christmas, when the trees are lit up, the windows decorated and shops open extra-late. It's coldest in January and February, coinciding with one of the few times to find bargains on flights and hotels, and in any case New York has some wonderful crisp and clear sunny days even then. Spring, early summer, and autumn are the most appealing times to visit, when temperatures can be comfortably warm. It's wise to avoid visiting between mid-July and August: the temperatures tend be sweltering and the humidity worse. On the other hand, locals tend to leave town then, so weekends are less crowded.

NEW YORK CITY AT A GLANCE

>>EATING

From street food to haute cuisine, it's here, it's excellent and it's in abundance. **Chinatown** is most accessible for ethnic eats. The **Lower East Side**, traditional home to Jewish food, now teems with fashionable restaurants, while the **East Village** is the locus for great late-night eats – bowls of ramen, slices of pizza and hot dogs. Some of the best and most expensive restaurants are just off **Madison Square Park**; continue up to **Midtown** for powerhouse names like *Aquavit* and *Oyster Bar*, one of the city's quintessential eateries. Further north, **Harlem** has fabulous soul food, barbecue and African restaurants.

>>DRINKING

Bars are everywhere and come in every stripe: pubs, dives, beer gardens, hidden speakeasies, exclusive hotel lounges. Drinkers descend on the **Lower East Side** and **East Village**, especially streets like Ludlow and Avenue A, which can seem like a carnival – but are good destinations nonetheless. Rocker hangouts and swanky wine bars also hover around **Union Square**, and **Ninth Avenue**, starting in **Chelsea** and moving up to **Hell's Kitchen**. The most exciting and characterful places are in the outer boroughs, specifically **Long Island City** and **Williamsburg**. Most bars and pubs are typically open till the wee hours of morning.

>>NIGHTLIFE

Clubbing hotspots jump around: the lower western edge of **Soho** one year, 27th Street in the far west of **Chelsea** another. The **East and West Villages** always offer a few standbys, and the **Meatpacking District** can be good if you're looking for busy places to put on your dancing shoes. Keep your ears open, get current listings magazines and generally aim downtown. Music venues are more established: the **West Village** and **Harlem** have historic venues for jazz; **Lincoln Center** holds top spots for classical music, dance and opera, with **Carnegie Hall** just a few blocks away; and the coolest rock clubs are mostly around the **Lower East Side**.

>>SHOPPING

For big-ticket retail, look no further than Midtown, specifically **Fifth Avenue**, where Saks, Bergdorf Goodman and many others congregate. **Madison Avenue** on the Upper East Side also has its share of famous brands. Somewhat edgier fashion can be found in **Soho** and **Nolita**: Prince and Spring streets are crammed with designer boutiques and hip jewellery and shoe shops. Those looking for vintage duds or the truly avant-garde might find the **Lower East Side** and **Williamsburg** more suitable. Antique hunters will have fun trolling around **Chelsea** and, on weekends, the **Hell's Kitchen Flea Market**.

OUR RECOMMENDATIONS ON WHERE TO EAT, DRINK AND SHOP ARE LISTED AT THE END OF EACH PLACES CHAPTER.

Day One in New York City

1 Starting point: Battery Park > p.38. Ferries set out from here to the Harbor Islands; leave early and plan on a full morning.

2 Statue of Liberty > p.40. One of the city's most potent symbols is just as exciting up close as from a distance, especially if you climb the steps to the crown.

3 Ellis Island > p.40. The sensitive and moving museum drives home New York's immigrant roots.

> p.43. Back on shore, stop for lunch at *Adrienne's Pizzabar* on pedestrianized Stone Street.

4 Stroll along **Wall Street** to see the buildings at the heart of world finance, then head up **Trinity Place** (Church Street) to the 1766 **St Paul's Chapel**, with its 9/11 exhibit. The **National September 11 Memorial** is across the street.

5 The High Line > p.92. If you've got the time on your way uptown, take a stroll along this elevated promenade on the West Side.

> For a pre-theatre meal, choose from traditional dining spots such as *Chez Napoleon* (p.128) and *Joe Allen* (p.129).

6 Taking in a Broadway play or musical is a must for theatre-lovers; any venue will suffice, as long as the show is up to standard.

> p.130. Atmospheric *Jimmy's Corner* is full of crusty barflies and boxing memorabilia; a drink at the bar provides a fitting end to a full day.

Day Two in New York City

1 Starting point: Zabar's > p.151. Pick up some provisions at *Zabar's* and enjoy them in the attached café or head for a picnic in Central Park.

2 Central Park > p.132. Wander across the park, starting at Strawberry Fields in the west, then walking along the Lake and across the Ramble or Great Lawn, emerging on the east side.

3 Metropolitan Museum of Art > p.138. Goya, Vermeer, the Hudson River School and the Temple of Dendur are among the highlights at this colossal museum.

4 Grand Central > p.109. Lunchtime tours (Wed & Fri) of Grand Central Terminal help illuminate the magnificent Main Concourse and other features of this architectural marvel.

Oyster Bar > p.120. Enjoy a late lunch in the bowels of Grand Central at this timeless Midtown hangout.

5 Empire State Building > p.103. The obligatory trip to the 320m-high viewing platform provides just what you'd expect: a great vantage point of the city.

6 Soho shopping > p.48. Prada and the Apple Store are destination shops, but there's plenty more to browse along Spring, Prince, Broadway and the smaller side streets.

> p.44. **Soho** and **Tribeca** are full of excellent high-end restaurants; if you can foot the bill, *Nobu*, *Bouley* or *Blue Ribbon Sushi* will certainly fit the bill.

2

3

5

Budget New York

New York can be an expensive place to visit, but there are a surprising number of inspiring sights and activities that are cheap or completely free.

1 Staten Island Ferry > p.39. The free boat ride across New York harbour offers mesmerizing views of the city and the Statue of Liberty.

2 Governors Island > p.40. Explore the historic houses, parks and galleries of this tranquil island – even the bikes are free.

Pizza slices at Artichoke > p.76. The iconic NYC budget snack is done to perfection at this tiny, low-key East Village pizza joint.

3 Chelsea art galleries > p.96. Wander a neighbourhood packed with cutting-edge contemporary art galleries (all free).

4 Free Fridays MoMA (p.116), the Morgan Library (p.108), Neue Galerie (p.140), the Whitney Museum of American Art (p.142) and the Asia Society (p.143) are free or donation only on Friday evenings.

4

Dinner in Chinatown > p.60. Best-value meals in Manhattan – eat like an emperor for less than $20 at *Great N.Y. Noodletown*.

1

Kids' New York

Most sights are perfectly appropriate for kids, but beyond the expected – such as the Statue of Liberty – you can easily tailor a day or two to their interests.

Good Enough to Eat > p.153. Load up with pancakes, French toast or corned beef hash at this relaxed restaurant.

1

1 Museum of Natural History > p.148. Go early to miss the crowds for the innovative special exhibits.

2 Carousel in Central Park > p.134. If the kids are too old for this, check out the skaters and performance artists at the nearby Mall or Sheep Meadow.

3 Flatiron and Chrysler and buildings > p.102 & p.110. Their supporting roles in *Spiderman* and other action movies should compensate for any initial reticence about checking out architecture.

4 Madison Square Park > p.102. Besides places to run and play, Madison Square boasts the *Shake Shack*, perfect for lunch or a midday snack.

5 Books of Wonder > p.104. If it's a weekend, you might hear a reading at this kids' book store; if not, browse then enjoy a cupcake for the road.

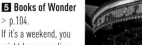

6 The Museum of the Moving Image > p.168. Swing a trip to Queens for interactive film fun, movie memorabilia and quirky screenings.

Zenon Taverna > p.172. Astoria is filled with cheerful, family-friendly Greek restaurants along the lines of this affordable spot.

2

BEST OF NEW YORK CITY

Big sights

1

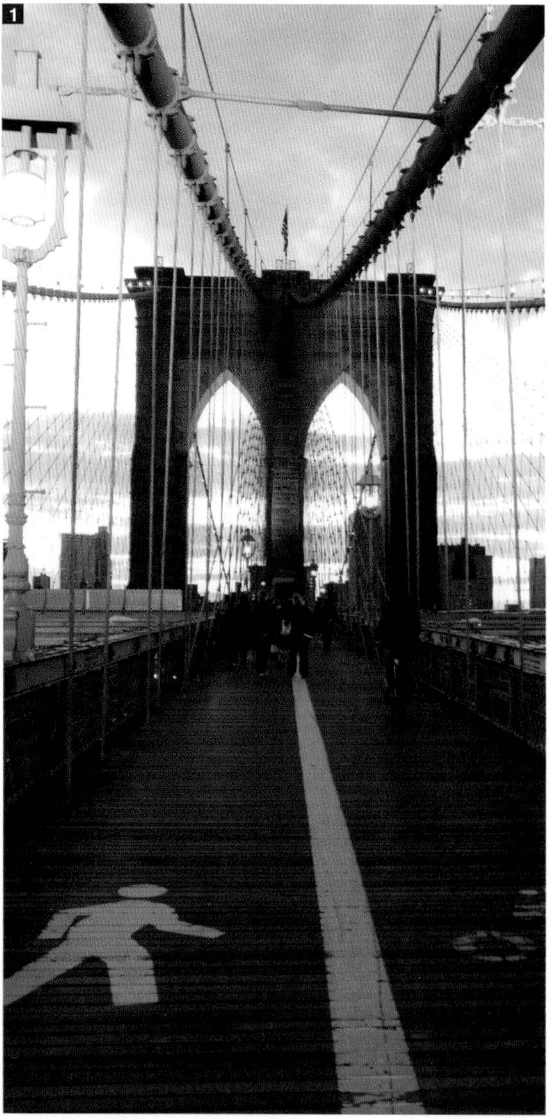

1 Brooklyn Bridge The elegant gateways, magnificent views and undeniable romance add up to a memorable walk whichever way you cross. > **p.42**

2

2 Central Park It's hard to imagine the city without this green and fantastically landscaped sanctuary. > **p.132**

3 The Met Spend a week exploring the museum's extensive holdings, or focus on a favourite section, such as the Vermeers or the Impressionist collection. > **p.138**

3

4

4 Statue of Liberty The views of Lower Manhattan and the trip to the crown make this the ultimate New York experience. > **p.40**

5 Empire State Building The king of Midtown's skyline, the Empire State is the skyscraper fixed in the public's imagination. > **p.103**

5

Hidden New York

1 Governors Island Wonderfully preserved campus-like retreat just across the harbour from downtown Manhattan, with parks, galleries and fine eighteenth-century houses. > **p.40**

2 Irish Hunger Memorial Haunting monument to Ireland's Great Famine in Battery Park City, topped by wild gardens and a ruined cottage from County Mayo. > **p.37**

3 Red Hook Off-the-beaten-path Brooklyn neighbourhood, with restored warehouses, whimsical boutiques, cafés, pubs and the best key lime pie in the northeast. > **p.164**

4 African Burial Ground National Monument This thought-provoking memorial recalls the largely forgotten history of New York's early African inhabitants. > **p.42**

5 Strivers' Row Some of New York's most alluring architecture: a quiet residential Harlem street dating back to the 1890s. > **p.160**

Museums and galleries

1

1 Frick Collection This Fifth Avenue mansion houses one of the city's most beautifully presented collections of fine art. > **p.138**

2 LES Tenement Museum
An apartment dwelling turned museum, this local treasure brilliantly captures the lives of three generations of immigrants. > **p.63**

3 Natural History Museum
One of the world's best natural history collections, with a first-class planetarium and a must-see ensemble of dinosaur fossils. > **p.148**

4 Ellis Island Museum of Immigration Illuminating memorial to US immigration, with fascinating exhibits, testimonials and artfully restored waiting rooms and halls. > **p.40**

5 MoMA Gallery of fabulous modern art and photography, from Monet and Cézanne to Picasso, Dalí, Rothko and Warhol. > **p.116**

Eating out

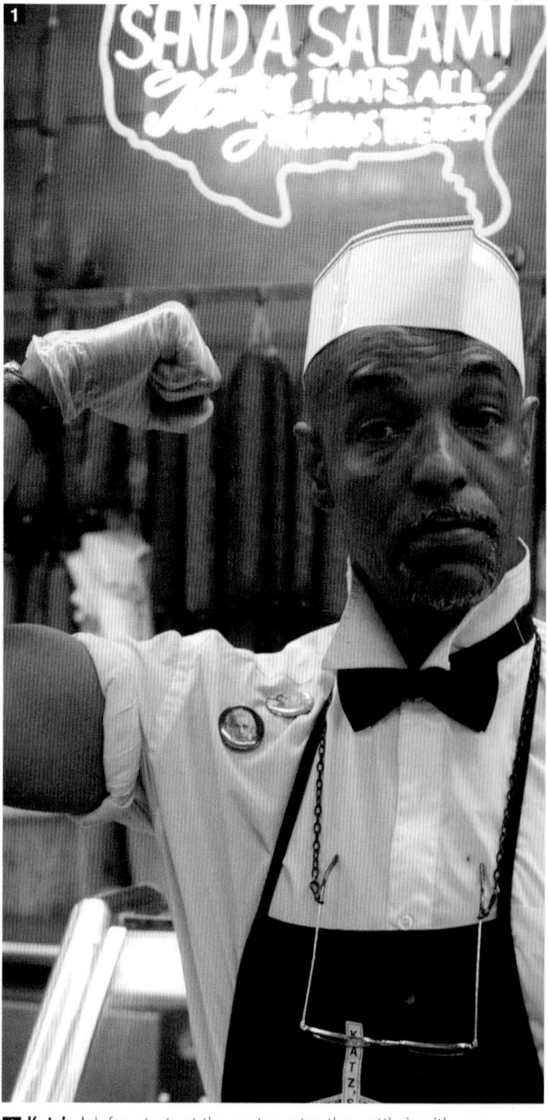

1 Katz's Ask for a taste at the meat counter, then settle in with your delicious, overstuffed pastrami sandwich. > **p.66**

2 Peter Luger Steak House In the face of relentless, newfangled competition, 125-year-old Peter Luger remains at the top of the steakhouse heap. > **p.172**

3 Red Rooster This Harlem game-changer offers a sophisticated take on Southern comfort food. > **p.161**

2

3

4 Maialino A smart Italian restaurant that feels accessible, doles out delicious food, and is situated by lovely Gramercy Park to boot. > **p.106**

4

5

5 Le Bernardin Prepare for a memorable night of flawless fish and sauce preparations, courtesy of Chef Eric Ripert. > **p.129**

Drinking

1

1 Bohemian Hall and Beer Garden This authentic Czech bar is New York's favourite beer garden, well worth a foray into Queens. > **p.172**

2

2 Pete's Candy Store Get a taste of the hip Williamsburg scene at this ex-candy store turned pub and music venue. > **p.173**

3 Balcony Bar and Roof Garden at the Met Romantic cocktail spots with gorgeous panoramas of Central Park, or a bird's-eye view of the Met's Great Hall. > **p.145**

3

4 King Cole Bar The iconic Midtown cocktail bar, inventor (probably) of the Bloody Mary, and home to that stunning Maxfield Parrish mural. > **p.121**

5 Ear Inn This cosy nineteenth-century seaman's pub is a neighbourhood classic. > **p.52**

5

4

Entertainment

1

1 Music Hall of Williamsburg An industrial vibe mingled with lounge space, solid acoustics and killer bookings, makes for an enjoyable night out. > **p.173**

2

3

2 Met Opera House The apogee of high culture in New York, fittingly expensive unless you can get hold of a last-minute standing room only ticket. > **p.155**

3 Lenox Lounge A lovingly restored Deco lounge, the Lenox feels like something between a dive bar and a jazz speakeasy. > **p.161**

4 Arlene's Grocery Charmingly grungy spot for some indie punk or to take your own turn on the stage during Monday's rock'n'roll karaoke. > **p.69**

5 Village Vanguard Probably the city's signature venue for jazz, the *Vanguard* has been showcasing big names for 75 years. > **p.91**

4

5

Shopping

1 Beacon's Closet Brooklyn's secondhand fashion paradise, specializing in high-quality modern labels as well as vintage attire. > **p.170**

2 Brooklyn Flea This weekend-only market has morphed into event shopping, with local gourmets providing gustatory accompaniment. > p.170

3 Apple Store All the latest laptops and iPods on display, as well as tech support at the "Genius Bar" and all kinds of tutorials. > p.118

4 Bloomingdale's Famous department store that stocks everything and somehow manages to remain the epitome of Upper East Side style. > p.118

5 Strand Bookstore This venerable book store with "18 miles of books" specializes in secondhand titles, recent review copies and new books at half price. > p.75

Outdoors

1 New York Botanical Garden If a Yankees game doesn't bring you to the Bronx, one of the country's finest botanical gardens surely should. > **p.169**

2

3

2 Brooklyn Bridge Park Sand volleyball, kayaking, outdoor movies, play spaces...the list of activities by DUMBO's shoreline keeps expanding > **p.163**

3 Ice skating in Bryant Park Renting blades to zoom around an ice rink with Midtown skyline architecture all around trumps most winter thrills. > **p.113**

4 Kayaking on the Hudson The active alternative to a ferry ride, kayak along the Hudson for free (on weekends) from Pier 40 in the West Village. > **p.86**

5 The High Line The newest (and still ongoing) addition to Manhattan's parks makes for an atmospheric stroll above the West Side. > **p.92**

4

5

PLACES

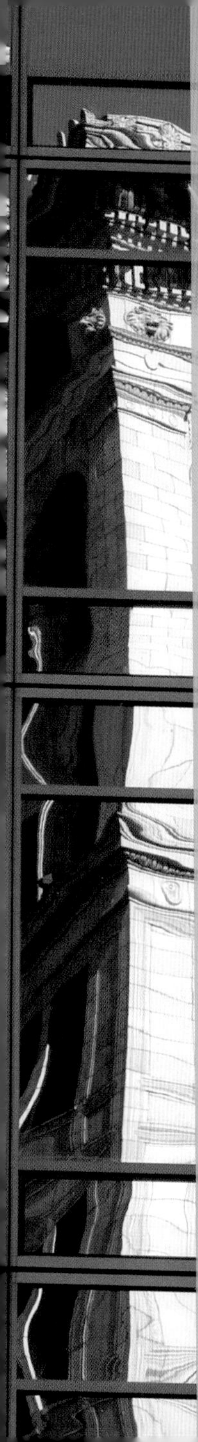

Financial District and the Harbor Islands

New York was born on the southern tip of Manhattan in the 1620s. Today, the heart of the world's financial markets is also home to some of the city's most historic streets, sights and Ground Zero, scene of the nation's biggest tragedy and now its most ambitious development. In recent years the neighbourhood has become increasingly residential, as former bank buildings are converted to luxury condos. To the north, City Hall Park remains the seat of New York's government, while the Brooklyn Bridge zooms eastward from here over the river. Take to the water to visit some of the city's offshore highlights and experience unbeatable views of Manhattan's celebrated skyline; just to the south of the Financial District, in New York Harbor, lies historic Ellis Island, the Statue of Liberty and the bucolic charms of Governors Island.

WALL STREET

Subway #4, #5, #2, #3 to Wall St. MAP P.34–35, POCKET MAP D23

Wall Street was named after the wooden stockade built by the Dutch at the edge of New Amsterdam in 1653, to protect themselves from the British colonies further north. The street has been associated with money for hundreds of years, and remains the apex of the global financial system thanks to the Stock Exchange. Yet Wall Street has gained a new leisurely air since much of it has been closed to traffic, and fitness studios have opened up in empty office spaces. The old Bank of Manhattan Trust at no. 40 was briefly the world's tallest building in 1930 (927ft) – today it's known as the Trump Building after the flamboyant tycoon who bought it in 1995.

WALL STREET

TRINITY CHURCH

79 Broadway at Wall St. Subway #4, #5 to Wall St ⓣ 212/602-0800, ⓦ www.trinitywallstreet.org. Mon–Fri 7am–6pm, Sat 8am–4pm, Sun 7am–4pm. Free. MAP P.34–35, POCKET MAP C23

Trinity Church held its first service at the western end of

Wall Street in 1698, but this striking Neo-Gothic version – the third model – only went up in 1846, and for fifty years was the city's tallest building. Trinity has the air of an English church (Richard Upjohn, its architect, was English), especially the sheltered graveyard; resting place of the first Secretary of the Treasury, Alexander Hamilton and steamboat king Robert Fulton.

NEW YORK STOCK EXCHANGE

11 Wall St. Subway #4, #5, #2, #3 to Wall St www.nyse.com. Closed to the public. MAP P.34-35, POCKET MAP D23

Behind the imposing Neoclassical facade of the **New York Stock Exchange** (on Broad St and usually draped with a giant US flag), the purse strings of the capitalist world are pulled. First established in 1817, two to three billion shares are now traded and $50 billion changes hands on an average day. Owing to security concerns, the public can no longer view the frenzied trading floor.

FEDERAL HALL NATIONAL MEMORIAL

26 Wall St. Subway #4, #5, #2, #3 to Wall St 212/825-6888, www.nps.gov/feha. Mon-Fri 9am–5pm. Free. MAP P.34-35, POCKET MAP D23

One of New York's finest examples of Greek Revival architecture, **Federal Hall** was completed in 1842 on the site of the old city hall, and is best known for the monumental statue of George Washington on its steps. Exhibits inside cover the heady days of 1789 when Washington was sworn in as America's first president here, as well as the later incarnations of the hall as US Customs House and Treasury. Washington's inaugural Bible is displayed,

NEW YORK STOCK EXCHANGE

and there are special exhibits on Alexander Hamilton.

THE MUSEUM OF AMERICAN FINANCE

48 Wall St. Subway #4, #5, #2, #3 to Wall St 212/908-4110, www.moaf.org. Tues–Sat 10am–4pm. $8. MAP P.34-35, POCKET MAP D23

Housed in the opulent banking hall of the former headquarters of the Bank of New York, the **Museum of American Finance** is the best place to gain an understanding of what's going on in the streets outside. Stocks, bonds and futures trading are demystified through multimedia presentations and a stack of rare artefacts, including a bond signed by Washington, and a stretch of ticker tape from the opening moments of 1929's Great Crash. Despite the inclusion of a detailed timeline of the 2008–2009 financial crisis, the overall message is unequivocally positive; that financial markets are a crucial factor in the development of modern society.

Financial District and the Harbor Islands

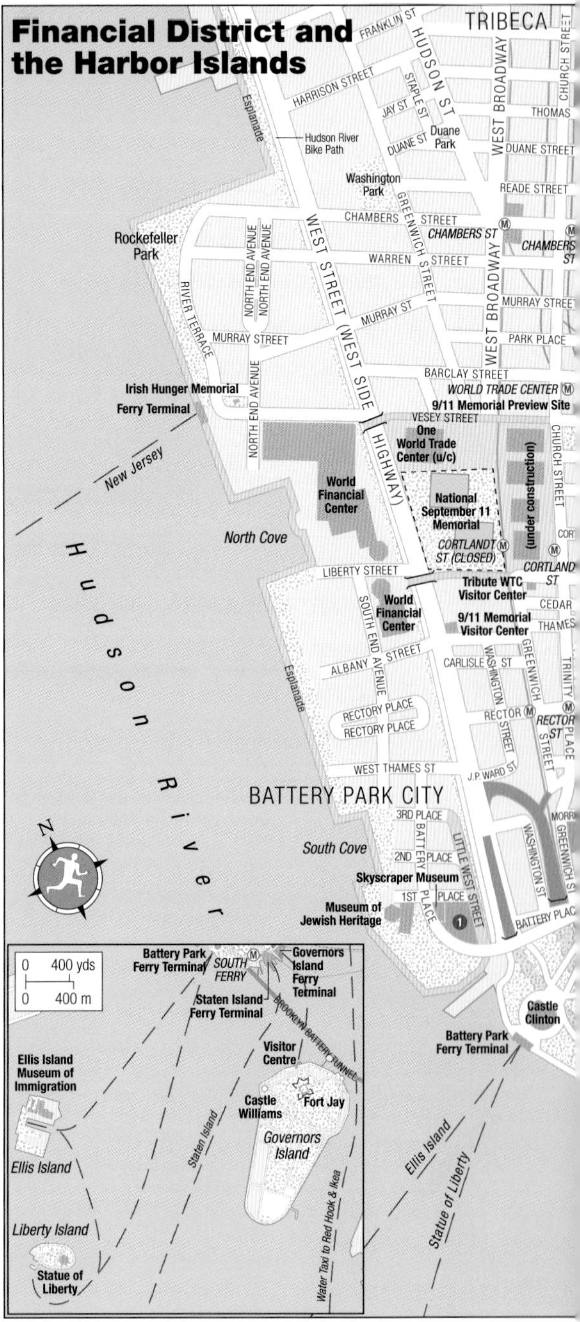
TRIBECA
FRANKLIN ST
HUDSON ST
HARRISON STREET
STAPLE ST
JAY ST
WEST BROADWAY
CHURCH STREET
THOMAS
Esplanade
Hudson River Bike Path
DUANE ST
Duane Park
DUANE STREET
Washington Park
READE STREET
CHAMBERS STREET
CHAMBERS ST
GREENWICH STREET
Rockefeller Park
NORTH END AVENUE
WEST STREET (WEST SIDE HIGHWAY)
WARREN STREET
MURRAY STREET
RIVER TERRACE
MURRAY ST
PARK PLACE
BARCLAY STREET
WORLD TRADE CENTER
Irish Hunger Memorial
Ferry Terminal
9/11 Memorial Preview Site
VESEY STREET
One World Trade Center (u/c)
New Jersey
World Financial Center
National September 11 Memorial
(under construction)
North Cove
CORTLANDT ST (CLOSED)
CORTLAND ST
LIBERTY STREET
Tribute WTC Visitor Center
CEDAR
SOUTH END AVENUE
9/11 Memorial Visitor Center
THAMES
Hudson River
ALBANY STREET
CARLISLE ST
WASHINGTON STREET
TRINITY PLACE
RECTOR ST
RECTOR PLACE
WEST THAMES ST
J.P. WARD ST
BATTERY PARK CITY
3RD PLACE
BATTERY PLACE
South Cove
2ND PLACE
LITTLE WEST STREET
WASHINGTON ST
GREENWICH ST
Skyscraper Museum
1ST PLACE
Museum of Jewish Heritage
BATTERY PLACE
N
0 400 yds
0 400 m
Battery Park Ferry Terminal
SOUTH FERRY
Governors Island Ferry Terminal
Staten Island Ferry Terminal
BROOKLYN BATTERY TUNNEL
Castle Clinton
Battery Park Ferry Terminal
Ellis Island Museum of Immigration
Visitor Centre
Castle Williams
Fort Jay
Governors Island
Ellis Island
Staten Island
Water Taxi to Red Hook & Ikea
Ellis Island
Statue of Liberty
Liberty Island
Statue of Liberty

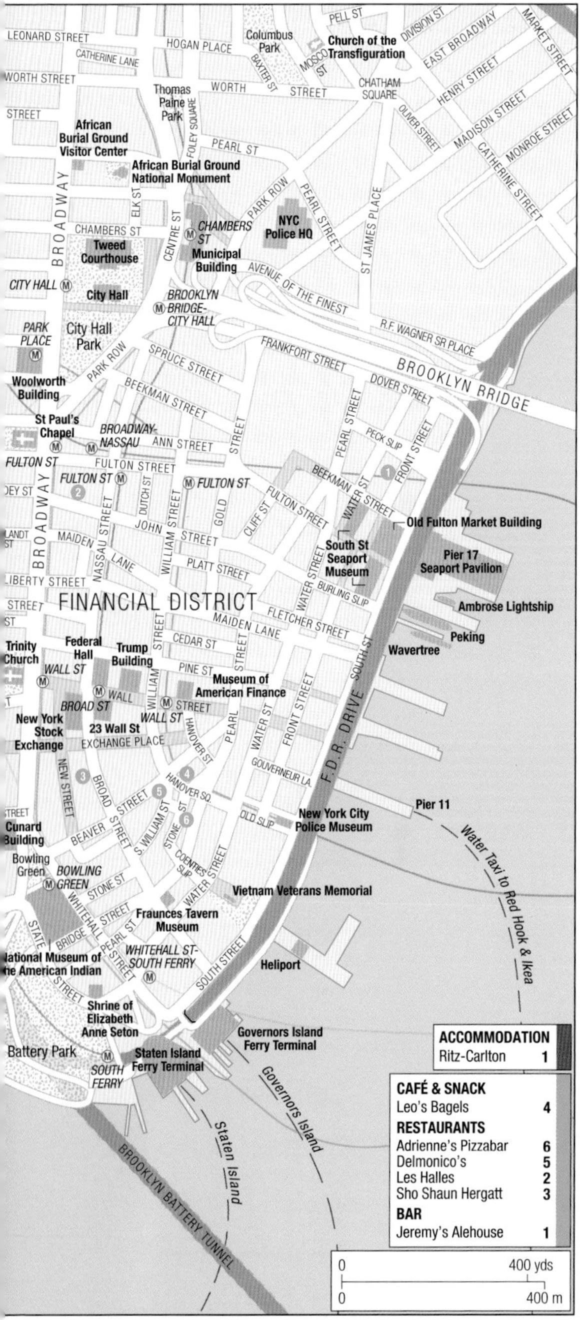
FINANCIAL DISTRICT
Columbus Park
Church of the Transfiguration
Thomas Paine Park
African Burial Ground Visitor Center
African Burial Ground National Monument
CHAMBERS ST
NYC Police HQ
Municipal Building
Tweed Courthouse
CITY HALL
City Hall
BROOKLYN BRIDGE-CITY HALL
PARK PLACE
City Hall Park
Woolworth Building
St Paul's Chapel
BROADWAY-NASSAU
FULTON ST
Old Fulton Market Building
South St Seaport Museum
Pier 17 Seaport Pavilion
Ambrose Lightship
Peking
Wavertree
Trinity Church
Federal Hall
Trump Building
WALL ST
Museum of American Finance
BROAD ST
New York Stock Exchange
23 Wall St
Pier 11
New York City Police Museum
Cunard Building
Bowling Green
BOWLING GREEN
Vietnam Veterans Memorial
Fraunces Tavern Museum
WHITEHALL ST-SOUTH FERRY
National Museum of the American Indian
Heliport
Shrine of Elizabeth Anne Seton
Governors Island Ferry Terminal
Battery Park
SOUTH FERRY
Staten Island Ferry Terminal
Water Taxi to Red Hook & Ikea
Governors Island
Staten Island
BROOKLYN BATTERY TUNNEL
BROOKLYN BRIDGE
F.D.R. DRIVE
LEONARD STREET
HOGAN PLACE
CATHERINE LANE
WORTH STREET
WORTH STREET
PELL ST
DIVISION ST
EAST BROADWAY
MARKET STREET
HENRY STREET
MADISON STREET
MONROE STREET
CATHERINE STREET
OLIVER STREET
CHATHAM SQUARE
BAXTER ST
MOSCO ST
FOLEY SQUARE
PEARL ST
ELK ST
CENTRE ST
PARK ROW
PEARL STREET
ST JAMES PLACE
AVENUE OF THE FINEST
R.F. WAGNER SR PLACE
FRANKFORT STREET
DOVER STREET
SPRUCE STREET
BEEKMAN STREET
ANN STREET
FULTON STREET
PECK SLIP
FRONT STREET
WATER ST
NASSAU STREET
DUTCH ST
WILLIAM STREET
GOLD
CLIFF ST
JOHN STREET
MAIDEN LANE
PLATT STREET
LIBERTY STREET
BURLING SLIP
FLETCHER STREET
CEDAR ST
PINE ST
SOUTH ST
BROADWAY
EXCHANGE PLACE
HANOVER ST
GOUVERNEUR LA.
NEW STREET
BROAD STREET
BEAVER STREET
S. WILLIAM ST
STONE ST
HANOVER SQ.
OLD SLIP
COENTIES SLIP
STONE ST
STATE
BRIDGE
WHITEHALL STREET
PEARL ST
SOUTH STREET
ACCOMMODATION
Ritz-Carlton 1
CAFÉ & SNACK
Leo's Bagels 4
RESTAURANTS
Adrienne's Pizzabar 6
Delmonico's 5
Les Halles 2
Sho Shaun Hergatt 3
BAR
Jeremy's Alehouse 1
0 400 yds
0 400 m

ST PAUL'S CHAPEL

209 Broadway at Fulton St. Subway E to World Trade Center; A, C, #4, #5 to Fulton St ☎ 212/233-4164, www.saintpaulschapel.org. Mon–Sat 10am–6pm, Sun 7am–3pm. Free. MAP P.34–35, POCKET MAP C22

St Paul's Chapel dates from 1766, making it almost prehistoric by New York standards. The main attraction inside is Unwavering Spirit, a poignant exhibition on 9/11. For eight months after the September 11 attacks, the chapel served as a sanctuary for rescue workers and the exhibit chronicles this period, with a moving ensemble of photos, artefacts and testimonies. Even George Washington's pew, preserved shrine-like from 1789, forms part of the exhibition (it served as a foot treatment chair for firefighters).

NATIONAL SEPTEMBER 11 MEMORIAL

Visitor Center at 90 West St (corner of Albany St). Subway R to Cortland St; #1 to Rector St; #4, #5 to Fulton St ☎ 212/266-5211, www.911memorial.org. Daily 10am–8pm (Oct–Feb till 6pm). Free. MAP P.34–35, POCKET MAP C22

Ground Zero remains a vast construction site, with hundreds of workers labouring away at the new World Trade Center – already the city's highest building. The poignant **National September 11 Memorial** opened in 2011, comprising two voids representing the footprints of the original towers, surrounded by oak trees and rings of water falling into illuminated pools. To visit, you must reserve a pass on the website, or visit the **9/11 Memorial Preview Site** (daily 9am–7.30pm, Oct–Feb till 7pm; free), 20 Vesey St (at Church St). The **9/11 Museum** is due to open by September 2012.

TRIBUTE WTC VISITOR CENTER

120 Liberty St. Subway R to Cortland St; #1 to Rector St; #4, #5 to Fulton St. ☎ 212/393-9160, www.tributewtc.com.

September 11 and the new World Trade Center

Completed in **1973**, the 110-storey Twin Towers of the World Trade Center were an integral part of New York's legendary skyline, a symbol of the city's social and economic success. At 1368 and 1362 feet – over a quarter of a mile high – the towers afforded mind-blowing views, and by 2001 they had become both a coveted workspace and a much-loved tourist destination. However, on **September 11, 2001**, two hijacked planes crashed into the towers just twenty minutes apart and all seven buildings of the complex eventually collapsed. Hundreds of firefighters, police officers and rescue workers were among the 2749 people who lost their lives.

In 2003, Polish-born architect Daniel Libeskind was named the overall designer for the new World Trade Center, though his plans were initially plagued with controversy and he's had little subsequent involvement with the project. In 2006 a modified design, still incorporating Libeskind's original 1776ft-high Freedom Tower (now "**One World Trade Center**"), was finally accepted and though financial disputes between the Port Authority and developer Larry Silverstein look set to continue, construction is now well under way under architect David Childs. The whole $12bn scheme, which also involves a Santiago Calatrava-designed transportation hub and four subsidiary towers, should be complete by 2014.

NATIONAL SEPTEMBER 11 MEMORIAL

Mon–Sat 10am–6pm, Sun 10am–5pm. $15 (tours $20). MAP P.34–35, POCKET MAP C23

Facing Ground Zero, the **Tribute WTC Visitor Center** commemorates the 9/11 attacks with a moving exhibit about the day itself, embellished with video and taped accounts of survivors. Items from the site make heart-rending symbols of the tragedy.

IRISH HUNGER MEMORIAL

290 Vesey St at North End Ave. Subway E to World Trade Center; #1, #2, #3 to Chambers St. Daily 8am–6.30pm. Free. MAP P.34–35, POCKET MAP B22

This sobering monument to the more than one million Irish people who starved to death during the Great Famine of 1845–1852 was designed by artist Brian Tolle in 2002. He transported an authentic famine-era stone cottage from County Mayo, and set it on a 25ft embankment overlooking the Hudson River. The passageway underneath echoes with haunting Irish folk songs, and there is a meandering path through the grassy garden.

MUSEUM OF JEWISH HERITAGE

36 Battery Place. Subway R, W to Whitehall St; #4, #5 to Bowling Green 646/437-4200, www.mjhnyc.org. Sun–Tues & Thurs 10am–5.45pm, Wed 10am–8pm, Fri 10am–5pm; Oct–March museum closes at 3pm on Fri. $12, free Wed 4–8pm. MAP P.34–35, POCKET MAP C24

This moving and informative museum begins with practical accoutrements of everyday Eastern European Jewish life, including photographs, before moving on to the horrors of the Holocaust. It ends with the establishment of Israel and subsequent Jewish achievements, even covering the successes of entertainers and artists like Samuel Goldwyn and Allen Ginsberg.

MUSEUM OF JEWISH HERITAGE

NATIONAL MUSEUM OF THE AMERICAN INDIAN

THE NATIONAL MUSEUM OF THE AMERICAN INDIAN

1 Bowling Green, the US Customs House. Subway R to Whitehall St; #4, #5 to Bowling Green ☎ 212/514-3700, www.nmai.si.edu. Daily 10am–5pm, Thurs 10am–8pm. Free. MAP P.34–35, POCKET MAP D24

Cass Gilbert's US Customs House is now home to the Smithsonian's **National Museum of the American Indian**, a thoughtful collection of artefacts from almost every tribe native to the Americas. The permanent collection includes intricate basketry and woodcarvings, quilled hides, feathered bonnets, and objects of ceremonial significance. Completed in 1907 and in use till 1973, the Beaux Arts **Customs House** is itself part of the attraction; the facade is adorned with elaborate statuary representing the major continents (carved by Daniel Chester French) and the world's great commercial centres, while the spectacular marble-clad Great Hall and Rotunda are beautifully decorated; the sixteen murals covering the 135ft dome were painted by Reginald Marsh in 1937.

THE FRAUNCES TAVERN MUSEUM

54 Pearl St at Broad St. Subway #1 to South Ferry; #4, #5 to Bowling Green; R to Whitehall St ☎ 212/425-1778, www.frauncestavernmuseum.org. Daily noon–5pm. $7. MAP P.34–35, POCKET MAP D24

Having survived extensive modification, several fires, and nineteenth-century use as a hotel, the three-storey, ochre-and-red-brick **Fraunces Tavern** was almost totally reconstructed in 1907 to mimic its appearance on December 4, 1783, when, after hammering the Brits, a weeping George Washington took leave of his assembled officers, intent on returning to rural life in Virginia. The **Long Room** where his speech was made has been decked out in the style of the time, while the adjacent Federal-style **Clinton Room** is smothered in florid French wallpaper from 1838. The tavern's upper floors contain exhibits tracing the site's history, two hundred flags and a collection of Revolutionary War artefacts; look out for the lock of Washington's hair.

BATTERY PARK

Subway #1 to South Ferry; #4, #5 to Bowling Green; R to Whitehall St. MAP P.34–35, POCKET MAP C24

Lower Manhattan lets out its breath in **Battery Park**, a bright and breezy landscaped

Visiting the Harbor Islands

The only way to get to any of the Harbor Islands is by **ferry**. Take the #1 train to South Ferry or the #4 or #5 trains to Bowling Green, then walk to the boat pier in Battery Park. From the pier, Statue Cruises go to **Liberty Island**, then on to **Ellis Island** (daily, every 30–45min, 9.30am–3.30pm; round-trip $13, $21 with audio guide). Note that you must be at security 30 minutes before departure. You can buy tickets at Castle Clinton (in the park), or buy them in advance (highly recommended) at ⓣ877/523-9849 or ⓦwww.statuecruises.com. The wait can be extremely long at any time of year (45min or more), but it's especially bad in the summer; you must line up to buy tickets, and then join another line to clear security before boarding the ferry. Start out as early as possible: keep in mind that if you take the last ferry of the day to Liberty Island, you won't be able to see Ellis.

Ferries to **Governors Island** (free) depart from the Battery Maritime Building just northeast of the Staten Island Ferry Terminal and Battery Park. Ferries depart on Fridays (every hour 10am–3pm; last ferry back 5pm), and Saturdays and Sundays (every hour 10am–5pm; last ferry back 7pm).

To simply get a closer view of the islands, catch the **Staten Island Ferry** (ⓣ212/639-9675, ⓦwww.siferry.com; free), which departs every 30 minutes from the terminal north of Battery Park. The 25-minute ride across to Staten Island provides a beautiful panorama of the harbour and downtown skyline.

area in which memorials and souvenir vendors lead up to a sweeping view of America's largest harbour. The squat 1811 **Castle Clinton** (daily 8am–5pm; free), on the west side of the park, is the place to buy tickets for and board ferries to the Statue of Liberty and Ellis Island, visible in the distance. At the bottom of Broadway, the park entrance holds the city's first official memorial to the victims of September 11; its focal point is the cracked 15ft steel-and-bronze sculpture *The Sphere* – designed by Fritz Koenig to represent world peace. The sculpture once stood in the WTC Plaza and survived the collapse of the towers.

LOWER MANHATTAN

THE STATUE OF LIBERTY

Liberty Island ☎ 212/363-3200, Ⓦ www.nps.gov/stli. Daily 9am–5.15pm. Free (with ferry ticket). MAP P.34–35, POCKET MAP A16

Standing tall and proud in the middle of New York Harbor, the **Statue of Liberty** has served as a symbol of the American Dream since its dedication in 1886. The monument was the creation of the French sculptor Frédéric Auguste Bartholdi, a gift of France in recognition of the fraternity between the French and American people. The 151ft statue (305ft with pedestal), which consists of thin copper sheets bolted together and supported by an iron framework designed by Gustave Eiffel (of Eiffel Tower fame), was built in Paris between 1874 and 1884.

The basic ferry ticket (see p.39) allows entry to Liberty Island's grounds only. The interior of the statue was closed throughout 2012 for renovation, but once it re-opens you'll be able to visit the museum inside and the pedestal observation deck (168 steps up) at no extra charge. To enjoy the spectacular views from the crown of the statue, you'll need to book a special ticket (extra charge) and climb 354 steps. You must pass another security screening at the statue itself.

WALL OF HONOR, ELLIS ISLAND

ELLIS ISLAND

☎ 212/363-3200, Ⓦ www.nps.gov/elis or Ⓦ www.ellisisland.org. Museum open daily 9am–5.15pm. Free. MAP P.34–35, POCKET MAP A15

Just across the water from Liberty Island, **Ellis Island** became an immigration station in 1892. It was the first stop for more than twelve million immigrants, all steerage-class passengers, and today some one hundred million Americans can trace their roots here. Closed in 1954, it reopened in 1990 as a **Museum of Immigration**, an ambitious project that eloquently recaptures the spirit of the place with artefacts, photographs, maps, and personal testimonies of the immigrants who passed through. On the first floor, the excellent permanent exhibit, "Peopling of America", chronicles four centuries of immigration, while the huge, vaulted Registry Room upstairs has been left imposingly bare.

GOVERNORS ISLAND

Ferry from 10 South St, Slip 7 ☎ 212/825-3045, Ⓦ www.nps.gov/gois or Ⓦ www.govisland.com. Late May to Sept Fri 10am–5pm, Sat & Sun 10am–7pm. Free. MAP P.34–35, POCKET MAP B15–16

Until the mid-1990s, **Governors Island** was the largest and most expensively run Coast-guard installation in the world, but today it's being developed into a leafy historical park, the island's bucolic village greens and colonial architecture reminiscent of a New England college campus. Many of the buildings are being restored as art galleries and craft stores,

THE PEKING, SOUTH STREET SEAPORT MUSEUM

and the **Historic Landmark District** at the northern end is managed by the National Park Service. Ferries arrive at Soissons Dock, where you'll find the small visitors' centre. From here it's a short stroll up to the solid walls of Fort Jay, completed in 1794, and the nearby shady lanes of Nolan Park, home to some beautifully preserved Neoclassical and Federal-style mansions. Other highlights include Castle Williams, a circular fort completed in 1811, but there are also plenty of green spaces in which to lounge in the sun, an artificial beach in the summer, and a breezy promenade with stellar views of Manhattan.

SOUTH STREET SEAPORT MUSEUM

12 Fulton St. Subway A, C, J, Z, #2, #3, #4, #5 to Fulton St ⓣ212/748-8600, ⓦwww.seany.org. April–Dec daily 10am–6pm; Jan–March Fri–Sun 10am–5pm, Mon 10am–5pm. $5. MAP P.34–35, POCKET MAP E22

The cobbled streets and busy promenade of **South Street Seaport** house all kinds of restaurants and shops, culminating in **Pier 17**, a touristy mall on the water.

You can take a number of boat trips here or visit the **Seaport Museum**, lodged in a series of painstakingly restored 1830s warehouses showing maritime art and trade exhibits. The museum was given a stylish makeover in 2012, with sixteen new galleries featuring photography, video and historic artefacts. Tickets also includes access to moored ships like the *Peking* (1911), the *Ambrose Lightship* (1908) and the *Wavertree* (1855).

CITY HALL

Subway J, Z to Chambers St; R to City Hall; #2, #3 to Park Place; #4, #5, #6 to Brooklyn Bridge-City Hall. MAP P.34–35, POCKET MAP D22

At the north end of City Hall Park sits graceful **City Hall**, completed in 1812; it still houses the mayor's office and city council. The sumptuous interior can be seen on free prearranged tours via the Art Commission (Thurs 10am; 1hr; ⓣ212/788-2656, ⓦwww.nyc.gov) or by just signing up for the public tours (Wed noon) at the tourist kiosk opposite the Woolworth Building.

WOOLWORTH BUILDING

THE WOOLWORTH BUILDING

233 Broadway between Barclay St and Park Place. Subway R to City Hall; #2, #3 to Park Place; #4, #5, #6 to Brooklyn Bridge-City Hall. Closed to the public.

MAP P.34–35, POCKET MAP C22

The world's tallest skyscraper until 1930, the **Woolworth Building** (792ft) exudes money, ornament and prestige. The soaring, graceful lines of Cass Gilbert's 1913 "Cathedral of Commerce" are fringed with Gothic-style gargoyles and elaborate decorations. Sadly, the ornate lobby is now closed to sightseers.

AFRICAN BURIAL GROUND NATIONAL MONUMENT

Monument at Duane St and Elk St; visitor centre at 290 Broadway. Subway J, Z to Chambers St; R to City Hall ⓣ 212/637-2019, Ⓦ www.nps.gov/afbg or Ⓦ www.africanburialground.gov. Daily 9am–5pm, visitor centre Tues–Sat 10am–4pm. Free.

MAP P.34–35, POCKET MAP D21

In 1991 construction workers uncovered the remains of 419 skeletons near Broadway, a tiny portion of an African burial ground that covered five blocks during the 1700s. After being examined, the skeletons were re-interred at this site in 2003, marked by seven grassy mounds and a highly polished black granite monument, a symbolic counterpoint to the infamous "gate of no return" on Gorée Island in Senegal. To learn more, walk around the corner to the visitor centre (look for the dedicated entrance). Videos, displays and replicas of the artefacts found here are used to recount the history of the site, and shed light on the brutal life of the city's oft forgotten enslaved population.

THE BROOKLYN BRIDGE

Subway (Manhattan) J, Z to Chambers St; #4, #5, #6 to Brooklyn Bridge-City Hall; (Brooklyn) A, C to High St. MAP P.34–35, POCKET MAP D22–F22

Completed in 1883, the **Brooklyn Bridge** was the first to connect what were the then two separate cities of New York and Brooklyn across the East River, and for twenty years after it was the world's longest suspension bridge. Indeed, the bridge's meeting of art and function, of romantic Gothic and daring practicality, became a sort of spiritual model for the next generation's skyscrapers. But the bridge didn't go up without difficulties: John Augustus Roebling, its architect and engineer, crushed his foot taking measurements and died of tetanus, and twenty workers perished during construction. The entrance to the boardwalk that carries walkers above the traffic is opposite City Hall Park. It's best not to look back till you're midway: the Financial District's giants cluster shoulder to shoulder through the spidery latticework of the cables, a mesmerizing glimpse of the twenty-first-century metropolis.

Cafés and snacks

LEO'S BAGELS

3 Hanover Sq at Stone St. Subway #2, #3 to Wall St. Daily 6am–5pm. MAP P.34–35, POCKET MAP D23

Get your bagel fix at this popular local joint, with the hand-rolled, chewy main event going for $1.15 or $2.50–4.75 with huge dollops of cream cheese and various *schmears*. Also does salads, soups and sandwiches.

Restaurants

ADRIENNE'S PIZZABAR

54 Stone St. Subway #2, #3 to Wall St ☎ 212/248-3838. Mon–Sat 11am–midnight, Sun 11am–10pm. MAP P.34–35, POCKET MAP D23

One of the better Italian restaurants downtown, with alfresco seating in the summer. Serves nonna-style square pizzas with a crispy crust; the crumbled sausage topping is especially tasty (from $18.50).

DELMONICO'S

56 Beaver St at S. William St. Subway #2, #3 to Wall St ☎ 212/509-1144. Mon–Fri 11.30am–10pm, Sat 5–10pm. MAP P.34–35, POCKET MAP D23

Many a million-dollar deal has been made at this 1837 landmark restaurant that features pillars from Pompeii and classics like lobster Newburg ($49) and succulent, pricey steaks (from $43); the small plates at *Next Door Grill Room* are much cheaper (from $13.29).

LES HALLES

15 John St between Broadway and Nassau St. Subway A, C, J, Z, #2, #3, #4, #5 to Fulton St ☎ 212/285-8585. Daily 11.30am–midnight. MAP P.34–35, POCKET MAP D22

This heady French bistro is the Rive Gauche fantasy of celebratory chef Anthony Bourdain, who churns out reasonably priced Gallic classics, such as escargots in garlic butter ($9), *moules* ($17.50) and steak frites ($20).

SHO SHAUN HERGATT

40 Broad St. Subway J, Z to Broad St; #2, #3 to Wall St ☎ 212/809-3993. Mon–Fri noon–2pm & 5.30–10pm, Sat 5.30–10pm. MAP P.34–35, POCKET MAP D23

Australian native Shaun Hergatt's stylish restaurant offers exceptional quality and value for money; the three-course prix-fixe lunch ($33) and four-course dinner ($85) include exquisite Aussie-influenced dishes like roasted pork loin and ocean trout tartare.

Bars

JEREMY'S ALEHOUSE

228 Front St at Peck Slip. Subway A, C, J, Z, #2, #3, #4, #5 to Fulton St. Mon–Fri 8am–4am, Sat & Sun 11am–4am. MAP P.34–35, POCKET MAP E22

This unpretentious local bar, with bras and ties hanging from the rafters (donated by happy patrons), serves well-priced pints of beer from $3.75 (served in plastic cups) and excellent burgers ($4) – happy hour Mon–Fri 4–6pm.

JEREMY'S ALEHOUSE

Soho and Tribeca

North of Ground Zero, Tribeca, the "Triangle Below Canal Street", is a former wholesale garment district that has been transformed into a gentrified community that mixes commercial establishments with loft residences, galleries, celebrity hangouts and chic restaurants. To the northeast, the historic district between Houston and Canal known as Soho (short for "South of Houston") owes its distinction to the cast-iron architecture used by nineteenth-century manufacturers and wholesalers. Decades after toiling immigrant women had left the premises, artists reclaimed the abandoned lofty factory floors as living spaces and studios in the 1960s. Since then, Soho has come to signify fashion chic, urbane shopping, and art, and its high-end chains attract celebrities and hordes of tourists; it's a grand place for brunch and browsing, and there are still a few good galleries to speak of.

DUANE PARK

Subway #1, #2, #3 to Chambers St. MAP P.45, POCKET MAP C21

Duane Park, at the confluence of Duane, Hudson and Greenwich streets, was the first open space acquired by the city specifically to be a public park. Once part of a 62-acre farm, the city bought the park in 1797 for $5, scaled it down and watched it go through various stages of beauty and neglect. From the 1940s, trees and flowers were replaced with patches of concrete, until the park became a scar of what it once was. The most recent restoration was completed in 1999, harking back to its genteel days of 1887 and the design of Samuel Parsons, Jr. and Calvert Vaux, famous for their work on Central Park. Wrought-iron fences are back, as are the World's Fair-style benches, historic-looking streetlights and cobblestones.

BROOME STREET, SOHO

Soho and Tribeca

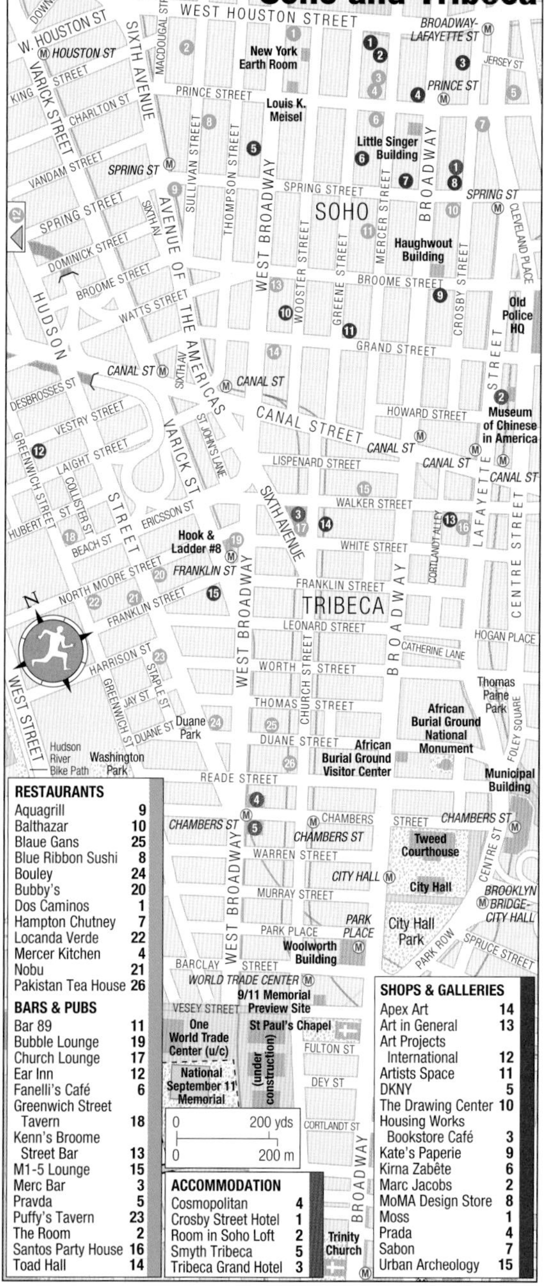

ROCKEFELLER PARK AND HUDSON RIVER PARK

Subway #1, #2, #3 to Chambers St.

MAP P.45, POCKET MAP B21

At the far western end of Chambers Street is **Rockefeller Park**, a charming parcel of lawn and gardens jutting into the Hudson River with fabulous views of New Jersey. In the summer, expect to see the wide lawn filled with sunbathers and the large playground jumping with children. From here you can stroll along **Hudson River Park**, a landscaped promenade that stretches north towards Chelsea and Midtown, or wander south to the tip of the island along the shady Battery Park City Esplanade.

WEST BROADWAY

Subway #1, #2, #3 to Chambers St.

MAP P.45, POCKET MAP C21

West Broadway is one of Tribeca's main thoroughfares, with several of the neighbourhood's best boutiques and restaurants, old and new. Across **West Broadway**, at 14 North Moore at the intersection of Varick, stands the New York Fire Department's **Hook and Ladder Company #8**, a nineteenth-century brick-and-stone firehouse that starred in the *Ghostbusters* movies (note the mural on the sidewalk outside), and played a crucial role in the rescue efforts of September 11. As it is a working firehouse, you can't do more than admire it externally.

Cast-iron architecture

Soho contains one of the largest collections of cast-iron buildings in the world, erected between 1869 and 1895. **Cast-iron architecture** was designed so that buildings could be assembled quickly and cheaply, with iron beams rather than heavy walls carrying the weight of the floors. The result was greater space for windows and remarkably decorative facades. Glorifying Soho's sweatshops, architects indulged themselves in Baroque balustrades, forests of Renaissance columns, and all the effusion of the French Second Empire. Many fine examples of cast-iron architecture can be glimpsed along **Broadway** and **Greene Street**.

ROCKEFELLER PARK

THE HAUGHWOUT BUILDING

488–492 Broadway. Subway R, N to Prince St; #6 to Spring St. MAP P.45, POCKET MAP D20

The magnificent 1857 **Haughwout Building** is perhaps the ultimate in the cast-iron architectural genre. Rhythmically repeated motifs of colonnaded arches are framed behind taller columns in this thin sliver of a Venetian-style palace – the first building ever to boast a steam-powered Otis elevator. The first two floors opened as a Bebe fashion store in 2010 (it's otherwise closed to the public).

HAUGHWOUT BUILDING

SPRING STREET

Subway R, N to Prince St; #6 to Spring St. MAP P.45, POCKET MAP C19–D19

Cutting across the heart of Soho, **Spring Street** east of Sixth Avenue is lined with old buildings, plush restaurants and boutiques; mostly high-end brands such as Chanel and John Varvatos, as well as trendy labels like Ben Sherman, especially as you get closer to Broadway. You'll find a few French bistros and cafés towards Sixth Avenue, while there's a small craft market on the corner of Wooster Street.

THE LITTLE SINGER BUILDING

561 Broadway. Subway R, N to Prince St; #6 to Spring St. MAP P.45, POCKET MAP D19

In 1904, Ernest Flagg took the possibilities of cast iron to their conclusion in this office and warehouse for the sewing machine company, a twelve-storey terracotta design whose use of wide window frames pointed the way to the glass curtain wall of the 1950s. The first floor is a Mango fashion store, but you won't get much sense of the building inside (the rest is off limits).

PRINCE STREET

Subway R, N to Prince St. MAP P.45, POCKET MAP C19–D19

The pulse beats here between Sixth Avenue and The Bowery, where the streets are always packed with shoppers looking to max-out their credit cards at the Apple Store, Camper and Michael Kors. In between the shops are small cafes and art galleries, such as **Louis K. Meisel** (where *Sex and the City* character Charlotte worked). On clear days, artists peddle original artwork and handmade jewellery from the sidewalks, though the crowds can get stifling at the weekends. The Belgian-block pavements of nearby Mercer and Greene streets retain the neighbourhood's historical charm. Just north of Prince Street at 141 Wooster Street, the **New York Earth Room** (Wed–Sun noon–3pm and 3.30–6pm; free; Ⓦ www.earthroom.org) is a permanent installation by land artist Walter de Maria; a second-floor loft completely covered in two feet of moist brown earth. The installation is usually closed in July and August.

Shops and galleries

APEX ART

291 Church St between Walker and White sts. Subway N, Q, R to Canal St; #1 to Franklin St. Tues–Sat 11am–6pm. MAP P.45, POCKET MAP C20

Founded in 1994, the thematic multimedia exhibits here are known for their intellectual diversity. Seven group exhibitions are presented each year, with a focus on contextualizing contemporary world art and culture.

ART IN GENERAL

79 Walker St near Broadway. Subway N, Q, R to Canal St. Tues–Sat noon–6pm. MAP P.45, POCKET MAP D20

This exhibition space, founded in 1981, is devoted to the unconventional art of emerging artists. Recent exhibits have featured audio installations set in an elevator, and a miniature theatre.

ART PROJECTS INTERNATIONAL

434 Greenwich St, at Vestry St. Subway #1 to Canal St. Tues–Sat 11am–6pm. MAP P.45, POCKET MAP B20

Highly respected for showing leading contemporary artists from Asia, this gallery's engaging exhibits are mostly in print and have featured artists like Zheng Xuewu, Gwenn Thomas and Richard Tsao. No sign – just walk in.

ARTISTS SPACE

38 Greene St. Subway A, C, E, N, R, Q to Canal St. Wed–Sun noon–6pm. MAP P.45, POCKET MAP C20

This video, performance art, architecture and design space has been a Soho mainstay for more than thirty years – contemporary artists dominate.

DKNY

420 West Broadway between Prince and Spring sts. Subway N, R to Prince St. Mon–Sat 11am–8pm, Sun noon–7pm. MAP P.45, POCKET MAP C19

This landmark store is great to wander, with enticing coffee-table books and houseware in addition to the expensive clothes.

THE DRAWING CENTER

35 Wooster St, between Grand and Broome sts. Subway A, C, E, N, R, Q to Canal St. Wed, Fri–Sun noon–6pm, Thurs noon–8pm. MAP P.45, POCKET MAP C20

Masters like Marcel Duchamp and Richard Tuttle, as well as emerging and unknown artists, are shown together at this committed nonprofit organization.

HOUSING WORKS BOOKSTORE CAFÉ

126 Crosby St between Houston and Prince sts. Subway B, D, F, M to Broadway-Lafayette; N, R to Prince St; #6 to Bleecker St. Mon–Fri 10am–9pm, Sat & Sun 10am–5pm. MAP P.45, POCKET MAP D19

Extra-cheap and secondhand books in a spacious and comfy environment, with a café at the back. Proceeds benefit AIDS charities.

MOSS

KATE'S PAPERIE

435 Broome St between Broadway and Crosby St. Subway #6 to Spring St. Mon–Sat 10am–8pm, Sun 11.30am–6pm. MAP P.45, POCKET MAP D20

Any kind of paper you can imagine or want, including great handmade cards, albums and exotic notebooks. If you can't find something – ask; they'll even custom-make stationery for you.

KIRNA ZABÊTE

96 Greene St between Spring and Prince sts. Subway N, R to Prince St. Mon–Sat 11am–7pm, Sun noon–6pm. MAP P.45, POCKET MAP C19

Fashion-forward store that stocks hand-picked highlights from hot designers such as Jason Wu, Rick Owens and Proenza Schouler.

MARC JACOBS

163 Mercer St between Prince and Houston sts. Subway N, R to Prince St. Mon–Sat 11am–7pm, Sun noon–6pm. MAP P.45, POCKET MAP D19

Doyen of the New York fashion world, Jacobs sells his women's ready-to-wear lines, accessories, shoes and men's clothes at this minimalist store.

MOMA DESIGN STORE

81 Spring St between Broadway and Crosby St. Subway N, R to Prince St; #6 to Spring St. Mon–Sat 10am–8pm, Sun 11am–7pm. MAP P.45, POCKET MAP D19

A trove of creatively designed goods that range from cheap to astronomical.

MOSS

150 Greene St at Houston St. Subway N, R to Prince St. Mon–Sat 11am–7pm. MAP P.45, POCKET MAP C19

Exceptionally curated gallery-boutique selling unusual examples of great contemporary industrial design – some at reasonable prices – but worth a look even if you're not buying.

SABON

PRADA

575 Broadway at Prince St. Subway N, R to Prince St. Mon–Sat 11am–8pm, Sun noon–7pm. MAP P.45, POCKET MAP D19

This jaw-dropping flagship store designed by Rem Koolhaas is as much of a sight as the famous clothes inside.

SABON

93 Spring St between Broadway and Mercer St. Subway R, N to Prince St; #6 to Spring St. Mon–Sat 10am–10pm, Sun 11am–8.30pm. MAP P.45, POCKET MAP D19

Luxury body and bath fragrances, soaps and aromatic oils from Israel; friendly assistants help you try the products at the old-fashioned sink in the middle of the store.

URBAN ARCHEOLOGY

143 Franklin St between Hudson and Varick sts. Subway #1 to Franklin St. Mon–Thurs 8am–6pm, Fri 8am–5pm. MAP P.45, POCKET MAP C21

Sensational finds for the home from salvaged buildings, including lighting fixtures and old-fashioned plumbing.

Restaurants

AQUAGRILL

210 Spring St at Sixth Ave. Subway C, E to Spring St ⓣ212/274-0505. Mon–Thurs noon–3pm & 6–10.45pm, Fri noon–3pm & 6–11.45pm, Sat noon–3.45pm & 6–11.45pm, Sun noon–3.45pm & 6–10.30pm. MAP P.45, POCKET MAP C19

At this enticing Soho spot, you'll find seafood so fresh it's still flapping. Russian Osetra Caviar chimes in at $155 per ounce, or try the grilled yellowfin tuna for $27. The excellent raw bar and Sunday brunch dishes are not prohibitively expensive, between $12.50 and $24.50. Reservations recommended.

BALTHAZAR

80 Spring St between Crosby St and Broadway. Subway #6 to Spring St ⓣ212/965-1414. Mon–Thurs 7.30am–midnight, Fri 7.30am–1am, Sat 8am–1am, Sun 8am–midnight. MAP P.45, POCKET MAP D19

Still one of the hottest reservations in town, *Balthazar*'s tastefully ornate Parisian decor and nonstop beautiful people keep your eyes busy until the food arrives. Then you can savour highlights such as the fresh oysters ($21) or exquisite pastries. Entrees $22–41.

BALTHAZAR

BLAUE GANS

139 Duane St between Church St and W Broadway. Subway A, C, #1, #2, #3 to Chambers St ⓣ212/571-8880. Daily 11am–midnight. MAP P.45, POCKET MAP C21

Poster-filled walls and a long bar made of zinc add personality to this bright Austro-German restaurant, with tasty *schnitzels*, goulash and fresh fish (entrees $19–30) the highlights of chef Kurt Gutenbruner's menu. The beer selection includes some unusual – and unusually tasty – German draughts.

BLUE RIBBON SUSHI

119 Sullivan St between Prince and Spring sts. Subway C, E to Spring St ⓣ212/343-0404. Daily noon–2am. MAP P.45, POCKET MAP C19

Widely considered one of the best and freshest sushi restaurants in New York, with fish flown in daily from Japan. Have some cold sake and dine at the sushi bar or in the cosy back room. Special rolls around $10, platters from $16.50.

BOULEY

163 Duane St at Hudson St. Subway #1, #2, #3 to Chambers St ⓣ212/964-2525. Mon–Sat 11.30am–11pm. MAP P.45, POCKET MAP C21

Modern French food made from the freshest ingredients by one of the city's most renowned chefs, David Bouley. Prices are fairly steep (entrees $38–45); soften costs by opting for one of the prix-fixe options (from $55). Jackets required.

BUBBY'S

120 Hudson St between Franklin and N Moore sts. Subway #1 to Franklin St ⓣ212/219-0666. Tues–Sun 24hr, Mon closes midnight. MAP P.45, POCKET MAP C21

A relaxed place serving American comfort food, like matzo-ball soup ($10) and barbecued meats ($27). It's the pies, though, that really pull in the crowds – try the Key Lime ($8).

DOS CAMINOS

475 W Broadway at Houston St. Subway #1 to Houston St ☎ 212/277-4300. Mon & Tues noon–10.30pm, Wed & Thurs noon–11pm, Fri noon–midnight, Sat 11.30am–midnight, Sun 11.30am–10.30pm. MAP P.45, POCKET MAP C19

Thoughtful, real-deal Mexican served with style – try the table-side guacamole. Brunch should set you back $12–16 per person, while dinner entrees range between $18 and $29.

HAMPTON CHUTNEY

68 Prince St at Crosby. Subway R, N to Prince St ☎ 212/226-9996. Daily 11am–9pm. MAP P.45, POCKET MAP D19

This place is all about dosas ($7.95), uttapas and naan breads, traditional south Indian fare, albeit with plenty of American ingredients. Orders are spiced up with a choice of fresh, home-made chutneys: cilantro, curry, mango, tomato, or peanut.

LOCANDA VERDE

377 Greenwich St at N Moore St. Subway #1 to Franklin St ☎ 212/925-3797. Daily 8am–3pm & 5.30–11pm. MAP P.45, POCKET MAP C21

This casual Italian taverna is a showcase for star chef Andrew Carmellini's exceptional creations; try the *porchetta* sandwich ($18), stuffed mountain trout ($26) or his fabulous pastas ($18–21).

MERCER KITCHEN

99 Prince St at Mercer St in Mercer Hotel. Subway R, N to Prince St ☎ 212/966-5454. Mon–Thurs 7am–midnight, Fri & Sat 7am–1am, Sun 7am–11pm. MAP P.45, POCKET MAP C19

This hip basement hangout and restaurant for hotel guests and scenesters entices with the casual culinary creations of star

DOS CAMINOS

chef Jean Georges Vongerichten, who makes ample use of his raw bar and wood-burning oven. Brunch will range between $12 and $24 per entree and dinner plates begin at $18.

NOBU

105 Hudson St at Franklin St. Subway #1 to Franklin St ☎ 212/219-0500. Mon–Fri 11.45am–2.15pm & 5.45–10.15pm, Sat & Sun 5.45–10.15pm. MAP P.45, POCKET MAP C21

Nobu Matsuhisa's lavish woodland decor complements his superlative Japanese cuisine. Try the black cod with miso ($32) and chilled sake served in hollow bamboo trunks. It's pricey and reservations are hard to get; if you can't get in, try your luck at the somewhat less expensive *Next Door Nobu*, literally next door.

PAKISTAN TEA HOUSE

176 Church St at Reade St. Subway A, C to Chambers St ☎ 212/240-9800. Mon–Sat 9am–4am. MAP P.45, POCKET MAP C21

Great, cheap Pakistani tandooris, baltis and curries. The staff will also create made-to-order naan. Main dishes average $8.

Bars and pubs

BAR 89

BAR 89

89 Mercer St between Spring and Broome sts. Subway R, N to Prince St; #6 to Spring St. Sun–Thurs noon–1am, Fri & Sat noon–2am. MAP P.45, POCKET MAP C19

Slick, modern lounge with soft blue light spilling down over the bar, giving the place a trippy, pre-dawn feel. Check out the clear liquid crystal bathroom doors that go opaque when shut ($10,000 each, reportedly). Strong, pricey drinks, try the chocolate martini, pay for them.

BUBBLE LOUNGE

228 W Broadway between Franklin and White sts. Subway #1 to Franklin St. Mon–Wed 5am–1am, Thurs 5pm–2am, Fri & Sat 5pm–4am. MAP P.45, POCKET MAP C20

A plush place to pop a cork or two. There's a long list of 300 champagnes and sparklers, as well as a tempting selection of signature cocktails on offer, but beware the skyrocketing tabs.

CHURCH LOUNGE

Grand Hotel, 2 Sixth Ave at White St. Subway A, C, E to Canal St; #1 to Franklin St ⓣ 212/519-6600. Daily 7am–1am. MAP P.45, POCKET MAP C20

Fabulous hotel bar, set at the bottom of the *Grand*'s spacious atrium – being surrounded by twinkling lights and beautiful people (it's much more atmospheric at night) eases the pain when it's time to pay.

EAR INN

326 Spring St between Washington and Greenwich sts. Subway C, E to Spring St; #1 to Houston St. Daily noon–4am. MAP P.45, POCKET MAP B20

"Ear" as in "Bar" with half the neon "B" chipped off. This historic pub near the Hudson opened in 1890 (the building dates from 1817). Its creaky interior is as cosy as a Cornish inn, with a good mix of beers on tap and basic, reasonably priced American food.

FANELLI'S CAFÉ

94 Prince St at Mercer St. Subway R, N to Prince St. Sun–Wed 10am–2am, Thurs–Sat 10am–4pm. MAP P.45, POCKET MAP D19

Established in 1922 (the building dates from 1853), *Fanelli's* is one of the city's oldest pubs, relaxed and informal and a favourite of the not-too-hip after-work crowd.

GREENWICH STREET TAVERN

399 Greenwich St at Beach St. Subway #1 to Franklin St. Mon–Fri 11am–11pm, Sat 4–11pm, Sun noon–8pm. MAP P.45, POCKET MAP B20

Friendly neighbourhood bar, refreshingly unpretentious for this part of town, with a solid menu of snack food, easy-going (generally male) clientele and beers for $3 in happy hour (Wed–Thurs 5–7pm).

KENN'S BROOME STREET BAR

363 W Broadway at Broome St. Subway #1 to Franklin St. Daily 11am–4am. MAP P.45, POCKET MAP C20

Open since 1972 but set in an

ageing 1825 Federal-style house, this comfortable bar offers 15 real ales (eight draughts), from Harpoon Winter Warm to Flying Dog Pale Ale (they also have Stella on tap), and serves food, including decent burgers from $9.25.

M1-5 LOUNGE

52 Walker St, between Church St and Broadway. Subway N, Q, R to Canal St. Mon–Fri 4pm–4am, Sat 7pm–4am. MAP P.45, POCKET MAP C20

Ultra hip lounge bar, with a decent range of beers, wines and cocktails to accompany the sleek design and good food. Live music and DJs set the scene.

MERC BAR

151 Mercer St between Houston and Prince sts. Subway R, N to Prince St. Sun–Wed 5pm–2am, Thurs–Sat 5pm–2am. MAP P.45, POCKET MAP D19

Soho's original cocktail lounge, this once super-trendy watering hole has aged nicely.

PRAVDA

281 Lafayette St between Prince and Houston sts. Subway R, N to Prince St. Mon–Wed 5pm–1am, Thurs 5pm–2am, Fri & Sat 5pm–3am, Sun 6pm–1am. MAP P.45, POCKET MAP D19

This chic Russian lounge serves caviar, stiff (and potent) vodka drinks and hard-boiled eggs for snacking. Now that its heyday has passed, there are fewer crowds competing to sample the 70 vodkas on offer, and there's a relaxed vibe.

FANELLI'S CAFÉ

PUFFY'S TAVERN

81 Hudson St between Harrison and Jay sts. Subway #1 to Franklin St. Daily 11.30am–4am. MAP P.45, POCKET MAP C21

Far from being P. Diddy's hangout, this small dive bar serves up cheap booze without an ounce of attitude, rare in this area. Italian sandwiches are served and its cool jukebox specializes in old 45s.

THE ROOM

144 Sullivan St between Houston and Prince sts. Subway C, E to Spring St. Daily 5pm–4am. MAP P.45, POCKET MAP C19

Dark, homey two-room bar with exposed brick walls and comfortable couches. No spirits, but an impressive array of domestic and international beers.

SANTOS PARTY HOUSE

96 Lafayette St, between Walker and White sts. Subway J, N, Q, R, Z, #6 to Canal St. Daily 7pm–4am. MAP P.45, POCKET MAP D20

Two-floor club and art space, with wild hip-hop, Latin and house most Thursdays to Saturdays; check the website for the current schedule.

TOAD HALL

57 Grand St between W Broadway and Wooster St. Subway A, C, E to Canal St. Daily noon–4am. MAP P.45, POCKET MAP C20

With a pool table, good service and excellent bar snacks, this stylish alehouse is a little less hip and a little more of a local hangout than some of its neighbours.

Chinatown, Little Italy and Nolita

Chinese immigrants have been coming to New York since the 1850s, making this Chinatown one of the oldest and biggest in the Western hemisphere. Indeed, with over 100,000 residents, Chinatown is Manhattan's most densely populated ethnic neighbourhood. Since the 1980s it has pushed across its traditional border on Canal Street into the smaller enclave of Little Italy, and has begun to sprawl east across Division Street and East Broadway into the Lower East Side. Little Italy itself, now squeezed into a narrow strip along Mulberry Street, is far more dependent on tourists than Chinatown, but both neighbourhoods are fun places to eat, with cheap noodles, roast duck, gelato and huge plates of pasta on offer. On the northern fringes of Little Italy, the hip quarter known as Nolita ("North of Little Italy") is home to a number of chic restaurants, bars and boutiques.

CANAL STREET

Subway A, C, E, J, N, Q, R, Z, #1, #6 to Canal St. MAP P.55, POCKET MAP D20–E20

Canal Street is Chinatown's main all-hours artery crammed with jewellery shops and kiosks hawking sunglasses, T-shirts and fake Rolexes. At the eastern end of the thoroughfare, the majestic Byzantine dome of the former Citizen's Savings Bank (now HSBC) and the 1909 Manhattan Bridge's grand Beaux Arts entrance seem out of place amid the neon signs and market stalls.

CHINATOWN

Chinatown, Little Italy and Nolita

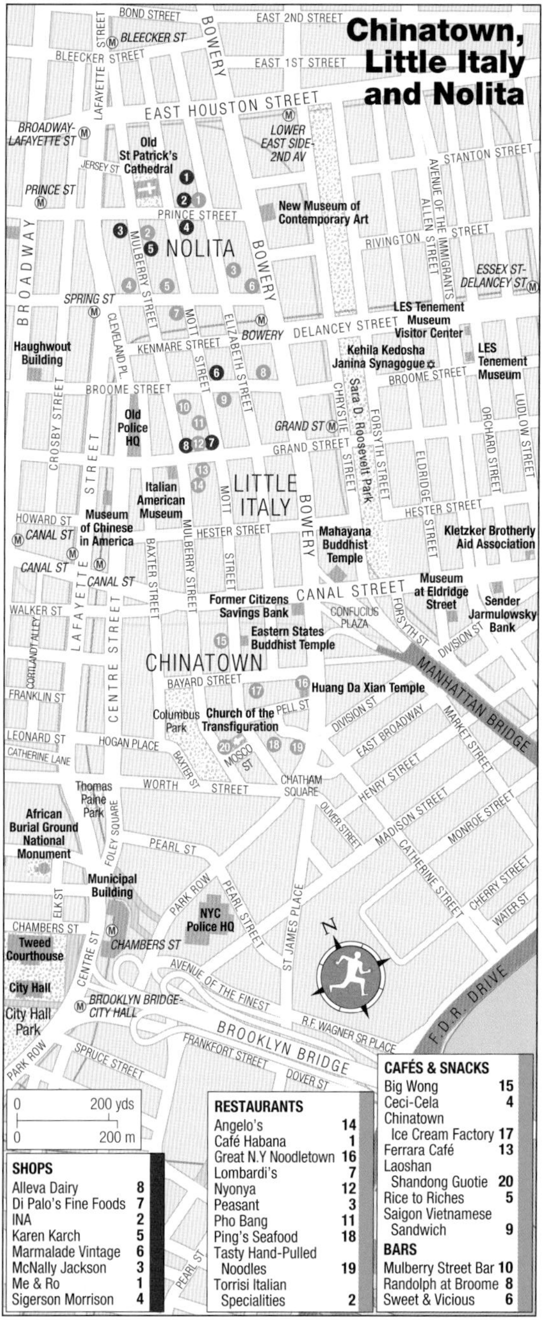

SHOPS

Alleva Dairy	8
Di Palo's Fine Foods	7
INA	2
Karen Karch	5
Marmalade Vintage	6
McNally Jackson	3
Me & Ro	1
Sigerson Morrison	4

RESTAURANTS

Angelo's	14
Café Habana	1
Great N.Y Noodletown	16
Lombardi's	7
Nyonya	12
Peasant	3
Pho Bang	11
Ping's Seafood	18
Tasty Hand-Pulled Noodles	19
Torrisi Italian Specialities	2

CAFÉS & SNACKS

Big Wong	15
Ceci-Cela	4
Chinatown Ice Cream Factory	17
Ferrara Café	13
Laoshan Shandong Guotie	20
Rice to Riches	5
Saigon Vietnamese Sandwich	9

BARS

Mulberry Street Bar	10
Randolph at Broome	8
Sweet & Vicious	6

CHURCH OF THE TRANSFIGURATION

29 Mott St. Subway J, N, Q, R, Z, #6 to Canal St ☎ 212/962-5157, Ⓦ www.transfigurationnyc.org. Sat 2–5pm, otherwise services only. Free. MAP P.55, POCKET MAP E21

This elegant green-domed Georgian edifice is known as the "church of immigrants" for good reason. Since opening in 1801 as a Lutheran parish, it has also served Irish and Italian church-goers. Today, Mass is said daily in Cantonese, English and Mandarin.

MOTT STREET

Subway J, N, Q, R, Z, #6 to Canal St. MAP P.55, POCKET MAP E20–21

Mott Street is Chinatown's most touristy restaurant row, although the streets around – Canal, Pell, Bayard, Doyers and Bowery – host a glut of good restaurants, tea and rice shops. Cantonese cuisine predominates, but many restaurants also specialize in spicier Sichuan and Hunan dishes. Most restaurants start closing around 10pm.

GRAND STREET

Subway B, D to Grand St. MAP P.55, POCKET MAP E20–F20

Grand Street was the city's Main Street in the mid-1800s, and nowadays you will find outdoor fruit, vegetable and

GRAND STREET

live seafood stands lining the curbs, offering bean curd, fungi and dried sea cucumbers. Ribs, whole chickens and roast ducks glisten in the storefront windows, alongside those of Chinese herbalists.

MUSEUM OF CHINESE IN AMERICA

215 Centre St between Howard and Grand sts. Subway J, N, Q, R, Z, #6 to Canal St ☎ 212/619-4785, Ⓦ www.mocanyc.org. Mon 11am–5pm, Thurs 11am–9pm, Fri 11am–5pm, Sat & Sun 10am–5pm. $7, free Thurs. MAP P.55, POCKET MAP D20

This fascinating museum opened in plush new premises in 2009, its core exhibition providing an historical overview of the Chinese in the US through evocative multimedia displays, artefacts

Chinatown temples

Chinatown is a good place to observe traditional Chinese temple rituals, though the architecture is usually modern – most temples occupy converted shopfronts. **The Eastern States Buddhist Temple**, 64 Mott St (daily 8am–6pm), was established in 1962 as a social club for elderly Chinese men. The main deity here is Sakyamuni Buddha, but there's also a glass-encased gold statue of the "four-faced Buddha", a replica of the revered image in Bangkok's Erawan Shrine. Chinese influence is more obvious at the gilded and peaceful **Mahayana Buddhist Temple**, 133 Canal St (daily 8am–6pm). Candlelight and blue neon glow around the giant gold Buddha on the main altar. At the corner of Pell St and the Bowery is one of Chinatown's few Taoist temples: **Huang Daxian Temple** (daily 9am–6pm).

and filmed interviews. Galleries are arranged around a sun-lit courtyard reminiscent of a traditional Chinese house.

ITALIAN AMERICAN MUSEUM AND MULBERRY STREET

155 Mulberry St. Subway J, N, Q, R, #6 to Canal St ☎ 212/965-9000, Ⓦ www.italianamericanmuseum.org. Mon–Fri by appointment, Sat 11am–6pm, Sun noon–6pm. Donation $5. MAP P.55, POCKET MAP D20

Little Italy's main strip, **Mulberry Street**, is home to many of the area's cafés and restaurants – and filled with tourists. There are no stand-out restaurants, although the former site of *Umberto's Clam House*, on the corner of Mulberry and Hester streets, was once notorious as the scene of the vicious gangland murder of Joe "Crazy Joey" Gallo in 1972. On the corner of Grand Street, the **Italian American Museum**, housed in the former 1885 Banca Stabile building, holds small exhibits on the old neighbourhood.

ST PATRICK'S OLD CATHEDRAL

263 Mulberry St at Prince St. Subway R, N to Prince St ☎ 212/226-8075, Ⓦ www.oldcathedral.org. Daily 8am–6pm. Free. MAP P.55, POCKET MAP D19

The first Catholic cathedral in the city, **St Patrick's Old Cathedral** began by serving the Irish immigrant community in 1809 and is the parent church to its much more famous offspring on Fifth Avenue and 50th Street.

NEW MUSEUM OF CONTEMPORARY ART AND THE BOWERY

235 Bowery at Prince St. Subway R, N to Prince St; #6 to Spring St ☎ 212/219-1222, Ⓦ www.newmuseum.org. Wed & Fri–Sun 11am–6pm, Thurs 11am–9pm. $14, free Thurs 7–9pm. MAP P.55, POCKET MAP E19

Powerful symbol of the Bowery's rebirth, this avant-garde art gallery is housed in a stack of seven shimmering aluminium boxes. The warehouse-like galleries are spacious, but still small enough to digest without overdosing on the diverse range of temporary exhibits inside. The **Bowery** itself was until relatively recently a byword for poverty and destitution, America's original skid row. At its peak, in 1949, around 14,000 homeless people could be found here, most dossing down in hostels known as flophouses. Today only eight flophouses remain, and the street is increasingly lined with smart, contemporary buildings, stores and bars.

NEW MUSEUM OF CONTEMPORARY ART

Shops

ALLEVA DAIRY

188 Grand St at Mulberry St. Subway J, Z, #6 to Canal St. Mon–Sat 8.30am–6pm, Sun 8.30am–3pm. MAP P.55, POCKET MAP D20

The oldest Italian *formaggiaio* (cheesemonger) and grocery in America (1892). Makes its own smoked mozzarella, provolone and ricotta.

DI PALO'S FINE FOODS

200 Grand St at Mott St. Subway B, D to Grand St. Mon–Sat 9am–6.30pm, Sun 9am–4pm. MAP P.55, POCKET MAP D20

Charming and authoritative family-run business, open since 1925, that sells some of the city's best ricotta, along with a fine selection of aged balsamic vinegars, oils and home-made pastas.

DI PALO'S

INA

21 Prince St between Elizabeth and Mott sts. Subway R, N to Prince St. Mon–Sat noon–8pm, Sun noon–7pm. MAP P.55, POCKET MAP D19

Favourite consignment shop selling recent season cast-offs. Full of bargains; there's a men's branch at 19 Prince St (next door; same hours).

KAREN KARCH

240 Mulberry St between Prince and Spring sts. Subway R, N to Prince St. Wed–Fri 1–6pm. MAP P.55, POCKET MAP D19

One of the city's most exclusive jewellery stores, where one-of-a-kind items are displayed amid breezy surroundings on dollhouse furniture.

MARMALADE VINTAGE

174 Mott St at Broome St. Subway J to Bowery, #6 to Spring St. Tues–Sun 1–7pm. MAP P.55, POCKET MAP D20

Fabulous vintage clothes from the 1940s to the 1990s; especially good for 1970s gear (including shoes and mink shawls).

MCNALLY JACKSON

52 Prince St, between Mulberry and Lafayette sts. Subway N, R to Prince St. Mon–Sat 10am–10pm, Sun 10am–9pm. MAP P.55, POCKET MAP D19

This independent Canadian book chain has a great café and excellent literary events, and arranges its books uniquely, by nation.

ME & RO

241 Elizabeth St between Houston and Prince sts. Subway B, D, F, M to Broadway-Lafayette; R, N to Prince St. Mon–Sat 11am–7pm, Sun noon–6pm. MAP P.55, POCKET MAP D19

The hottest, most distinctive jewellery designer in Manhattan, with tasteful Modernist designs inspired by the traditions of China, India and Tibet.

SIGERSON MORRISON

28 Prince St at Mott St. Subway R, N to Prince St. Mon–Sat 11am–7pm, Sun noon–6pm. MAP P.55, POCKET MAP D19

Timeless, elegant shoes for women by Kari Sigerson and Miranda Morrison, a real pilgrimage for any shoe lover.

Cafés and snacks

BIG WONG

67 Mott St between Bayard and Canal sts. Subway J, N, Q, R, Z, #6 to Canal St. Daily 7.30am–10pm. MAP P.55, POCKET MAP D21

This cafeteria-style Cantonese BBQ joint serves some of Chinatown's tastiest duck and congee (savoury rice stew), all for $5.25–9.75.

CECI-CELA

55 Spring St between Mulberry and Lafayette sts. Subway #6 to Spring St. Mon–Sat 7am–10pm, Sun 8am–8pm. MAP P.55, POCKET MAP D19

Tiny French patisserie with tables in the back, selling delectable baked goods. Divine almond croissants and palmiers (elephant-ear-shaped, sugar-coated pastries).

CHINATOWN ICE CREAM FACTORY

65 Bayard St between Mott and Elizabeth sts. Subway J, N, Q, R, Z, #6 to Canal St. Daily 11am–11pm. MAP P.55, POCKET MAP D21

An essential stop after dinner at one of the restaurants nearby. Specialties include green tea, ginger and almond cookie ice cream.

FERRARA CAFÉ

195 Grand St between Mott and Mulberry sts. Subway J, N, Q, R, Z, #6 to Canal St; B, D to Grand St. Sun–Fri 8am–midnight, Sat 8am–1am. MAP P.55, POCKET MAP D20

The best-known and most traditional of Little Italy's coffeehouses, this neighbourhood landmark has been around since 1892. Try the New York cheesecake, hand-dipped chocolate *cannoli*, or, in summer, *granite* (Italian ices). Outdoor seating is available in warmer weather.

FERRARA CAFÉ

LAOSHAN SHANDONG GUOTIE

106 Mosco St. Subway J, Z, #6 to Canal St. Daily 8am–9pm. MAP P.55, POCKET MAP D21

Identified simply by a "Fried Dumpling" sign in English, this bargain hole-in-the-wall specializes in pan-fried dumplings characteristic of northern China ($1 for 5).

RICE TO RICHES

37 Spring St between Mott and Mulberry sts. Subway #6 to Spring St. Sun–Thurs 11am–11pm, Fri & Sat 11am–1am. MAP P.55, POCKET MAP D19

Utterly irresistible rice pudding, served up in this fashionable space in a variety of sweet flavours, from peanut butter and choc chip, to mango and cinnamon. Bowls start at $7.

SAIGON VIETNAMESE SANDWICH

369 Broome St at Mott St. Subway #6 to Spring St. Daily 8am–8pm. MAP P.55, POCKET MAP D20

One of the best makers of Vietnamese sandwiches (known as *bánh mì*) in the city. The classic is a large chunk of French bread stuffed with pork, sausage and pickled vegetables – all for $4.50.

Restaurants

ANGELO'S

146 Mulberry St between Hester and Grand sts. Subway N, R, #6 to Canal St. Tues–Thurs & Sun noon–11.30pm, Fri noon–12.30am, Sat noon–1am. MAP P.55, POCKET MAP D20

Little Italy's red-sauce restaurants cater firmly to tourists these days, but this 1902 classic is the best place to get a sense of the area's original style and flavours.

CAFÉ HABANA

17 Prince St at Elizabeth St. Subway R to Prince St ☎ 212/625-2001. Daily 9am–midnight. MAP P.55, POCKET MAP D19

Small and always crowded, this Cuban–South American option features some of the best skirt steak and fried plantains this side of Cuba. A takeout window next door serves great *café con leche*.

GREAT N.Y. NOODLETOWN

28 Bowery at Bayard St. Subway B, D to Grand St; J, Z, #6 to Canal St ☎ 212/349-0923. Daily 9am–4am. MAP P.55, POCKET MAP E20.

Despite the name, noodles aren't the real draw at this down-to-earth restaurant – the soft-shell crabs (in season) are crisp, salty and delicious. Good roast meats (try the baby pig) and soups too.

PING'S SEAFOOD

LOMBARDI'S

32 Spring St at Mott St. Subway #6 to Spring St ☎ 212/941-7994. Sun–Thurs 11.30am–11pm, Fri & Sat 11.30am–midnight. MAP P.55, POCKET MAP D19

The oldest pizzeria in the US (since 1905) serves some of the best pies in town, including an amazing clam pizza; no slices, though. Ask for roasted garlic on the side.

NYONYA

199 Grand St between Mott and Mulberry sts. Subway B, D to Grand St; J, Z, #6 to Canal St ☎ 212/334-3669. Sun–Thurs 11am–11.30pm, Fri & Sat 11am–midnight. MAP P.55, POCKET MAP D20

Superb Malaysian grub at wallet-friendly prices. Try the chicken curry, spicy squid or clay-pot noodles. Cash only.

PEASANT

194 Elizabeth St between Prince and Spring sts. Subway R, N to Prince St; J, Z to Bowery; #6 to Spring St ☎ 212/965-9511. Tues–Sun 6pm–2am. MAP P.55, POCKET MAP D19

A bit of a hangout after hours for city chefs, here you'll pay around $22–39 for Frank De Carlo's beautifully crafted Italian food such as *porchetta arrosto* (roasted suckling pig) or $11–14 for brick-oven-fired pizzas.

PHO BANG

157 Mott St between Grand and Broome sts. Subway B, D to Grand St J, Z, #6 to Canal St ☎ 212/966-3797. Daily 10am–10pm. MAP P.55, POCKET MAP D20

One of the most popular Vietnamese restaurants in the city, often packed at weekends. The main event is *pho*, Vietnamese beef noodle soup, which comes in several varieties, but the crispy spring

LOMBARDI'S

rolls and chicken curry are also excellent.

PING'S SEAFOOD

22 Mott St between Chatham Square and Pell St. Subway R, N, J, Z, #6 to Canal St ☎ 212/602-9988. Daily 10.30am–midnight. MAP P.55, POCKET MAP E21

While this Hong Kong seafood restaurant is good anytime, it's most enjoyable on weekends for dim sum, when carts of tasty, bite-size delicacies whirl by for the taking every thirty seconds. This place offers superb bang for your buck.

TASTY HAND-PULLED NOODLES

1 Doyers St at the Bowery. Subway J, N, Q, R, Z, #6 to Canal St ☎ 212/791-1817. Daily 10.30am–10.30pm. MAP P.55, POCKET MAP E21

Freshly cooked and delicious hand-pulled noodles made to order – choose from seven different types, then opt for pan-fried or boiled noodles with pork, fish, beef, chicken, shrimp and several other combos.

TORRISI ITALIAN SPECIALTIES

250 Mulberry St, between Prince and Spring sts. Subway N, R to Prince St ☎ 212/965-0955. Mon–Wed & Sun 5.30–11pm, Thurs–Sat noon–2pm & 5.30–11pm. MAP P.55, POCKET MAP D19

This vaunted modern Italian restaurant is great for a splurge (no reservations; $60 prix-fixe), while its sister joint, *Parm*, next door (daily 11am–midnight), knocks out great sandwiches.

Bars

MULBERRY STREET BAR

176-1/2 Mulberry St between Broome and Grand sts. Subway J, Z to Bowery; #6 to Canal St. Daily 11.30am–2am. MAP P.55, POCKET MAP D20

Donnie Brasco and *The Sopranos* had scenes shot in this favourite local dive bar, located in the heart of Little Italy. Formerly known as *Mare Chiaro*, the wooden bar, subway tile floor and pressed tin roof have barely changed since it opened in 1908.

RANDOLPH AT BROOME

349 Broome St, between Elizabeth St and the Bowery. Subway J, Z to Bowery; B, D to Grand St. Mon–Fri 7am–4am, Sat & Sun 8am–4am. MAP P.55, POCKET MAP D20

Friendly European café that serves artisanal cocktails and gourmet coffee from the Brooklyn Roasting Company (till 5pm). Happy hour is daily noon–8pm, and there's a cosy outdoor patio at the front.

SWEET & VICIOUS

5 Spring St between Bowery and Elizabeth St. Subway J, Z to Bowery. Daily 3pm–4am. MAP P.55, POCKET MAP D19

This bar is a neighbourhood favourite and the epitome of rustic chic, with exposed brick and wood and antique chandeliers. The tempting cocktail list features such delicious concoctions as a berry Cosmopolitan and a lemondrop Martini. A back garden and a cosy atmosphere add to its charm.

The Lower East Side

Historically the epitome of the American ethnic melting pot, the Lower East Side has been a revolving door for immigrants since the 1830s, when Irish and German populations moved in. The second wave came from Southern Italian and Eastern European Jewish communities arriving in the 1880s. By 1915, Jews had the largest representation in the Lower East Side, numbering more than 320,000. While a fair proportion of inhabitants today are working-class Latino or Asian, you are just as likely to find students, moneyed artsy types and other refugees from the overly-gentrified areas of Soho and the nearby East Village, a blend that makes this one of the city's most enthralling neighbourhoods and one of its hippest areas for shopping, drinking, dancing and – what else? – food.

ORCHARD STREET

Subway F, J, M, Z to Delancey St/Essex St; B, D to Grand St. MAP P.63, POCKET MAP E19

The centre of the Lower East Side's so-called Bargain District, Orchard is best visited on weekends, when filled with stalls and storefronts hawking discounted designer clothes and bags, though note that many Jewish-owned stores are closed on Saturdays. The rooms above the stores used to house sweatshops, so named because whatever the weather, a stove had to be kept warm for pressing the clothes made there. Much of the garment industry moved uptown ages ago, and the rooms are a bit more salubrious now – often home to pricey apartments.

LOWER EAST SIDE TENEMENT MUSEUM

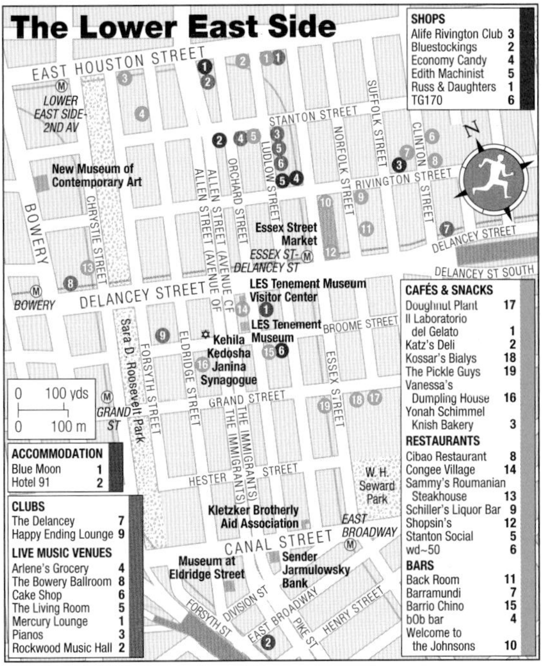

LOWER EAST SIDE TENEMENT MUSEUM

97 Orchard St between Broome and Delancey sts. Subway B, D to Grand St; F, J, M, Z to Delancey St/Essex St ☎ 212/982-8420, Ⓦ www.tenement.org. $22; for tickets go to the visitor centre at 103 Orchard St (daily 10am–6pm). MAP P.63, POCKET MAP E20

This illuminating museum offers a glimpse into the crumbling and claustrophobic interior of an 1863 tenement, with its deceptively elegant, though ghostly, entry hall and two communal toilets for every four families. Museum guides expertly bring to life the building's past and present, aided by documents, photographs and artefacts found on-site, and concentrating on the area's multiple ethnic heritages.

Various apartments inside have been renovated with period furnishings to reflect the lives of tenants, from the mid-nineteenth century to the mid-twentieth century – when many families ran cottage industries from home.

The tenement is accessible only by themed **guided tours** (1hr, every 15–30 min; daily 10.30am–5pm). These include "Hard Times", which focuses on a German-Jewish family and Italian family during the economic depressions of 1863 and 1935; "Irish Outsiders", which examines the grim life of the Irish Moore family from 1868–69; and "Sweatshop Workers", a visit to the Levine family's garment workshop and the Rogarshevskys' Sabbath table at the turn of the twentieth century. "Foods of the Lower East Side" ($45) is a two-hour tour of the neighbourhood (Fri & Sat only).

ESSEX STREET MARKET

120 Essex St at Delancey St. Subway F, J, M, Z to Delancey St/Essex St ☎ 212/388-0449, www.essexstreetmarket.com. Mon–Sat 8am–7pm. MAP P.63, POCKET MAP E19

On the north side of Delancey Street sprawls the **Essex Street Market**, erected under the aegis of Mayor LaGuardia in the 1930s. Here you'll find all sorts of fresh fruit, fish and vegetables, along with artisan chocolates, cheese and *Shopsin's* restaurant (p.67).

ESSEX STREET MARKET

MUSEUM AT ELDRIDGE STREET

12 Eldridge St between Canal and Division sts. Subway B, D to Grand St; F to East Broadway ☎ 212/219-0302, www.eldridgestreet.org. Mon–Thurs & Sun 10am–5pm, Fri 10am–3pm by tour only, every 30min (1hr); $10. MAP P.63, POCKET MAP E20

Built in 1887, this wonderfully restored synagogue is one of the neighbourhood jewels: a brick and terracotta hybrid of Moorish and Gothic influences, with rich woodwork and stained-glass windows, including the west-wing rose window – a spectacular Star of David roundel. The synagogue is still in use, but tours visit the main sanctuary upstairs, while exhibits introduce the history of the building and the area.

Exploring the Jewish Lower East Side

Though its Jewish population has dwindled, the Lower East Side retains a rich legacy of Jewish food, stores and, especially, Jewish buildings. Several synagogues are well maintained and most accept visitors Sun–Thurs. Perhaps the best preserved is the Museum at Eldridge St (see above), but you can also visit the 1927 **Kehila Kedosha Janina Synagogue and Museum** (☎ 212/431-1619, www.kkjsm.org. Sun 11am–4pm; free; Map p.63, Pocket map E20) at 280 Broome St (at Allen St), home of the Romaniote Jews from Greece, an obscure branch of Judaism with roots in the Roman era. Enthusiastic volunteers introduce Jewish art and various exhibits. Further south at 54–58 Canal St is the ornate facade of the **Sender Jarmulowsky Bank**. Founded in 1873 by a Russian peddler who made his fortune reselling ship tickets, the bank catered to the financial needs of the area's non-English-speaking immigrants (the building dates from 1912). In 1914, the bank collapsed; on its closure, thousands lost what little savings they had accumulated. At the corner of Canal and Ludlow streets, the **Kletzker Brotherly Aid Association building** at no. 41 (now a Chinese funeral home) is a relic of a time when Jewish towns set up their own lodges (in this case, the town was Kletzk, in modern-day Belarus) to provide services such as community healthcare and burials. For more in-depth tours contact the Lower East Side Jewish Conservancy (☎ 212/374-4100, www.nycjewishtours.org).

Shops

ALIFE RIVINGTON CLUB

158 Rivington St at Clinton St. Subway J, M, Z to Essex St; F to Delancey St. Mon–Sat noon–7pm, Sun noon–6pm. MAP P.63, POCKET MAP F19

A shrine to designer sneakers, with special edition Nikes going for as much as $900, as well as $150 sunglasses and other accessories for sale. The hip T-shirts are "just" $35.

BLUESTOCKINGS

172 Allen St, between Rivington and Stanton sts. Subway F to Lower East Side-Second Ave. Daily 11am–11pm. MAP P.63, POCKET MAP E19

Bluestockings sells new and used books on gay and gender studies, feminism, police and prisons, democracy studies and black liberation.

ECONOMY CANDY

108 Rivington St between Essex and Ludlow sts. Subway J, M, Z to Essex St; F to Delancey St. Mon 10am–6pm, Tues–Fri & Sun 9am–6pm, Sat 10am–5pm. MAP P.63, POCKET MAP E19

Old-fashioned sweet store that sells hundreds of kinds of chocolates, candies, nuts, dried fruits and halvah.

EDITH MACHINIST

104 Rivington St at Ludlow St. Subway J, M, Z to Essex St; F to Delancey St. Mon–Fri 1–8pm, Sat noon–8pm, Sun noon–7pm. MAP P.63, POCKET MAP E19

This trendy used clothes store holds some exceptional finds (particularly shoes and top designers) but at a fraction of their Fifth Avenue price tags.

RUSS & DAUGHTERS

179 E Houston St between Allen and Orchard sts. Subway F to Lower East Side-2nd Ave. Mon–Fri 8am–8pm, Sat 9am–7pm, Sun 8am–5.30pm. MAP P.63, POCKET MAP E19

The original Manhattan gourmet shop, it was set up in 1914 to sate the appetites of homesick immigrant Jews with smoked fish, pickled vegetables, cheese and amazing bagels with smoky lox; expect to pay $11.25 for the latter, though.

TG170

77 Ludlow St, at Broome St. Subway F to Lower East Side-Second Ave. Daily noon–8pm. MAP P.63, POCKET MAP E20

Terri Gillis's women's clothing boutique is a magnet for fashionistas hunting for independent and emerging local designers.

RUSS & DAUGHTERS

Cafés and snacks

DOUGHNUT PLANT

379 Grand St between Essex and Norfolk sts. Subway J, M, Z to Essex St; F to Delancey St. Tues–Sun 6.30am–6.30pm. MAP P.63, POCKET MAP F20

Serious (and seriously delicious) doughnuts; make sure you sample the seasonal flavours and glazes, including pumpkin and passion fruit.

IL LABORATORIO DEL GELATO

188 Ludlow St, at Houston St. Subway J, Z to Essex St; F to Delancey St. Mon–Thurs 7.30am–10pm, Fri 7.30am–midnight, Sat 10am–midnight, Sun 10am–10pm. MAP P.63, POCKET MAP E19

This shrine to cream and sugar serves up over 230 flavours (48 weekly; $4.25–6.75), from honey lavender and toasted sesame to tarragon pink pepper.

KATZ'S DELI

205 E Houston St at Ludlow St. Subway F to Lower East Side-Second Ave. Sun, Wed, Thurs 8am–10.45pm, Mon & Tues 8am–9.45pm, Fri & Sat 8am–2.45am. MAP P.63, POCKET MAP E19

Venerable Lower East Side Jewish deli since 1888, serving archetypal overstuffed pastrami and corned-beef sandwiches, bagels, hot dogs and Ruebens (sandwiches $16.95). Famous for the faux-gasm scene from *When Harry Met Sally*.

KOSSAR'S BIALYS

367 Grand St between Essex and Norfolk sts. Subway J, M, Z to Essex St; F to Delancey St. Mon–Thurs, Sun 6am–8pm, Fri 6am–3pm. MAP P.63, POCKET MAP F20

A generations-old kosher treasure serves, bar none, the city's best bagels and bialys ($0.90), a flattened savoury dough traditionally topped with onion or garlic.

KATZ'S DELI

THE PICKLE GUYS

49 Essex St at Grand St. Subway R, N, J, Z, #6 to Canal St. Daily 10.30am–midnight. MAP P.63, POCKET MAP E20

Come here for fresh home-made pickles, olives and other yummy picnic staples from huge barrels of garlicky brine.

VANESSA'S DUMPLING HOUSE

118A Eldridge St between Grand and Broome sts. Subway B, D to Grand St. Mon–Sat 7.30am–10.30pm, Sun 7.30am–10pm. MAP P.63, POCKET MAP E20

This always busy Chinese restaurant knocks out various combinations of steamed or fried pork, shrimp and vegetable dumplings at the bargain price of $1 for 4.

YONAH SCHIMMEL KNISH BAKERY

137 E Houston St between First and Second aves. Subway F to Lower East Side-second Ave. Sun–Thurs 9am–7pm, Fri & Sat 9am–10pm. MAP P.63, POCKET MAP E19

This place has been making and selling some of New York's best knishes ($3.50–4) since 1910: rounds of vegetable- or meat-stuffed dough, baked fresh on the premises, as are the wonderful bagels.

Restaurants

CIBAO RESTAURANT

72 Clinton St at Rivington St. Subway J, M, Z to Essex St; F to Delancey St ☎ 212/228-0703. Daily 6am–2am. MAP P.E20, POCKET MAP F19

El Cibao is the best Dominican restaurant on the Lower East Side. Hearty portions of rice and beans ($6) and huge sandwiches, particularly the Cubano ($4.50), are bargains.

CONGEE VILLAGE

100 Allen St at Delancey St. Subway J, M, Z to Essex St; F to Delancey St ☎ 212/941-1818. Daily 10.30am–2am. MAP P.63, POCKET MAP E19

This Cantonese restaurant is a shrine to the eponymous fragrant, soupy rice dish and a wide range of other Hong Kong favourites for less than $10.

SAMMY'S ROUMANIAN STEAKHOUSE

157 Chrystie St at Delancey St. Subway B, D to Grand St; J, Z to Bowery; F to Lower East Side-Second Ave ☎ 212/673-0330. Mon–Thurs 4–10pm, Fri & Sat 4–11pm, Sun 3–9.30pm. MAP P.63, POCKET MAP E19

This basement Jewish steakhouse gives diners more than they bargained for: schmaltzy songs, delicious food (topped off by home-made *rugalach* and egg creams for dessert) and chilled vodka.

SCHILLER'S LIQUOR BAR

SCHILLER'S LIQUOR BAR

131 Rivington St at Norfolk St. Subway F to Delancey St; J, M, Z to Essex St ☎ 212/260-4555. Mon–Thurs 11am–1am, Fri 11am–3am, Sat 10am–3am, Sun 10am–1am. MAP P.63, POCKET MAP F19

Trendy bistro with beautiful clientele. The menu features salads and good steaks with classic sauces ($16–31).

SHOPSIN'S

Stall 16, Essex St Market, 120 Essex St. Subway F to Delancey St; J, M, Z to Essex St. (no phone). Wed–Sat 9am–2pm, Sun 10am–2pm. MAP P.63, POCKET MAP F19

A New York institution, Kenny Shopsin ran his idiosyncratic diner in the West Village for years, but was forced down here by high rents. His addictive creations – like peanut-butter-filled pancakes – have a loyal following.

STANTON SOCIAL

99 Stanton St, between Ludlow and Orchard sts. Subway F to Lower East Side-Second Ave ☎ 212/995-0099. Mon–Fri 5pm–1am, Sat 11.30am–1am, Sun 11.30am–11pm. MAP P.63, POCKET MAP E19

Chandeliers, lizard-skin banquettes and retro booths draw a young, hip crowd to this restaurant-cum-lounge bar. Food, such as zesty snapper tacos with mango salsa, is designed for sharing.

WD-50

50 Clinton St between Rivington and Stanton sts. Subway F to Delancey St; J, M, Z to Essex St ☎ 212/477-2900. Mon–Sat 6–10.30pm, Sun 6–10pm. MAP P.63, POCKET MAP F19

Celebrated chef Wylie DuFresne attracts crowds with experimental haute cuisine such as venison tartare with edamame ice cream and pork belly with black soy beans and turnips. Reservations required.

Bars

BACK ROOM

102 Norfolk St between Delancey and Rivington sts. Subway F to Delancey St; J, M, Z to Essex St. Tues–Sat 7.30pm–4am. MAP P.63, POCKET MAP F19

With a hidden, back-alley entrance, this former speakeasy was reputedly once a haunt of gangster Meyer Lansky. Booze is served in teacups as a nod to its Prohibition days.

BARRAMUNDI

67 Clinton St between Stanton and Rivington sts. Subway F to Delancey St; J, M, Z to Essex St. Daily 6pm–4am. MAP P.63, POCKET MAP F19

Laidback bar with a magical, fairy-lit garden that provides sanctuary from the increasingly hip surroundings. Come 10pm though, the garden closes and you've got to move inside.

BARRIO CHINO

253 Broome St at Orchard St. Subway B, D to Grand St. Mon 5.30pm–1am, Tues–Thurs & Sun 11.30am–1am, Fri & Sat 11.30am–2am. MAP P.63, POCKET MAP F19

Don't be confused by the Chinese lanterns or drink umbrellas – the speciality here is tequila, and there are over fifty to choose from. Shots are even served with the traditional sangria chaser.

BOB BAR

233 Eldridge St between Houston and Stanton sts. Subway F to Lower East Side-Second Ave. Tues–Sun 7pm–4am. MAP P.63, POCKET MAP E19

This cosy bar turns into one of the best dance parties in town after midnight, with DJs spinning a mix of hip-hop, reggae and R&B.

WELCOME TO THE JOHNSONS

123 Rivington St between Essex and Norfolk sts. Subway F to Delancey St; J, M, Z to Essex St. Mon–Fri 3pm–4am, Sat & Sun noon–4pm. MAP P.63, POCKET MAP E19

This 1970s throwback dive bar is all about rockin' out and chillin' out, and you can do both without any friction. Good beers, great bartenders.

Clubs

THE DELANCEY

168 Delancey St at Clinton St. Subway F to Delancey St; J, M, Z to Essex St www.thedelancey.com. Daily 5pm–4am. MAP P.63, POCKET MAP F19

Williamsburg hipsters meet Lower East Side chic at this rooftop lounge and nightclub. Things can get frisky in the basement, which pulsates with loud music and live acts.

HAPPY ENDING LOUNGE

302 Broome St between Eldridge and Forsythe sts. Subway J, Z to Bowery; B, D to Grand St. Tues 10pm–4am, Wed–Sat 7pm–4am. MAP P.63, POCKET MAP E20

This former erotic massage parlour (Xie He Health) has been reborn as an exceptionally cool bar and club, with the original tiled sauna rooms converted to cosy booths.

HAPPY ENDING LOUNGE

Live music

ARLENE'S GROCERY

95 Stanton St between Ludlow and Orchard sts. Subway F to Lower East Side-Second Ave ☎ 212/358-1633, 🌐 www.arlenesgrocery.net. Daily 5pm–2am. MAP P.63, POCKET MAP E19

This intimate venue hosts free gigs by local indie talent every night. Monday (free) is "Rock and Roll Karaoke" night, when you can wail along (with a live band) to your favourite songs. Tues–Sun cover $8–10.

THE BOWERY BALLROOM

6 Delancey St at the Bowery. Subway J, Z to Bowery; B, D to Grand St ☎ 212/533-2111, 🌐 www.boweryballroom.com. Daily from 7pm. MAP P.63, POCKET MAP E19

Great acoustics make this a favourite local venue to see well-known indie rock bands. Shows cost $15–55. Pay in cash at the *Mercury Lounge* box office (see opposite), at the door, or through Ticketweb.

CAKE SHOP

152 Ludlow St between Rivington and Stanton sts. Subway F to Delancey St; J, M, Z to Essex St ☎ 212/253-0036 🌐 www.cake-shop.com. Sun–Thurs 9am–2am, Fri & Sat 9am–4am. MAP P.63, POCKET MAP E19

This unassuming coffee shop and record store becomes a cutting-edge venue for indie rock most evenings – cover ranges from $7–10.

THE LIVING ROOM

154 Ludlow St between Stanton and Rivington sts. Subway F to Delancey St; J, M, Z to Essex St ☎ 212/533-7235, 🌐 www.livingroomny.com. Sun–Thurs 6pm–2am, Fri & Sat 6pm–4am. MAP P.63, POCKET MAP E19

Comfortable couches and a friendly bar make for a relaxed setting in which to hear local, low-key folk and acoustic rock. Shows are usually free ($10 donation), with a one-drink minimum.

MERCURY LOUNGE

MERCURY LOUNGE

217 E Houston St between Ludlow and Essex sts. Subway F to Lower East Side-Second Ave ☎ 212/260-4700, 🌐 www.mercuryloungenyc.com. Daily shows from 7pm. MAP P.63, POCKET MAP E19

The dark, medium-sized space showcases local, national and international pop and rock acts. Events cost around $10–25. Pay in cash at the box office, at the door or via Ticketweb.

PIANOS

158 Ludlow St at Rivington St. Subway F to Delancey St; J, M, Z to Essex St ☎ 212/505-3733, 🌐 www.pianosnyc.com. Daily 3pm–4am. MAP P.63, POCKET MAP E19

This converted piano factory hosts an endless roster of mostly rock bands (expect four choices nightly) in the back room ($8–10) and excellent DJs from 10pm.

ROCKWOOD MUSIC HALL

196 Allen St between Houston and Stanton sts. Subway F to Lower East Side-Second Ave ☎ 212/614-2494, 🌐 rockwoodmusichall.com. Mon–Fri 6pm–4am, Sat & Sun 3pm–4am. MAP P.63, POCKET MAP E19

Come early: though there are no bad seats in the house, seven nights of live music draw locals to this tiny space.

The East Village

Once a solidly working-class refuge of immigrants, the East Village, ranging east of Broadway to Avenue D between Houston and 14th streets, became home to New York's nonconformist intelligentsia in the early part of the twentieth century; in the 1950s, it was one of the main haunts of the Beat poets – Kerouac, Burroughs, Ginsberg. By the 1980s it was home to radical artists, including Keith Haring, Jeff Koons and Jean-Michel Basquiat, while gay icon Quentin Crisp lived on East 3rd St from 1981 till his death in 1999. During the Nineties, escalating rents forced many people out, and the East Village is no longer the hotbed of dissidence and artistry that it once was. Nevertheless, it remains one of downtown Manhattan's most vibrant neighbourhoods, with boutiques, thrift stores, record shops, bars and restaurants, populated by old-world Ukrainians, students, punks, artists and burn-outs.

ASTOR PLACE

Subway N, R to 8th St; #6 to Astor Place. MAP P.70–71, POCKET MAP D18

Astor Place marks the western fringe of the East Village, named after real-estate tycoon John Jacob Astor. Infamous for his greed, Astor was the wealthiest person in the US at the time of his death in 1848 (worth $115bn in modern terms). Beneath the replicated old-fashioned kiosk of the Astor Place subway station, the platform walls sport reliefs of beavers, recalling Astor's first big killings – in the fur trade. The teen hangout here is the balancing black steel cube *Alamo* (1967) by Tony Rosenthal, which dominates the centre of the intersection. In the 1830s, **Lafayette St**, which runs south from Astor Place, was home to the city's wealthiest residents; **Colonnade Row**, a strip of four 1833 Greek-Revival houses with Corinthian columns, is all that remains.

The stocky brownstone-and-brick building across Lafayette was once the **Astor Library**. Built with a bequest from Astor between 1853 and 1881, it was the first public library in New York. It became the Public Theater in 1967. **Astor Place Opera House** was erected on the corner of Astor Place and East 8th Street in 1847, infamous as the site of the Astor Place Riot two years later. Supporters of local stage-star Edwin Forrest tried to stop the performance of English Shakespearean actor William Macready, and in the resulting clashes 22 people died. The theatre closed in 1850.

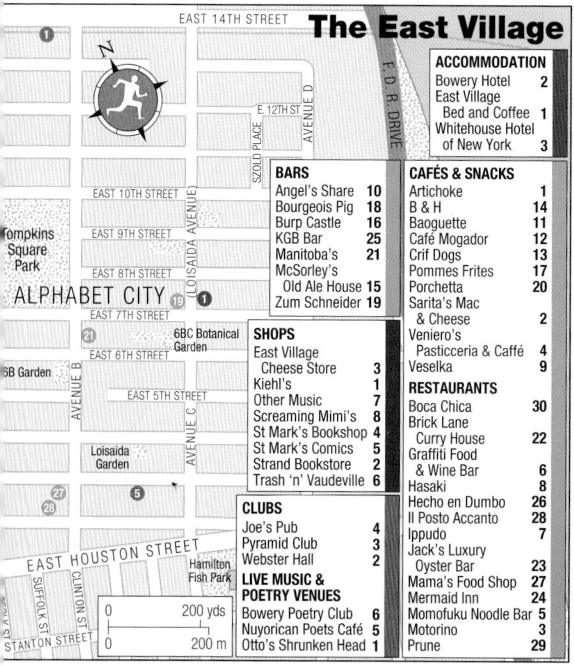

GRACE CHURCH

802 Broadway at E 10th St. Subway N, R to 8th St ☎ 212/254-2000, www.gracechurchnyc.org. Daily noon–5pm. Free. MAP P.70–71, POCKET MAP D17

The lacy marble of **Grace Church** was built and designed in 1846 by James Renwick (of St Patrick's Cathedral fame) in a delicate Neo-Gothic style. Dark and aisled, with a flattened, web-vaulted ceiling, it was something of a society church in its day. Nowadays it is one of the city's most secretive escapes, and frequently offers shelter to the less fortunate.

MERCHANT'S HOUSE MUSEUM

29 E 4th St between Lafayette St and the Bowery. Subway B, D, F, M to Broadway-Lafayette; N, R to 8th St; #6 to Astor Place ☎ 212/777-1089, www.merchantshouse.com. Thurs–Mon noon–5pm. $10. MAP P.70–71, POCKET MAP D18

Constructed in 1832, this elegant Federal-style rowhouse offers a rare and intimate glimpse of domestic life in New York during the 1850s. The house was purchased by Seabury Tredwell in 1835, a successful metal merchant, when the area was an up-and-coming suburb for the middle class. Remarkably, much of the mid-nineteenth-century interior remains in pristine condition, largely thanks to Seabury's daughter Gertrude, who lived here until 1933 – it was preserved as a museum three years later. Highlights include furniture fashioned by New York's best cabinetmakers, the mahogany four-poster beds, and the tiny brass bells in the basement, used to summon the servants.

GRACE CHURCH

COOPER UNION – FOUNDATION BUILDING

7 E 7th St, Cooper Square, between Third and Fourth aves. Subway N, R to 8th St; #6 to Astor Place ☎ 212/353-4100, www.cooper.edu. MAP P.70–71, POCKET MAP D18

Erected in 1859 by wealthy industrialist Peter Cooper (1791–1883) as a college for the poor, the **Foundation Building of Cooper Union** is best known as the place where, in 1860, Abraham Lincoln wowed an audience of top New Yorkers with his so-called "right makes might" speech, in which he boldly criticized the pro-slavery policies of the Southern states – an event that helped propel him to the White House later that year. In 1909 it was also the site of the first open meeting of the NAACP (National Association for the Advancement of Colored People), chaired by W.E.B. Du Bois. Today, Cooper Union is a prestigious art, engineering and architecture school, whose nineteenth-century glory is evoked with a statue of the benevolent Cooper by Augustus Saint-Gaudens just in front of the hall. From the entrance hall the guards normally allow you to walk downstairs to the Great Hall, where historical exhibits are displayed in the gallery outside.

ST MARK'S PLACE

Subway N, R to 8th St; #6 to Astor Place. MAP P.70–71, POCKET MAP D18–E18

The East Village's main drag gets a name, not a number (it could have been called East 8th Street). **St Mark's Place** stretches east from Cooper Union to Tompkins Square Park. Between Third Avenue and Avenue A it's lined with souvenir stalls, punk and hippie-chic clothing shops and newly installed chain restaurants, signalling the end of the gritty atmosphere that had dominated this thoroughfare for years.

ST MARK'S CHURCH IN-THE-BOWERY

131 E 10th St at Second Ave. Subway N, R to 8th St; #6 to Astor Place ⓣ 212/674-6377, ⓦ www.stmarksbowery.org. MAP P.70–71, POCKET MAP D17

In 1660, New Amsterdam Director-General Peter Stuyvesant built a small chapel here close to his farm, and was buried inside in 1672 (his tombstone is now set into the outer walls). The box-like Episcopalian house of worship that currently occupies this space was completed in 1799 over his tomb, and sports a Neoclassical portico that was added fifty years later. The church is still used for services and is normally locked – walk up to the office on the second floor (side door) and someone will let you in to see the vivid stained-glass windows. The church was home to Beat poetry readings in the 1950s, and in the 1960s the **St Mark's Poetry Project** (ⓦ www.poetryproject.com) was founded here to ignite artistic and social change. It remains an important cultural rendezvous, with poetry readings Monday, Wednesday

RUSSIAN & TURKISH BATHS

and Friday evenings at 8pm, dance performances by the Danspace Project (ⓦ www.danspaceproject.org) and plays from the Incubator Arts Project (ⓦ www.incubatorarts.org).

UKRAINIAN MUSEUM

222 E 6th St between Second and Third aves. Subway N,R to 8th St; #6 to Astor Place ⓣ 212/228-0110, ⓦ www.ukrainianmuseum.org. Wed–Sun 11.30am–5pm. $8. MAP P.70–71, POCKET MAP D18

Dedicated to chronicling the history of the Ukrainian immigrant community. The varied collection contains ethnic items such as Ukrainian costumes and examples of the country's famous painted eggs; lectures are also held here.

RUSSIAN & TURKISH BATHS

268 E 10th St between First Ave and Ave A. Subway L to First Ave ⓣ 212/674-9250, ⓦ www.russianturkishbaths.com. Mon, Tues, Thurs, Fri noon–10pm, Wed 10am–10pm, Sat 9am–10pm, Sun 8am–10pm. $35. MAP P.70–71, POCKET MAP E17

A neighbourhood landmark that's still going strong, with a an ice-cold pool, Russian sauna (filled with 20,000lbs of red-hot rocks), a modern cherry-wood sauna and a Turkish steam room, as well as massage rooms and a restaurant. Free soap, towel, robe and slippers. Check the website for details of mixed and single-sex sessions.

TOMPKINS SQUARE PARK

Subway L to First Ave; N, R to 8th St; #6 to Astor Place. MAP P.70–71, POCKET MAP F17–F18

Fringed by avenues A and B and East 7th and East 10th streets, **Tompkins Square Park** was one of the city's great centres for political protest and homes of radical thought. In the Sixties, regular demonstrations were organized here, and during the 1980s, the park was more or less a shantytown until the homeless were kicked out in 1991. Today it has a playground, dog run and a summer jazz festival. The famous saxophonist and composer Charlie "Bird" Parker lived at 151 Avenue B, a simple whitewashed 1849 house with a Gothic doorway (closed to the public). The Bird lived here from 1950 until 1954, when he died of a pneumonia-related haemorrhage.

ALPHABET CITY

Subway L to First Ave; N, R to 8th St; #6 to Astor Place. MAP P.70–71, POCKET MAP F18

Named after the avenues known as A–D, where the island bulges east beyond the city's grid structure, **Alphabet City** was not long ago a notoriously unsafe patch, with burnt-out buildings that were well-known dens for the brisk heroin trade. Now it's one of the most dramatically revitalized areas of Manhattan: crime is down, many of the vacant lots have been made into community gardens, and the streets have become the haunt of moneyed twenty-somethings and daring tourist youth. Only **Avenue D** might still give you some pause; the other avenues have some of the coolest bars, cafés and stores in the city.

COMMUNITY GARDENS

Subway L to First Ave; N, R to 8th St; #6 to Astor Place. MAP P.70–71, POCKET MAP F18

In the 1970s, huge parts of the East Village burned to the ground after cuts in the city's fire-fighting budget closed many of the local firehouses. Green Thumb, founded in 1978, helped locals transform vacant lots into vibrant green spaces, turning the rubble-filled messes into some of the prettiest and most verdant spaces in lower Manhattan. Of particular note is the **East 6th Street and Avenue B** affair, overgrown with wildflowers, vegetables, trees and roses. Other gardens include the very serene **6 B/C Botanical Garden** on East 6th Street between B and C and **Loisaida Garden** on East 4th Street between B and C.

TOMPKINS SQUARE PARK

Shops

EAST VILLAGE CHEESE STORE

40 Third Ave between E 9th and 10th sts. Subway R to 8th St; #6 to Astor Place. Daily 8.30am–6.30pm. MAP P.70–71, POCKET MAP D17

The city's most affordable source for cheese; its front-of-the-store bins sell pungent blocks and wedges starting at just a few dollars (cash only).

KIEHL'S

109 Third Ave at E 13th St. Subway L to Third Ave St. Mon–Sat 10am–8pm, Sun 11am–6pm. MAP P.70–71, POCKET MAP E17

An exclusive 150-year-old pharmacy that sells its own range of natural ingredient-based classic creams, soaps and oils.

OTHER MUSIC

15 E 4th St between Broadway and Lafayette St. Subway #6 to Astor Place. Mon–Fri 11am–9pm, Sat noon–8pm, Sun noon–7pm. MAP P.70–71, POCKET MAP D18

The city's most engaging and curious indie-rock and avant-garde collection. Records here are divided into categories like "In", "Out", and "Then".

SCREAMING MIMI'S

382 Lafayette St at E 4th St. Subway #6 to Bleecker St or Astor Place. Mon–Sat noon–8pm, Sun 1–7pm. MAP P.70–71, POCKET MAP D18

One of the most established vintage stores in Manhattan, Screaming Mimi's offers reasonably priced clothes, bags, shoes and housewares.

ST MARK'S BOOKSHOP

31 Third Ave at E 9th St. Subway #6 to Astor Place. Mon–Sat 10am–midnight, Sun 11am–midnight. MAP P.70–71, POCKET MAP D18

Founded in 1977 to serve the erudite community of NYU, these bookworms specialize in

ST MARK'S BOOKSHOP

cultural theory, graphic design, poetry, film and foreign press.

ST MARK'S COMICS

11 St Mark's Place between Second and Third aves. Subway #6 to Astor Place. Mon & Tues 10am–11pm, Wed 9am–1am, Thurs–Sat 10am–1am, Sun 11am–11pm. MAP P.70–71, POCKET MAP D18

Pilgrimage site for comic, manga and graphic novel fans from all over the world, with plenty of rare memorabilia.

STRAND BOOKSTORE

828 Broadway at E 12th St. Subway N, R, Q, L, #4, #5, #6 to Union Square. Mon–Sat 9.30am–10.30pm, Sun 11am–10.30pm. MAP P.70–71, POCKET MAP D17

With about eighteen miles of books and a stock of more than 2.5 million, this is the largest book operation in the city.

TRASH 'N' VAUDEVILLE

4 St Mark's Place between Second and Third aves. Subway #6 to Astor Place. Mon–Thurs noon–8pm, Fri 11.30am–8.30pm, Sat 11.30am–9pm. Sun 1–7.30pm. MAP P.70–71, POCKET MAP D18

Actually two shops, on top of each other, this has been a Goth and punk mecca since the 1970s. Great clothes, new and "antique", in the true East Village spirit.

Cafés and snacks

ARTICHOKE

328 E 14th St between First and Second aves. Subway L to First Ave. Daily 11am–5am. MAP P.70–71, POCKET MAP E17

Fabulous late-night pizza slices to take away in the early hours, with just four choices: sumptuous cheese-laden Sicilian ($4), Margherita ($4), crab ($4.50) or the trademark artichoke-spinach pie, topped with a super-creamy sauce ($4.50).

B & H

127 Second Ave between E 7th St and St Mark's Place. Subway #6 to Astor Place. Daily 7am–11pm. MAP P.70–71, POCKET MAP E18

Good veggie choice, this tiny luncheonette serves home-made soup, *challah* and *latkes*. You can also create your own juice combination to stay or go.

BAOGUETTE

37 St Mark's Place at Second Ave. Subway #6 to Astor Place. Sun–Thurs 11am–midnight, Fri & Sat 11am–2am. MAP P.70–71, POCKET MAP E18

Tiny modern takeaway specializing in richly flavoured Vietnamese *banh mi* sandwiches for $6.50 – they also do a great spicy catfish version ($7.50), fried noodles and rice plates (from $9).

CAFÉ MOGADOR

101 St Mark's Place between First Ave and Ave A. Subway #6 to Astor Place. Sun–Thurs 9am–1am, Fri & Sat 9am–2pm. MAP P.70–71, POCKET MAP E18

Young hipster-types frequent this romantic, Moroccan-themed mainstay. Expect crowds and stalled service, but the food is more than worth the wait. Try the *charmoulla* with either chicken or lamb. The brunch (Sat–Sun 9am–4pm) is especially good, with a choice of delicate mains such as *eggs champignon* (eggs, mushrooms and cheese) served with orange juice, coffee or tea for just $12.

CRIF DOGS

113 St Mark's Place between First Ave and Ave A. Subway #6 to Astor Place. Sun–Thurs noon–2am, Fri & Sat noon–4am. MAP P.70–71, POCKET MAP E18

Hot-dog aficionados swear by these deep-fried, shiny wieners bursting with flavour (from $2.75), enjoyed Philly-steak style, smothered in cheese, or topped with avocado and bacon.

POMMES FRITES

123 Second Ave between E 7th St and St Mark's Place. Subway #6 to Astor Place. Sun–Thurs 11.30am–1am, Fri & Sat 11.30am–3.30am. MAP P.70–71, POCKET MAP E18

Arguably the best fries in the city, with gooey, Belgian-style toppings available; try the rosemary garlic mayo or curry ketchup ($4.50–7.75).

VENIERO'S

PORCHETTA

110 E 7th St, between First Ave and Ave A. Subway #6 to Astor Place. Sun–Thurs 11.30am–10pm, Fri & Sat 11.30am–11pm. MAP P.70–71, POCKET MAP E18

This tiny takeaway shop (with a few stools and counter inside) has developed a loyal following for its luscious Tuscan *porchetta* sandwiches ($10), thick slabs of roasted and seasoned pork in a ciabatta roll.

SARITA'S MAC & CHEESE

345 E 12th St between Second and First aves. Subway L to First Ave. Daily 11am–11pm. MAP P.70–71, POCKET MAP E17

Indulge your macaroni and cheese cravings at this homey joint, with ten creative varieties on offer, blending cheddar, gruyère, brie and goat's cheese with herbs and meats. Pick your portion sizes: nosh, major munch or mongo ($4.75–19).

VENIERO'S PASTICCERIA & CAFFÉ

342 E 11th St between First and Second aves. Subway L to First Ave; #6 to Astor Place. Sun–Thurs 8am–midnight, Fri & Sat 8am–1am. MAP P.70–71, POCKET MAP E17

A beloved East Village institution, tempting the neighbourhood with heavenly cheesecake ($4.50), tiramisu ($5.25) and Italian pastries since 1894 – the almond torte ($4.75) is their most famous snack. Sit inside the old-world marble-floor café, or takeaway.

VESELKA

144 Second Ave, corner of E 9th St. Subway #6 to Astor Place. Daily 24hr. MAP P.70–71, POCKET MAP E17

This popular Ukrainian diner has been an East Village institution since the 1960s, offering fine home-made borscht from $4.75, *kielbasa* sausage ($15.95), *pierogi* ($6.95) and great burgers.

VESELKA

Restaurants

BOCA CHICA

13 First Ave at E 1st St. Subway F to Lower East Side-Second Ave. Mon–Thurs 5–11pm, Fri & Sat 5–11.30pm, Sun noon–11pm. MAP P.70–71, POCKET MAP E19

This is authentic Latin American food, piled high and washed down with black beer and tropical drinks. Everything is good, but the shrimp dishes are exceptional.

BRICK LANE CURRY HOUSE

306 E 6th St between First and Second aves. Subway #6 to Astor Place ☎ 212/979-8787. Sun–Thurs noon–11pm, Fri & Sat noon–1am. MAP P.70–71, POCKET MAP E18

Hands-down the best Indian in the East Village thanks to its expanded selection of traditional favourites ($14–20).

GRAFFITI FOOD & WINE BAR

244 E 10th St between First and Second aves. Subway L to First Ave; #6 to Astor Place ☎ 212/677-0695. Tues & Sun 5.30–10.30pm, Wed–Sat 5.30–11.45pm. MAP P.70–71, POCKET MAP E17

Pastry chef Jehangir Mehta cooks up a fusion of Chinese, American and Indian flavours in this artsy space, with four tables and courses costing $7–15, including chili pork dumplings and foie gras raspberry crostini.

HASAKI

210 E 9th St at Stuyvesant St. Subway #6 to Astor Place ☎212/473-3327. Mon & Tues 5.30–11pm, Wed–Fri noon–3pm & 5.30–11pm, Sat & Sun 1–4pm & 5.30–11.30pm. MAP P.70–71, POCKET MAP D17

Some of the best sushi in the city is served at this popular but mellow downstairs cubbyhole. Sit at the bar and the chefs will try to tempt you with a variety of improvised dishes (five pieces from $23).

HECHO EN DUMBO

354 Bowery between Great Jones and E 4th sts. Subway #6 to Astor Place ☎212/937-4245. Mon–Thurs 11.30am–4pm & 5.30pm–midnight, Fri & Sat 11.30am–4pm & 5.30pm–2am, Sun 11.30am–4pm & 5.30–11pm. MAP P.70–71, POCKET MAP D18

This authentic Mexican diner migrated across the East River in 2010, but it still knocks out wonderful small plates ($8–12) and Mexico City contemporary cuisine such as house-cured beef, lamb shank confit and an innovative selection of tacos and burritos ($9–13).

IL POSTO ACCANTO

190 E 2nd Street between aves A and B. Subway F to Lower East Side-Second Ave ☎212/228-3562. Mon 5.30pm–3am, Tues–Fri noon–3am, Sat & Sun noon–3.30pm & 5.30pm–3am. MAP P.70–71, POCKET MAP E18

Nab a spot at a high wooden table at this small, intimate wine bar and restaurant serving a vast array of Italian reds by the glass. You can easily make a meal from the excellent small plates of pasta ($12–15), panini ($8) and the like. Can get crowded, like its popular parent restaurant next door (*Il Bagatto*).

IPPUDO

65 Fourth Ave, between E 9th and E 10th sts. Subway #6 to Astor Place ☎212/388-0088. Mon–Fri 11am–3.30pm & 5–11.30pm, Sat & Sun 11am–12.30am. MAP P.70–71, POCKET MAP D17

The first overseas outpost of Fukuoka-based "ramen king" Shigemi Kawahara, this popular Japanese ramen shop offers steaming bowls of classic *tonkotsu*-style noodles for $15, as well as tasty pork buns.

JACK'S LUXURY OYSTER BAR

101 Second Ave at 6th St. Subway #6 to Astor Place ☎212/979-1012. Mon–Thurs 6–11pm, Fri & Sat 6pm–midnight. MAP P.70–71, POCKET MAP E18

Deconstructed dishes, such as savoury octopus spread and aphrodisiacal oyster plates, and a 24-seat dining room, make eating here an intimate and full-on romantic experience.

MAMA'S FOOD SHOP

200 E 3rd St between aves A and B. Subway F to Lower East Side-Second Ave ☎212/777-4425. Tues–Fri 4–11pm, Sat & Sun 4–11pm. MAP P.70–71, POCKET MAP F18

Whopping portions of tasty and cheap home-cooked soul food. Hearty plates of fried chicken and pan-seared tilapia start at $12.50 with one side (think sweet potatoes and mac and cheese). Other specialties; include home-made meatloaf and roasted vegetables.

MAMA'S

IL POSTO ACCANTO

MERMAID INN

96 Second Ave between E 5th and 6th sts. Subway #6 to Astor Place ☎212/674-5870. Mon 5.30–10pm, Tues–Thurs 5.30–11pm, Fri & Sat 5–11.30pm, Sun 5–10pm. MAP P.70–71, POCKET MAP E18

Serious seafood restaurant serving simple and fresh dishes in a Maine boathouse atmosphere. There's an excellent raw bar, and specials change daily depending on the catch; highlights include the littleneck clams ($10) and lobster sandwich ($26).

MOMOFUKU NOODLE BAR

171 First Ave between E 10th and E 11th sts. Subway L to First Ave; #6 to Astor Place ☎212/777-7773. Mon–Thurs & Sun noon–4.30pm & 5.30–11pm, Fri & Sat noon–4.30pm & 5.30pm–2am. MAP P.70–71, POCKET MAP E17

Celebrated chef David Chang's first restaurant, where his simplest creations are still the best: silky steamed pork buns with hoisin sauce and pickled cucumbers ($10), or steaming bowls of chicken and pork ramen noodles ($16). If you're in the neighbourhood, it's worth checking out Chang's other ventures: the *Momofuku Bakery & Milk Bar* (251 E 13th St, at Second Ave; daily 9am–midnight) serves sweet treats.

MOTORINO

349 E 12th St, near First Ave. Subway L to First Ave ☎212/777-2644. Mon–Thurs & Sun 11am–midnight, Fri & Sat 11am–1am. MAP P.70–71, POCKET MAP E17

Some of the best pizza in the city, with a tongue-tingling Stracciatella (basil, olive oil and sea salt) and a cherry stone clam masterpiece.

PRUNE

54 E 1st St between First and Second aves. Subway F to Lower East Side-Second Ave ☎212/677-6221. Mon–Fri 11.30am–3.30pm & 5.30–11pm, Sat & Sun 10am-3.30pm & 5.30–11pm. MAP P.70–71, POCKET MAP E19

Cramped, yet adventurous and full of surprises, this modern American bistro delivers one of the city's most exciting dining experiences, serving dishes such as sweetbreads wrapped in bacon, seared sea bass with Berber spices, and buttermilk ice cream with pistachio puff pastry. A choice of over ten Bloody Marys gives weekend brunch a bit of a kick.

Bars

ANGEL'S SHARE

8 Stuyvesant St between E 9th St and Third Ave. Subway #6 to Astor Place. Sun–Wed, 6pm–2.30am, Thurs 6pm–2am, Fri & Sat 6pm–1.30am. MAP P.70–71, POCKET MAP D17
This serene, Japanese-style haven is a great date spot and the cocktails are some of the best in the city. It can be hard to find, though: walk through the *Yokocho* restaurant, up the stairs.

ANGEL'S SHARE

BOURGEOIS PIG

111 E 7th St between First Ave and Ave A. Subway L to First Ave; #6 to Astor Place. Sun–Thurs 5pm–2am, Fri & Sat 5pm–3am. MAP P.70–71, POCKET MAP E18
The decadent Versailles theme at this funky wine bar, replete with wall-size mirrors and crimson satin couches, is backed by an extensive cocktail menu (from $12).

BURP CASTLE

41 E 7th St between Second and Third aves. Subway #6 to Astor Place. Mon–Fri 5pm–4am, Sat & Sun 4pm–4am. MAP P.70–71, POCKET MAP D18
The bartenders wear monks' habits, choral music is piped in, and you are encouraged to speak in tones below a whisper. Oh, and there are over 550 different types of beer.

KGB BAR

85 E 4th St at Second Ave. Subway F to Lower East Side-Second Ave; #6 to Astor Place. Daily 7pm–4am. MAP P.70–71, POCKET MAP E18
A dark bar on the second floor, which was the Ukrainian Labor Home social club in the 1950s, but is better known now for its marquee literary readings.

MANITOBA'S

99 Ave B between E 6th and 7th sts. Subway L to First Ave; #6 to Astor Place. Daily 2pm–4am. MAP P.70–71, POCKET MAP F19
Run by Dick Manitoba, lead singer of the punk group The Dictators, the kickin' jukebox and rough-and-tumble vibe at this spot make it a drinkers' favourite.

MCSORLEY'S OLD ALE HOUSE

15 E 7th St between Second and Third aves. Subway #6 to Astor Place. Mon–Sat 11am–1am, Sun 1pm–1am. MAP P.70–71, POCKET MAP D18
Yes, it's often full of tourists and NYU students, but you'll be drinking in history at this landmark bar that opened in 1854 – it's the oldest pub in the city. Today, it only pours its own ale – light or dark.

ZUM SCHNEIDER

107 Ave C at E 7th St. Subway L to 1st Ave; #6 to Astor Place. Mon–Thurs 5pm–1am, Fri 4pm–4am, Sat 1pm–4am, Sun 1pm–1am. MAP P.70–71, POCKET MAP F18
A German beer hall (and indoor garden) with a mega-list of brews from the Fatherland, and wursts too.

Clubs

JOE'S PUB

Public Theater, 425 Lafayette St between Astor Place and E 4th St. Subway #6 to Astor Place ☎ 212/539-8770. MAP P.70–71, POCKET MAP D18
The word "pub" is a misnomer

for this swanky nightspot that features a vast array of musical, cabaret and dramatic performances. Shows nightly at 7.30pm, 9.30pm and 11pm (cover $6–50).

PYRAMID CLUB

101 Ave A between E 6th and 7th sts. Subway L to First Ave; #6 to Astor Place ☎212/228-4888. Tues & Thurs–Sat 8pm–4am, Sun 9pm–1am. MAP P.70–71, POCKET MAP E18

This small club has been an East Village standby for years. Saturday is New Wave and Britpop ($6), Tuesday is an open-mike music competition ($10), but it's the insanely popular 1980s Dance Party on Thursday that is not to be missed ($7).

WEBSTER HALL

125 E 11th St, between Third and Fourth aves. Subway N, Q, R, L, #4, #5, #6 to Union Square ☎212/353-1600, www.websterhall.com. Club nights Thurs–Sat 10pm–4am. Cover $10–35. MAP P.70–71, POCKET MAP D17

Four floors, a hip, young crowd and a big electro mash-up on Fridays and Saturdays make this a solid bet for a good night out.

Live music and poetry venues

BOWERY POETRY CLUB

308 Bowery at Bleeker St. Subway F to Lower East Side-Second Ave; #6 to Bleecker St ☎212/614-0505, www.bowerypoetry.com. Mon–Fri 4pm–4am, Sat & Sun noon–4am. MAP P.70–71, POCKET MAP D19

Terrifically welcoming lit joint featuring Urbana Poetry Slam every Tuesday night at 7pm ($7); an event dedicated to showcasing the city's most innovative and current voices in poetry.

ZUM SCHNEIDER

NUYORICAN POETS CAFÉ

236 E 3rd St between aves B and C. Subway F to Lower East Side-Second Ave ☎212/505-8183, www.nuyorican.org. Shows Tues–Sun from 7pm. MAP P.70–71, POCKET MAP F18

The godfather of all slam venues often features stars of the poetry world who pop in unannounced. SlamOpen on Wednesdays 9pm (except the first Wednesday of every month) and the Friday Night Slam (10pm) cost $7 and $10 respectively.

OTTO'S SHRUNKEN HEAD

538 E 14th St, between aves A and B. Subway L to First Ave ☎212/228-2240, www.ottosshrunkenhead.com. Mon–Fri noon–4am, Sat & Sun 4pm–4am. MAP P.70–71, POCKET MAP F17

This East Village joint is hard to pigeonhole; a Tiki bar that hosts live indie and punk rock bands, as well as some of the most popular club nights on the island. Weekends also see a host of rock/punk parties. Usually no cover.

The West Village

For many visitors, the West Village, Greenwich Village – or simply "the Village" – is the most-loved neighbourhood in New York. It sports refined Federal and Greek Revival townhouses and a busy late-night streetlife, while cosy restaurants, bars and cafés clutter every corner – many of the attractions that first brought bohemians here around the start of World War I. The area proved fertile ground for struggling artists and intellectuals, and the neighbourhood's clubs and off-Broadway theatres came to define Village life, laying the path for rebellious, countercultural groups and musicians in the 1960s; John Coltrane, Bob Dylan and Jimmy Hendrix all built their early careers here. Today, the central part of the Village is dominated by the sprawling New York University campus, adding a youthful edge to this fashionable, historic and increasingly expensive corner of Manhattan.

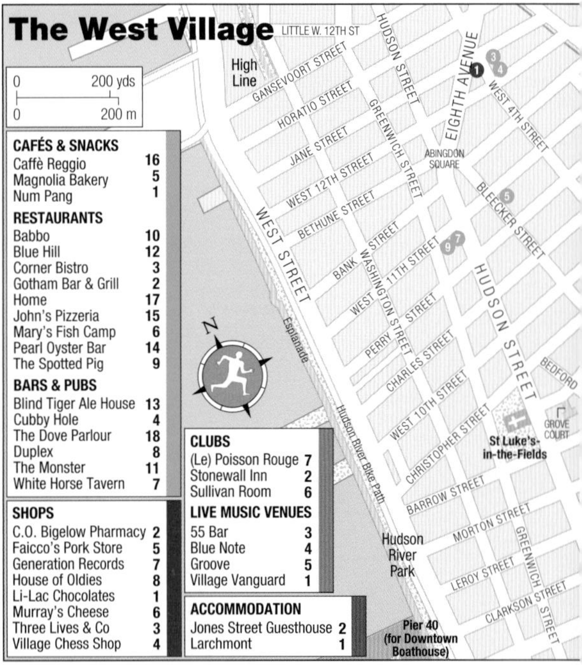

WASHINGTON SQUARE PARK

Subway A, B, C, D, E, F to West 4th St; N, R to 8th St. MAP P.82–83, POCKET MAP C18

The natural centre of the Village is **Washington Square Park**. Memorialized in Henry James's 1880 novel *Washington Square*, the city completed an extensive renovation of the park in 2012, though only the row of elegant Greek Revival mansions on its northern edge – the "solid, honourable dwellings" that James described – remind visitors of the area's more illustrious past.

Today, all these buildings belong to New York University (NYU). The most imposing monument in the park is Stanford White's **Washington Arch**, built in 1892 to commemorate the centenary of George Washington's presidential inauguration.

PLAYING CHESS IN WASHINGTON SQUARE PARK

During the spring and summer months, the square becomes a combination of a running track, performance venue, giant chess tournament and social club; boiling over with life as skateboards flip, dogs run and guitar notes crash through the urgent cries of performers calling for the crowd's attention.

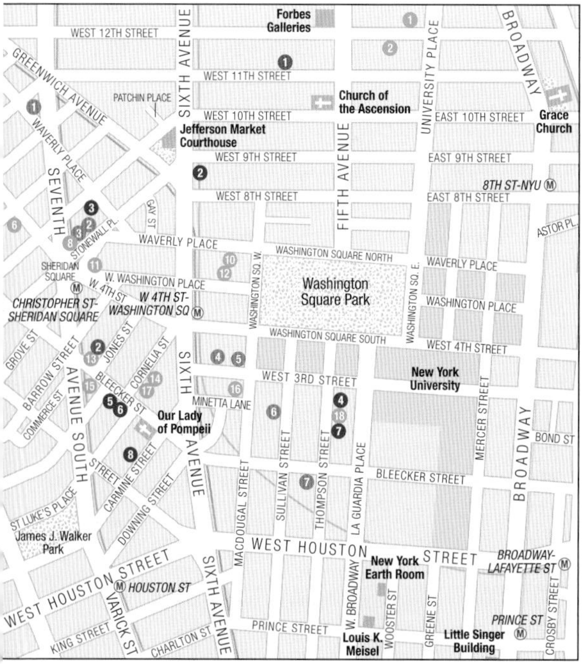

CHURCH OF THE ASCENSION

Fifth Ave and W 10th St. Subway N, Q, R, L, #4, #5, #6 to Union Square; F, L at 14th St ☎ 212/254-8620, 🌐 www.ascensionnyc.org. Mon–Sat noon–1pm, Sun services only at 9am, 11am, 6pm. Free. MAP P.82–83, POCKET MAP C17

A small, restored structure originally built in 1841 by Richard Upjohn (architect of Trinity Church), the **Church of the Ascension** was later redecorated by Stanford White. Duck inside to see the gracefully toned La Farge altar painting and some fine stained glass on view.

THE FORBES GALLERIES

62 Fifth Ave at W 12th St. Subway N, Q, R, L, #4, #5, #6 to Union Square; F, L at 14th St ☎ 212/206-5548, 🌐 www.forbesgalleries.com. Tues, Wed, Fri & Sat 10am–4pm. Free. MAP P.82–83, POCKET MAP C17

This museum contains a rather whimsical collection of treasures assembled by the Forbes family, owners of the publishing empire. The 10,000-strong host of tin soldiers, over 500 model boats and early Monopoly boards, will appeal primarily to aficionados and kids, though the galleries also hold temporary exhibitions of a diverse range of artwork, from cartoons to rare Art Deco gems.

JEFFERSON MARKET COURTHOUSE AND PATCHIN PLACE

425 Sixth Ave at W 10th St. Subway A, B, C, D, E, F, M to West 4th St; #1 to Christopher St-Sheridan Sq ☎ 212/243-4334. Library open Mon, Wed 9am–8pm, Tues, Thurs 9am–7pm, Fri, Sat 10am–5pm. MAP P.82–83, POCKET MAP B17

Known for its unmistakable clock tower, the nineteenth-century **Jefferson Market Courthouse** is an imposing High Victorian–style edifice, complete with gargoyles, which first served as an indoor market but went on to be a firehouse, jail, and finally a women's detention centre before enjoying its current incarnation as a public library. Adjacent to it and opening onto West 10th Street, **Patchin Place** (closed to the public) is a tiny mews constructed in 1848, whose neat rowhouses were home to the reclusive Djuna Barnes for more than forty years. Patchin Place has also been home to e.e. cummings, Marlon Brando, Ezra Pound and Eugene O'Neill.

BLEECKER STREET

Subway A, B, C, D, E, F to West 4th St; #1 to Christopher St-Sheridan Sq. MAP P.82–83, POCKET MAP B18

Cutting across from the Bowery to Hudson Street,

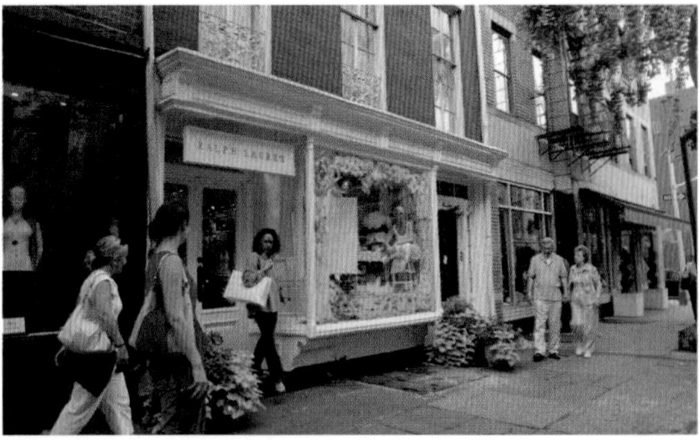

BLEECKER STREET

CHRISTOPHER STREET

Bleecker Street, with its touristy concentration of shops, bars, and restaurants, is to some extent the Main Street of the Village. It has all the best reasons you come to this part of town: all-day cafés, late-night bars, cheap record stores, traditional bakeries and food shops, and the occasional good restaurant or pizzeria.

At Sixth Avenue, the Italian-Renaissance style **Our Lady of Pompeii Church**, built in 1929, hints at the area's Italian past; *Faicco's* butchers and *Rocco's* (best known for its crunchy nut *cannoli*) are still here, as well as celebrated deli *Murray's Cheese* (see p.87). Bob Dylan lived for a time at 161 West 4th St, and the cover of his 1963 *Freewheelin'* album was shot a few paces away on Jones St, just off Bleecker.

SHERIDAN SQUARE AND CHRISTOPHER PARK

Subway #1 to Christopher St-Sheridan Sq. MAP P.82–83, POCKET MAP B18

Confusingly, **Christopher Park** holds a pompous-looking statue of Civil War cavalry commander General Sheridan, though **Sheridan Square** is actually the next space down, where West 4th Street meets Washington Place. Historically, the area is better known, however, as the scene of one of the worst and bloodiest of New York's Draft Riots, when a marauding mob assembled here in 1863 and attacked members of the black community. Violence also erupted here in 1969 during the Stonewall Riots. The event is commemorated by George Segal's **Gay Liberation Monument**, unveiled in 1992. Further north, 66 Perry St, between Bleecker and West 4th Street, was used as the exterior of Carrie's apartment in *Sex and the City*, while there's almost always a line of people waiting outside lauded *Magnolia Bakery* at Bleecker and West 11th St (see p.88). The historic *White Horse Tavern*, over at West 11th Street and Hudson, is where legend claims Dylan Thomas had his last drink (see p.90).

CHRISTOPHER STREET

Subway #1 to Christopher St-Sheridan Sq. MAP P.82–83, POCKET MAP B18

The Village's main gay artery runs from Sixth Avenue to West Street passing by many a gay bar, sex toy shop and café. The lively street's weekend cruise scene is still strong, although the domain is by no means as exclusively gay as it once was.

BEDFORD STREET

BEDFORD STREET

Subway #1 to Christopher St-Sheridan Sq.
MAP P.82–83, POCKET MAP B18

Bedford Street runs west off Seventh Avenue to become one of the quietest and most desirable Village addresses. Edna St Vincent Millay, the young poet and playwright, lived at no. 75 1/2. At only 9ft wide, it is one of the narrowest houses in the city. The brick and clapboard structure next door at no. 77 is the **Isaacs-Hendricks House**, built in 1799 and the oldest house in the Village. The building at no. 90, right on the corner of Grove Street (above the *Little Owl*), served as the exterior for Monica's apartment in *Friends*, though the TV series was shot entirely in L.A. studios. Opposite is 17 Grove Street, built in 1822 and one of the most complete wood-frame houses in the city.

GROVE STREET

Subway #1 to Christopher St-Sheridan Sq.
MAP P.82–83, POCKET MAP B18

Turn left down **Grove Street** from the *Little Owl* and you'll find Grove Court just off the street, one of the neighbourhood's most attractive and exclusive little mews. Heading back to Seventh Avenue on Grove Street, keep an eye out for *Marie's Crisis Café* at no. 59. Now a gay piano bar, this was the site of the rented rooms where English revolutionary writer and philosopher Thomas Paine died in 1809. Paine, who was reviled in England for his support of both the American and French revolutions, was the author of the eighteenth century's three bestselling pamphlets; *Common Sense*, published in 1776, is generally credited with turning public opinion in favour of US independence. The current building dates from 1839, the café named in part after Paine's masterful essay *The American Crisis*.

ST LUKE'S PLACE

Subway #1 to Christopher St-Sheridan Sq.
MAP P.82–83, POCKET MAP B18

One block south of Bedford Street is a section of Leroy Street known as **St. Luke's Place**; no. 10 was used as the exterior of the Cosby house (from the famous 1980s TV show), while no. 6 is the former residence of Jimmy Walker, an extravagant mayor of New York in the 1920s.

DOWNTOWN BOATHOUSE

Pier 40, end of Houston St ⓣ 212/229-2114, ⓦ www.downtownboathouse.org. Mid-May to mid-Oct. MAP P.82–83, POCKET MAP A19

This volunteer organization offers free weekend kayaking on the **Hudson River**, at the edge of the West Village. You can only paddle around the piers in the immediate vicinity, but the sensational views and the chance to work off all those cupcakes make this a fabulous deal (children under 16 must be accompanied by an adult).

Shops

C.O. BIGELOW PHARMACY

414 Sixth Ave between W 8th and 9th sts. Subway A, B, C, D, E, F, M to W 4th St; #1 to Christopher St. Mon–Fri 7.30am–9pm, Sat 8.30am–7pm, Sun 8.30am–5.30pm. MAP P.82–83, POCKET MAP C17

Established in 1882, this is the oldest apothecary in the country – and that's exactly how it looks, with the original Victorian shop-fittings still in place. Specializes in homeopathic remedies.

FAICCO'S PORK STORE

260 Bleecker St between Morton and Leroy sts. Subway A, B, C, D, E, F, M to W 4th St. Tues–Fri 8.30am–6pm, Sat 8am–6pm, Sun 9am–2pm. MAP P.82–83, POCKET MAP B18

This old-school Italian butcher serves some of the best-value meats, Italian products and sandwiches in the city.

GENERATION RECORDS

210 Thompson St between Bleecker and W 3rd sts. Subway A, B, C, D, E, F, M to W 4th St. Sun–Thurs 11am–10pm, Fri & Sat 11am–11pm. MAP P.82–83, POCKET MAP C18

MURRAY'S CHEESE

The focus here is on hardcore, metal and punk, with some indie rock thrown in. New CDs, vinyl and records on offer.

HOUSE OF OLDIES

35 Carmine St between Bleecker St and Bedford St. Subway A, B, C, D, E, F, M to W 4th St; #1 to Houston St. Tues–Sat 10am–5pm. MAP P.82–83, POCKET MAP B18

This shop specializes in rare and out-of-print vinyl records from the 1950s, 1960s and 1970s.

LI-LAC CHOCOLATES

40 Eighth Ave at Jane St. Subway A, C, E, L, #1, #2, #3 to 14th St. Mon–Sat noon–8pm, Sun noon–5pm. MAP P.82–83, POCKET MAP B17

Delicious chocolates handmade on the premises since 1923, including fresh fudge and hand-moulded Liberties and Empire States.

MURRAY'S CHEESE

254 Bleecker St at Cornelia St. Subway A, B, C, D, E, F, M to W 4th St; #1 to Christopher St. Mon–Sat 8am–8pm, Sun 10am–7pm. MAP P.82–83, POCKET MAP B18

The exuberant and entertaining staff make any visit to this cheese-lovers' mecca a treat.

THREE LIVES & CO

154 W 10th St at Waverly Place. Subway A, B, C, D, E, F, M to W 4th St; #1 to Christopher St. Sun noon–7pm, Mon & Tues noon–8pm, Wed–Sat 11am–8.30pm. MAP P.82–83, POCKET MAP B18

Excellent literary bookstore that has an especially good selection of books by and for women, as well as general titles.

VILLAGE CHESS SHOP

230 Thompson St between W 3rd and Bleecker sts. Subway A, B, C, D, E, F, M to W 4th St. Daily 24hr. MAP P.82–83, POCKET MAP C18

Every kind of chess set for every kind of pocket since 1972. Usually packed with people playing.

Cafés and snacks

CAFFÈ REGGIO

119 MacDougal St between Bleecker and W 3rd sts. Subway A, B, C, D, E, F to W 4th St. Mon–Thurs 8am–3am, Fri & Sat 8am–4.30am, Sun 9am–3am. MAP P.82–83, POCKET MAP C18
Oldest coffee shop in the Village, dating back to 1927, and embellished with all sorts of Italian antiques, paintings and sculpture.

MAGNOLIA BAKERY

401 Bleecker St at W 11th St. Subway #1 to Christopher St. Mon–Thurs & Sun 9am–11.30pm, Fri & Sat 9am–12.30am. MAP P.82–83, POCKET MAP B18
There are lots of baked goods on offer at this very popular bakery, but everyone comes for the good but slightly overrated cupcakes (celebrated on *Sex and the City*), $3 each.

NUM PANG

21 E 12th St at University Place. Subway L, N, Q, R, #4, #5, #6 to Union Square ☎ 212/255-3271. Mon–Sat 11am–10pm, Sun noon–9pm. MAP P.82–83, POCKET MAP C17
Superb Cambodian-style sandwiches served on freshly toasted semolina flour baguettes with chilli mayo and home-made pickles; try the pulled duroc pork ($7.75).

Restaurants

BABBO

110 Waverly Place between MacDougal St and Sixth Ave. Subway A, B, C, D, E, F, M to W 4th St; #1 to Christopher St ☎ 212/777-0303. Mon–Sat 5.30–11.30pm, Sun 5–11pm. MAP P.82–83, POCKET MAP C18
Some of the best pasta in the city; this Mario Batali mecca for Italian food-lovers is a must. Try the mint love letters or goose liver ravioli – they're worth the pinch on your wallet.

BLUE HILL

75 Washington Place between Sixth Ave and Washington Square Park. Subway A, B, C, D, E, F to W 4th St; #1 to Christopher St ☎ 212/539-1776. Mon–Sat 5.30–11pm, Sun 5.30–10pm. MAP P.82–83, POCKET MAP C18
Rustic American and New England fare, including parsnip soup and braised cod, made with seasonal upstate ingredients. Don't miss the rich chocolate bread pudding.

CORNER BISTRO

331 W 4th St at Jane St. Subway A, C, E, L to 14th St ☎ 212/242-9502. Mon–Sat 11.30am–4am, Sun noon–4am. MAP P.82–83, POCKET MAP B17
Popular no-frills tavern serving cheap beer and some of the best burgers ($6.75) in town. An excellent place to unwind and refuel in a friendly atmosphere.

GOTHAM BAR & GRILL

12 E 12th St between Fifth Ave and University Place. Subway L, N, Q, R, #4, #5, #6 to Union Sq ☎ 212/620-4020. Mon–Thurs noon–2.15pm & 5.30–10pm, Fri noon–2.15pm & 5.30–11pm, Sat 5–11pm, Sun 5–10pm. MAP P.82–83, POCKET MAP C17
One of the city's best restaurants, the *Gotham* features marvellous American food; at the very least, it's worth a drink at the bar to see the city's beautiful people drift in.

MAGNOLIA BAKERY

HOME

20 Cornelia St between Bleecker and W 4th sts. Subway A, B, C, D, E, F, M to W 4th St; #1 to Christopher St ☎ 212/243-9579. Mon–Fri 11.30am–11pm, Sat 10.30am–11pm, Sun 10.30am–10pm. MAP P.82–83, POCKET MAP B18

One of those rare restaurants that manages to pull off cosy with flair. The creative and reasonably priced American food is always fresh and tasty, though it may be a better deal for lunch (around $20) than dinner ($30–40).

JOHN'S PIZZERIA

278 Bleecker St between Sixth and Seventh aves. Subway A, B, C, D, E, F, M to W 4th St; #1 to Christopher St ☎ 212/243-1680. Daily 11.30am–11.30pm. MAP P.82–83, POCKET MAP B18

This full-service restaurant serves some of the city's most popular pizzas, thin with a coal-charred crust ($13.75). Be prepared to wait in line for a table; they don't do slices.

MARY'S FISH CAMP

64 Charles St at W 4th St. Subway #1 to Christopher St ☎ 646/486-2185. Mon–Sat noon–3pm & 6–11pm. MAP P.82–83, POCKET MAP B18

Lobster rolls, *bouillabaisse* and seasonal veggies adorn the menu at this intimate spot, where you can almost smell the salt air. Go early, as the line lasts into the night (no reservations).

PEARL OYSTER BAR

18 Cornelia St between Bleecker and W 4th sts. Subway A, B, C, D, E, F, M to W 4th St; #1 to Christopher St ☎ 212/691-8211. Mon–Fri noon–2.30pm & 6–11pm, Sat 6–11pm. MAP P.82–83, POCKET MAP B18

Upmarket version of a New England fish shack, best known for its lemony-fresh lobster roll. You may have to fight for a table here, but the thoughtfully executed seafood dishes are well worth it.

PEARL OYSTER BAR

THE SPOTTED PIG

314 W 11th St at Greenwich St. Subway #1 to Christopher St ☎ 212/620-0393. Mon–Fri noon–2am, Sat & Sun 11am–2am. MAP P.82–83, POCKET MAP A18

New York's first gastro-pub, courtesy of chef Mario Batali. The menu is several steps above ordinary bar food – featuring smoked-haddock chowder and sheep's ricotta *gnudi* – and the wine list is excellent. Entrees $17–31, with lunch plates under $20.

THE SPOTTED PIG

Bars and pubs

BLIND TIGER ALE HOUSE

281 Bleecker St at Jones St. Subway A, B, C, D, E, F, M to W 4th St; #1 to Christopher St. Daily 11.30am–4am. MAP P.82–83, POCKET MAP B18

This wood-panelled pub is the home of serious ale connoisseurs, with 28 rotating draughts (primarily US microbrews such as Sixpoint and Smuttynose for around $6.50), a couple of casks and loads of bottled beers – they also serve cheese plates from Murray's. The prime location means it tends to get packed.

CUBBY HOLE

281 W 12th St at W 4th St. Subway A, C, E, L to 14th St. Mon–Fri 4pm–4am, Sat & Sun 2pm–4am. MAP P.82–83, POCKET MAP B17

This pocket-sized lesbian bar is warm and welcoming, with a busy festive atmosphere and unpretentious clientele.

THE DOVE PARLOUR

228 Thompson St between Bleecker and W 3rd sts. Subway A, B, C, D, E, F, M to W 4th St. Daily 4pm–4am. MAP P.82–83, POCKET MAP C18

A relaxed subterranean bar for the post-college crowd with jazzy happy hours spilling into upbeat late nights.

WHITE HORSE TAVERN

DUPLEX

61 Christopher St at Seventh Ave S. Subway A, B, C, D, E, F, M to W 4th St; #1 to Christopher St. Daily 4pm–4am. MAP P.82–83, POCKET MAP B18

A village institution, this entertaining piano bar/cabaret elevates gay bar culture to a new level. A fun place for anyone, gay or straight, to stop for a tipple.

THE MONSTER

80 Grove St between Waverly Place and W 4th St. Subway A, B, C, D, E, F, M to W 4th St; #1 to Christopher St ⓣ 212/924-3558, ⓦ manhattan-monster.com. Mon–Fri 4pm–4am, Sat & Sun 2pm–4am. MAP P.82–83, POCKET MAP B18

Large, campy gay bar with drag cabaret, piano and downstairs dancefloor. Very popular, especially with tourists, yet has a strong neighbourhood feel. Cover $4–8.

WHITE HORSE TAVERN

567 Hudson St at W 11th St. Subway #1 to Christopher St. Daily 11am–3am. MAP P.82–83, POCKET MAP A18

Village institution, opening in 1880: Dylan Thomas supped his last here before being carted off to the hospital with alcohol poisoning. The beer and food are cheap and palatable, and there's outside seating in the summer.

Clubs

(LE) POISSON ROUGE

158 Bleecker St at Thompson St. Subway A, B, C, D, E, F, M to W 4th St ⓣ212/505-3474, ⓦwww.lepoissonrouge.com. Daily 5pm–2am, Fri & Sat 5pm–4am. Cover $5 (Wed)–$20 (Fri). MAP P.82–83, POCKET MAP C18

Club and live music venue (live rock, folk, pop and electronica), with dance nights most Wednesdays, Fridays and Saturdays ("Freedom Party" is the city's longest running weekly Friday night dance party).

STONEWALL INN

53 Christopher St between Seventh Ave and Waverly Place. Subway A, B, C, D, E, F, M to W 4th St; #1 to Christopher St ☎ 212/488-2705, Ⓦ www.thestonewallinnnyc.com. Daily 2pm–4am. MAP P.82–83, POCKET MAP B18

The gay civil-rights movement began outside this bar/club in the late 1960s and despite a few revamps hasn't changed much since. The crowd is mostly tourists and men, but everyone is made welcome.

SULLIVAN ROOM

218 Sullivan St at Bleecker St. Subway A, B, C, D, E, F, M to W 4th St ☎ 212/252-2151, Ⓦ www.sullivanroom.com. Thurs–Sat 10pm–5am. MAP P.82–83, POCKET MAP C18

Hidden basement club for serious dancing. Fri and Sat, popular with students from nearby NYU, are good for house music. The only downside: two bathrooms for the whole place. Cover $10–15.

Live music venues

55 BAR

55 Christopher St at Seventh Ave. Subway #1 to Christopher St. Daily 4.30pm–4am. MAP P.82–83, POCKET MAP B18

A gem of an underground jazz bar that's been around since the days of Prohibition, with a great jukebox, congenial clientele, and live jazz every night.

BLUE NOTE

131 W 3rd St between Sixth Ave and MacDougal St. Subway A, B, C, D, E, F, M to W 4th St; #1 to Christopher St ☎ 212 475 8592, Ⓦ www.bluenote.net. Sun–Thurs 6pm–1am, Fri & Sat 6pm–3am. MAP P.82–83, POCKET MAP C18

Open since 1981 (and unrelated to the record label), this jazz institution regularly hosts top international performers, with the likes of Sarah Vaughan, Dizzy Gillespie and Oscar Peterson making lauded appearances over the years ($15–25).

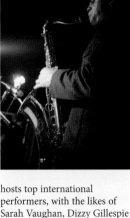

VILLAGE VANGUARD

GROOVE

125 MacDougal St at W 3rd St. Subway A, B, C, D, E, F, M to W 4th St ☎ 212/254-9393, Ⓦ www.clubgroove.com. Daily 4pm–4am. MAP P.82–83, POCKET MAP C18

This lively joint features live rhythm & blues and soul music every night; it's one of the best bargains around. Sets at 7pm and 9.30pm. No cover Sun–Thurs.

VILLAGE VANGUARD

178 Seventh Ave S between W 11th and Perry sts. Subway #1, #2, #3 to 14th St. ☎ 212/255-4037, Ⓦ www.villagevanguard.com. Daily 8pm–1am. MAP P.82–83, POCKET MAP B17

A NYC jazz landmark, the *Village Vanguard* celebrated its seventieth anniversary in 2005. Sonny Rollins made a legendary recording here in 1957, John Coltrane followed in 1961 and there's still a regular diet of big names. Cover is $25, including a one drink minimum ($5–16).

Chelsea and the Meatpacking District

A grid of tenements, rowhouses and warehouses west of Sixth Avenue between West 14th and 30th streets, Chelsea came to life with the gay community's arrival, beginning in the late Seventies. New York's art scene further transformed the neighbourhood in the Nineties with an explosion of galleries between Tenth and Twelfth avenues. Superstore retail sticks to Sixth Avenue, while Eighth is lined with cafés and bars. The triangular wedge of land created by Fourteenth, Gansevoort and West streets, aka the Meatpacking District, is a trendy place for shopping and clubbing. North of Chelsea in the West 30s, the ever-diminishing Garment District offers little to see.

THE HIGH LINE

Gansevoort St to W 30th St, roughly along Tenth Ave; entrances at Gansevoort, 14th, 16th, 18th, 20th, 23rd, 26th, 28th and 30th sts. Subway A, C, E to 14th St; C, E to 23rd St Ⓦ www.thehighline.org. Daily: April, May, Oct & Nov 7am–10pm; June–Sept 7am–11pm; Dec–March 7am–7pm.. MAP P.93, POCKET MAP B10

An ambitious urban renewal project that spans the Meatpacking District and West Chelsea, the **High Line** opened in 2009. It's a stunning transformation of a disused railway that once moved goods and produce around lower Manhattan, then spent years threatened with demolition.

Basically an elevated promenade-cum-public park, it pays proper homage to its history – steel rails peek out from the ground; smooth pavement and wood echo the lines of train tracks; and wild growth patches have been left intact. The first stretch, from Gansevoort to 20th Street, has a subtle water feature between 14th and 15th streets and an amphitheatre a few blocks north. Between 20th and 30th streets the walkway feels narrower; at one point it is elevated on a metal catwalk right in the trees.

THE HIGH LINE

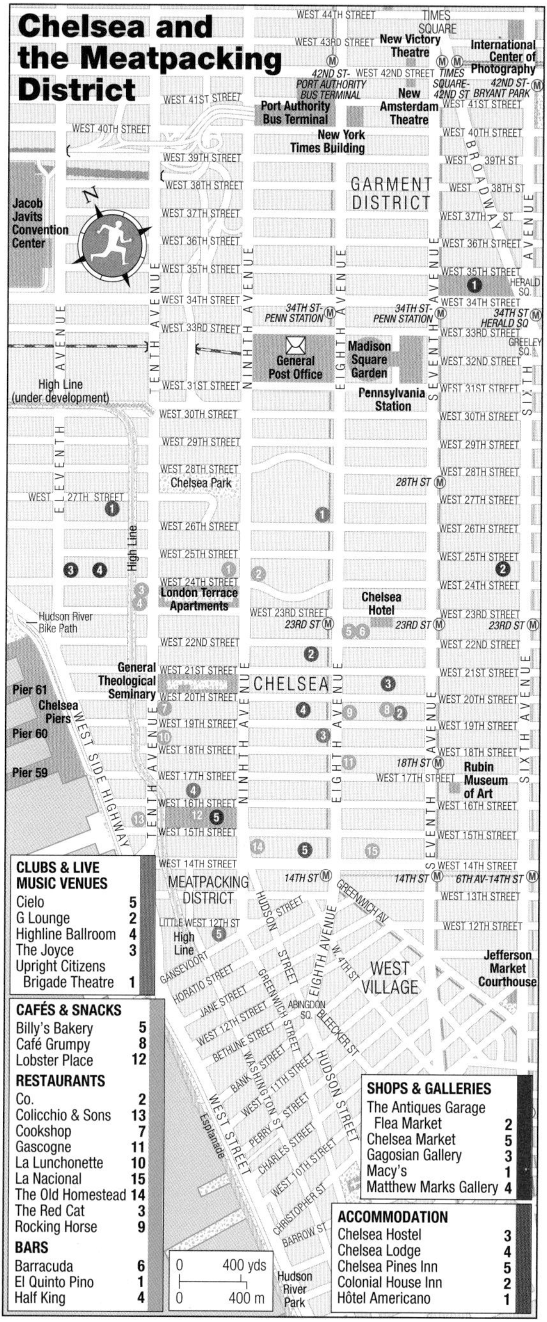
Chelsea and the Meatpacking District
WEST 44TH STREET
TIMES SQUARE
WEST 43RD STREET
New Victory Theatre
International Center of Photography
42ND ST- PORT AUTHORITY BUS TERMINAL
WEST 42ND STREET
TIMES SQUARE- 42ND ST
42ND ST- BRYANT PARK
WEST 41ST STREET
Port Authority Bus Terminal
New Amsterdam Theatre
New York Times Building
WEST 40TH STREET
WEST 39TH STREET
WEST 38TH STREET
WEST 37TH STREET
WEST 36TH STREET
WEST 35TH STREET
WEST 34TH STREET
WEST 33RD STREET
WEST 32ND STREET
WEST 31ST STREET
WEST 30TH STREET
WEST 29TH STREET
WEST 28TH STREET
WEST 27TH STREET
WEST 26TH STREET
WEST 25TH STREET
WEST 24TH STREET
WEST 23RD STREET
WEST 22ND STREET
WEST 21ST STREET
WEST 20TH STREET
WEST 19TH STREET
WEST 18TH STREET
WEST 17TH STREET
WEST 16TH STREET
WEST 15TH STREET
WEST 14TH STREET
WEST 13TH STREET
WEST 12TH STREET
BROADWAY
GARMENT DISTRICT
Jacob Javits Convention Center
HERALD SQ.
34TH ST- PENN STATION
34TH ST HERALD SQ
GREELEY SQ.
General Post Office
Madison Square Garden
Pennsylvania Station
ELEVENTH AVENUE
TENTH AVENUE
NINTH AVENUE
EIGHTH AVENUE
SEVENTH AVENUE
SIXTH AVENUE
High Line (under development)
High Line
Chelsea Park
28TH ST
London Terrace Apartments
Hudson River Bike Path
Chelsea Hotel
23RD ST
General Theological Seminary
CHELSEA
Pier 61
Chelsea Piers
Pier 60
Pier 59
WEST SIDE HIGHWAY
18TH ST
Rubin Museum of Art
14TH ST
6TH AV-14TH ST
MEATPACKING DISTRICT
LITTLE WEST 12TH ST
HUDSON STREET
GREENWICH AV
EIGHTH AVENUE
W. 4TH ST
WEST VILLAGE
Jefferson Market Courthouse
GANSEVOORT
HORATIO STREET
JANE STREET
WEST 12TH STREET
GREENWICH STREET
ABINGDON SQ.
BLEECKER ST
BETHUNE STREET
WASHINGTON ST
BANK STREET
WEST 11TH STREET
HUDSON STREET
WEST STREET
Esplanade
PERRY ST
CHARLES STREET
WEST 10TH STREET
CHRISTOPHER ST
BARROW ST
Hudson River Park
0 400 yds
0 400 m
CLUBS & LIVE MUSIC VENUES
Cielo 5
G Lounge 2
Highline Ballroom 4
The Joyce 3
Upright Citizens Brigade Theatre 1
CAFÉS & SNACKS
Billy's Bakery 5
Café Grumpy 8
Lobster Place 12
RESTAURANTS
Co. 2
Colicchio & Sons 13
Cookshop 7
Gascogne 11
La Lunchonette 10
La Nacional 15
The Old Homestead 14
The Red Cat 3
Rocking Horse 9
BARS
Barracuda 6
El Quinto Pino 1
Half King 4
SHOPS & GALLERIES
The Antiques Garage Flea Market 2
Chelsea Market 5
Gagosian Gallery 3
Macy's 1
Matthew Marks Gallery 4
ACCOMMODATION
Chelsea Hostel 3
Chelsea Lodge 4
Chelsea Pines Inn 5
Colonial House Inn 2
Hôtel Americano 1

RUBIN MUSEUM OF ART

150 W 17th St, between Sixth and Seventh aves. Subway #1 to 18th St; F, M to 14th St ⓣ 212/620-5000, ⓦ www.rmany.org. Mon & Thurs 11am–5pm, Wed 11am–7pm, Fri 11am–10pm, Sat & Sun 11am–6pm, closed Tues. $10, free on Fri 6–10pm. MAP P.93, POCKET MAP D10

The serene **Rubin Museum** is one of the city's lesser-visited gems, a collection of two thousand paintings, sculptures and textiles from the Himalayas and surrounding regions. The permanent exhibits on the second and third floors are organized and labelled with great care and thought, essential for a subject that will be familiar to few. While a few pieces manage to stand out, the thrust is less about individual artists and objects and more about understanding how and why art is created. A stylish ground-floor café, the *K2 Lounge*, hosts performances on Friday nights.

THE CHELSEA HOTEL

222 W 23rd St between Seventh and Eighth aves. Subway C, E to 23rd St ⓦ www.hotelchelsea.com. MAP P.93, POCKET MAP C10

Built as a luxury cooperative apartment in 1884 and converted to a hotel in 1903, the **Chelsea Hotel** has served as undisputed home to the city's harder-up literati and its musical vagabonds. Eugene O'Neill, Arthur Miller and Tennessee Williams lived here, and Brendan Behan and Dylan Thomas staggered in and out during their New York visits. Legend has it that Jack Kerouac typed *On the Road* nonstop onto a 120ft roll of paper while here, though most agree that took place at 454 W 20th Street, over a six-week period (and from existing journals, not just the top of his head). Bob Dylan wrote songs in and about the hotel, and Sid Vicious stabbed Nancy Spungen to death in 1978 in their suite, a few months before his own life ended with an overdose of heroin.

The hotel's future, at press time, was murky; purchased by a secretive developer in late 2011, the hotel stopped accepting guests as it was tearing up the art-filled lobby and working on extensive renovations. Check the website or do some research into current goings-on before making plans to do anything more than scoping out the red-brick exterior.

HISTORIC CHELSEA ROWHOUSES

GENERAL THEOLOGICAL SEMINARY

440 W 21st St between Ninth and Tenth aves. Subway C, E to 23rd St ☎ 212 243-5150, www.gts.edu. Mon–Sat 10am–3pm; later in summer, but always call ahead. MAP P.93, POCKET MAP C10

Founded in 1817, this is a Chelsea secret, a harmonious assemblage of Gothic structures that feel like part of a college campus. Though the buildings still house a working Episcopalian seminary – the oldest in the US – it's possible to explore the grounds and small chapel. You'll need to get a special pass to check out their collection of Latin Bibles, one of the largest in the world.

LONDON TERRACE APARTMENTS

405 and 465 W 23rd St between Ninth and Tenth aves. Subway C, E to 23rd St. MAP P.93, POCKET MAP C10

Surrounding a private garden, these rows of 1930s apartment buildings got their name because the management made the original doormen wear London bobby uniforms. However, they were later nicknamed "The Fashion Projects" for their retinue of big-time designer, photographer and model residents (including Isaac Mizrahi, Annie Leibovitz and Deborah Harry) and their proximity to Chelsea's real housing projects.

CHELSEA PIERS

W 17th to W 23rd St along Hudson River. Subway C, E to 23rd St ☎ 212 336-6666, www.chelseapiers.com. Hours vary according to activity. MAP P.93, POCKET MAP B11

First opened in 1910, this was where the great transatlantic liners would disembark their passengers (it was en route to the **Chelsea Piers** in 1912 that the *Titanic* sank). By the 1960s, however, the piers had fallen into neglect. Reopened in 1995,

THE GENERAL POST OFFICE

the new Chelsea Piers stretches between piers 59 to 62 as a sports complex, with ice rinks and open-air roller rinks, as well as a skate park, bowling alley and a golf range. There's a nice waterfront walkway at the end of **Pier 62**.

THE GENERAL POST OFFICE

421 Eighth Ave at W 33rd St. Subway A, C, E to 34th St ☎ 212/330-3296. Mon–Fri 7am–10pm, Sat 9am–9pm, Sun 11am–7pm. MAP P.93, POCKET MAP C9

The 1913 **General Post Office**, officially the James A Farley Station (named after a well-regarded postmaster general), is a relic from when municipal pride was all about making statements. Twenty huge columns stand beneath the sonorous inscription: "Neither snow nor rain nor heat nor gloom of night stays these couriers from the swift completion of their appointed rounds." The McKim, Mead and White building is being refitted to transform the Post Office into Moynihan Station and use it as an entrance to Amtrak and LIRR trains at Penn Station; in the meantime, duck inside to see a few historical postal exhibits.

Shops and galleries

THE ANTIQUES GARAGE FLEA MARKET

112 W 25th St between Sixth and Seventh aves. Subway F, M #1 to 23rd St. Sat & Sun 9am–5pm. MAP P.93, POCKET MAP D10

Packed into a bi-level garage, vendors come to peddle all sorts of old knick-knacks, antique jewellery, framed items, toys, cigarette lighters and more.

CHELSEA MARKET

75 Ninth Ave between W 15th and 16th sts. Subway A, C, E to 14th St. Mon–Sat 7am–9pm, Sun 8am–7pm. MAP P.93, POCKET MAP A17

A nice array of food shops lines this former Nabisco factory warehouse's ground floor; go for *pad thai*, panini, chewy breads, sinful brownies or kitchenware.

GAGOSIAN GALLERY

555 W 24th St between Tenth and Eleventh aves, other locations at 522 W 21st St and 980 Madison Ave Subway C, E to 23rd St ⓣ212/741-1111, ⓦwww.gagosian.com. Tues–Sat 10am–6pm. MAP P.93, POCKET MAP B10

This art world powerbroker shows heavyweights such as Richard Serra and Damien Hirst.

MACY'S

CHELSEA MARKET

MACY'S

151 Broadway at W 34th St at Herald Square. Subway B, D, F, M, N, Q, R to 34th St. Mon–Sat 10am–9.30pm, Sun 11am–8.30pm. MAP P.93, POCKET MAP D9

One of the world's largest department stores, Macy's stocks fairly mediocre brands (except for the excellent Cellar houseware department). If you're from abroad, head to the Visitor Center (Balcony Level) to receive a ten percent discount; bring your passport.

MATTHEW MARKS GALLERY

522 W 22nd St between Tenth and Eleventh aves, with three other branches in Chelsea. Subway C, E to 23rd St ⓣ212/243-0200, ⓦwww.matthewmarks.com. Tues–Sat 11am–6pm. MAP P.93, POCKET MAP B10

The centrepiece of Chelsea's art scene, showcasing pieces by artists such as Cy Twombly and Ellsworth Kelly.

Cafés and snacks

BILLY'S BAKERY

184 Ninth Ave between 21st and 22nd sts; two other locations. Subway C, E and #1 to 23rd St. Mon–Thurs 8.30am–11pm, Fri & Sat

8.30am–midnight, Sun 9am–10pm. MAP P.93, POCKET MAP C10

This retro pastry shop is an excellent alternative to overcrowded *Magnolia Bakery* (see p.88). Owned by a former employee of *Magnolia*, it doles out wonderful cupcakes and a tangy Key Lime Pie, in a much more sedate setting.

CAFÉ GRUMPY

224 W 20th St between Seventh and Eighth aves; three other city locations. Subway C, E to 23rd St. Mon–Thurs 6.30am–8pm, Sat 7.30am–8pm, Sun 7am–7.30pm. MAP P.93, POCKET MAP C10

It's uncertain which will take longer, choosing a coffee – the selections described as if they were wines – or getting your fix, as each cup comes made to order. But you'll be able to taste the difference; it's as good as it gets. The original *Grumpy* is over in Brooklyn's Greenpoint.

LOBSTER PLACE

75 Ninth Ave, between 15th and 16th sts. Subway A, C, E to 14th St. Mon–Sat 9.30am–8pm, Sun 10am–7pm. MAP P.93, POCKET MAP C11

A Chelsea Market fishmonger with a sandwich window at the back; take your chowder (small portion $3.50), fresh sushi meal or picnic box ($10.95–19.95) up to the High Line for lunch.

Restaurants

CO.

230 Ninth Ave at W 24th St. Subway C, E to 23rd St ☎212/243-1105. Mon 5–11pm, Tues–Sat 11.30am–11pm, Sun 11am–10pm. MAP P.93, POCKET MAP C10

Fashionable new wave pizzeria. Start with the crostini ($4) and an escarole salad ($8), then share a few of the oddly shaped pizzas, like shiitake and rosemary ($16), and meatball ($18).

COLICCHIO & SONS

85 Tenth Ave at W 15th St. Subway A, C, E to 14th St; L to Eighth Ave ☎212/400-6699. Tap Room Mon–Thurs noon–3pm & 5.30–10pm, Fri noon–3pm & 5.30–11pm, Sat 11am–3pm & 5–11pm, Sun 11am–3pm & 5–10pm; dining room Mon–Thurs 6–10pm, Fri 5.30–11pm, Sat 5–11pm, Sun 5–9pm. MAP P.93, POCKET MAP A17

Celebrity chef Tom Colicchio strikes again, offering a menu of unusual, delicious combinations, such as butter-poached oysters with celery root pasta and caviar, in a somewhat overwrought dining area. *The Tap Room* at the front offers an excellent prix-fixe lunch ($25), more casual dinner options and a warmer vibe.

COOKSHOP

156 Tenth Ave at 20th St. Subway C, E to 23rd St ☎212/924-4440. Mon–Fri 8am–4pm & 5.30–11.30pm, Sat 11am–4pm & 5.30–11.30pm, Sun 11am–3pm & 5.30–10pm. MAP P.93, POCKET MAP C10

Part of the Marc Meyer stable, with ever-busy street-side tables and a menu of seasonal, contemporary American fare – dishes always showcase the food's provenance; entrees might include pheasant pasta, grilled rabbit from the Hudson Valley and Vermont suckling pig (most $25–30); there are interesting brunch options and inventive Bloody Marys, too.

GASCOGNE

158 Eighth Ave between 17th and 18th sts. Subway A, C, E to 14th St; #1 to 18th St ☎212/675-6564. Tues–Thurs noon–3pm & 5.30–10.30pm, Fri noon–3pm & 5.30–11pm, Sat noon–11pm, Sun noon–10.30pm. MAP P.93, POCKET MAP C11

The beautiful backyard garden is the perfect setting for hearty dishes from southwest France like *cassoulet* and *foie gras* (around $25–30). Various prix-fixes are available, with an especially good four-course Monday night deal ($30).

LA LUNCHONETTE

130 Tenth Ave at W 18th St. Subway A, C, E to 14th St ☎ 212/675-0342. Mon–Thurs & Sun 11.30am–3.30pm & 5.30–10.30pm, Fri–Sat 11.30–3.30pm & 5.30–11.30pm. MAP P.93, POCKET MAP C11

Unpretentious and comfortable real-deal French bistro in an old Polish bar. Sample delicious lamb sausages or skate wing.

LA NACIONAL

239 W 14th St between Seventh and Eighth aves. Subway A, C, E, L, #1, #2, #3 to 14th St ☎ 212/243-9308. Mon–Wed & Sun noon–10pm, Thurs–Sat noon–11pm. MAP P.93, POCKET MAP B17

Home of the Spanish Benevolent Society, *La Nacional* retains the feel of a club while being open to anyone who enters. Try very reasonably priced *croquetas*, shrimp with garlic sauce and top-notch *paella*.

THE OLD HOMESTEAD

56 Ninth Ave between W 14th and 15th sts. Subway A, C, E to 14th St ☎ 212/242-9040. Mon–Thurs noon–10.45pm, Fri noon–11.45pm, Sat 1–11.45pm, Sun 1–9.45pm. MAP P.93, POCKET MAP A17

Steak. Period. But really gorgeous steak, served in an almost comically old-fashioned walnut dining room by waiters in black vests. Huge portions, but expensive – roughly $45 per steak.

THE OLD HOMESTEAD

THE RED CAT

227 Tenth Ave between W 23rd and 24th sts. Subway C, E to 23rd St ☎ 212/242-1122. Mon 5–11pm, Tues–Thurs noon–2.30pm, 5–11pm, Fri & Sat noon–2.30pm & 5pm–midnight, Sun 5–10pm. MAP P.93, POCKET MAP B10

Superb service, a fine American–Mediterranean kitchen, diverse wine list and cosy atmosphere all make for a memorable dining experience.

ROCKING HORSE

182 Eighth Ave between W 19th and 20th sts. Subway C, E to 23rd St; #1 to 18th St. ☎ 212/463-9511. Mon–Thurs noon–11pm, Fri noon–midnight, Sat 11am–midnight, Sun 11am–11pm. MAP P.93, POCKET MAP C11

The high-end Mexican cuisine served at *Rocking Horse* is very inventive – seared salmon Napoleon, jalapeno-braised brisket – while the mojitos and margaritas pack a punch.

Bars

BARRACUDA

275 W 22nd St between Seventh and Eighth aves. Subway C, E, #1 to 23rd St. Daily 4pm–4am. MAP P.93, POCKET MAP C10

A favourite bar in New York's gay scene, and pretty laidback for Chelsea, though drag shows and DJs perk things up in the later hours.

EL QUINTO PINO

401 W 24th St at Ninth Ave. Subway C, E to 23rd St. Mon–Thurs 5pm–midnight, Fri & Sat 5pm–1am, Sun 5–11pm. MAP P.93, POCKET MAP C10

There are relatively few seats in this elegant tapas bar, so come early to nibble on pork cracklings ($6)and an uncanny sea urchin sandwich ($15), paired up with a good selection of Spanish wines.

THE JOYCE

HALF KING

505 W 23rd St between Tenth and Eleventh aves. Subway C, E to 23rd St. Daily 11am–2am. MAP P.93, POCKET MAP B10

This popular Irish pub, owned by a small group of writer/artists, features decent food and regular literary events.

Clubs and live music venues

CIELO

18 Little W 12th St at Ninth Ave. Subway A, C, E to 14th St T 212/645-5700, W www.cieloclub.com. Mon & Wed–Sat 10pm–4am. $10–25. MAP P.93, POCKET MAP A17

Expect velvet rope-burn at this super-exclusive place: there's only room for 250 people. DeepSpace Mondays, a reggae and dub party hosted by the French DJ Francois K, are the highlight.

G LOUNGE

225 W 19th St between Seventh and Eighth aves. Subway #1 to 18th St T 212/929-1085, W glounge.com. Daily 4pm–4am. MAP P.93, POCKET MAP C11

At Chelsea's friendliest gay lounge, it's all about Martinis and preening. Go during weeknights when things are less hectic.

HIGHLINE BALLROOM

431 W 16th St between Ninth and Tenth aves. Subway A, C, E to 14th St. T 212/414-5994, W www.highlineballroom.com. $10 minimum for table seating during shows. MAP P.93, POCKET MAP C11

One of the newer venues in town, with table seating available (full dinner if you like) for shows – acts run from indie rock to hip-hop, reggae and big band. DJ sets too.

THE JOYCE

175 Eighth Ave at W 19th St. Subway #1 to 18th St; C, E to 23rd St T 212/691-9740, W www.joyce.org. MAP P.93, POCKET MAP C11

The Joyce was created by dancers in 1982 to showcase dance. Touring companies both local and from around the world keep this Art Deco-style theatre in brisk business.

UPRIGHT CITIZENS BRIGADE THEATRE

307 W 26th St between Eighth and Ninth aves. Subway C, E to 23rd St T 212/366-9176, W www.ucbtheatre.com. Cover free to $10. MAP P.93, POCKET MAP C10.

Consistently hilarious sketch-based and improv comedy, seven nights a week. You can sometimes catch *Saturday Night Live* members in the ensemble.

Union Square, Gramercy Park and the Flatiron District

For a glimpse of well-preserved nineteenth-century New York, it's definitely worth a jaunt around the more genteel parts of the east-side neighbourhoods that surround Union Square and Gramercy Park. Madison Square Park and the decidedly anorexic Flatiron Building anchor the amorphous area of the Flatiron District, which veers up and down Broadway and takes in a number of elegant facades; things take on more of a high-rise, Midtown flavour the closer you get to the Empire State Building. Some of the best and most expensive restaurants in the city call this stretch home; wander east to the high 20s around Lexington Avenue, a little Indian area called Curry Hill, for wallet relief in the kosher vegetarian restaurants and *chaat* cafés frequented by taxi drivers.

UNION SQUARE

Bordered by Broadway, Park Avenue S, 14th and 17th sts. Subway L, N, Q, R,#4, #5, #6 to Union Square. MAP P.101, POCKET MAP D11

Founded as a park in 1813, **Union Square** lies between E 14th and E 17th streets, interrupting Broadway's diagonal path. The park was the site of many political protests and workers' rallies between the Civil War and the early twentieth century. Later, the area evolved into an elegant theatre and shopping district. The leafy and bench-lined square is best known for its **Farmers' Market**, held Monday, Wednesday, Friday

UNION SQUARE

and Saturday from 8am to 6pm; there's tons of local produce, cheese, meat, even wine. Craft vendors, none too special, line the southwest side, though they're taken over by a popular holiday market as Christmas approaches.

IRVING PLACE

Subway L, N, Q, R, #4, #5, #6 to Union Square. MAP P.101, POCKET MAP E11

This graceful six-block stretch was named after author Washington Irving, though the claims that he lived at no. 49 are spurious; he did, at the least, frequently visit a nephew who lived in the area. Regardless, it's a lovely walk from the Con Ed building at the south end up to Gramercy Park; the intersection with 19th Street – and that sidestreet itself – is especially evocative.

THEODORE ROOSEVELT BIRTHPLACE

28 E 20th St between Park Ave S and Broadway. Subway N, R, #6 to 23rd St ☎ 212/260-1616. Tues–Sat 9am–5pm, tours on the hour 10am–4pm (except noon). Free. MAP P.101, POCKET MAP D10

Theodore Roosevelt's birthplace was restored in 1923 to the way it would have been when he was born there in 1858; the family moved uptown when he was fourteen. The rather sombre mansion contains mostly original furnishings – a brilliant chandelier in the parlour and "Teedie's" crib – viewable on an obligatory guided tour; it doesn't take more than fifteen minutes to see it all. You might spend as much time in the attached galleries looking at hunting trophies and documents from Roosevelt's life.

GRAMERCY PARK

Irving Place between 20th and 21st sts. Subway #6 to 23rd St. MAP P.101, POCKET MAP E10

A former "little crooked swamp", **Gramercy Park** is one of the city's prettiest squares. The city's last private park, it is accessible only to those rich or fortunate enough to live here – or those staying at the nearby *Gramercy Park Hotel* (see p.178). Inside the gates stands a statue of the actor Edwin Booth, brother of Lincoln's assassin, John Wilkes Booth. The private **Players Club**, at 15 Gramercy Park, was founded by Booth and sits next door to the prestigious **National Arts Club** at no. 16, another members-oriented place, though you can sneak inside in the afternoons for the free art exhibits. The brick-red structure at no. 34 was one of the city's very first building cooperatives.

THE FLATIRON BUILDING

At Broadway, Fifth Ave and 23rd St. Subway N, R to 23rd St. MAP P.101, POCKET MAP D10

Set on a triangular, or iron-shaped, plot of land, the lofty, elegant 1902 **Flatiron Building** is covered with terracotta Medusa heads and other striking ornamentation. The uncommonly thin, tapered shape of this Daniel Burnham-designed skyscraper (tall for the time, at 307ft) caused consternation regarding its stability and wind-tunnel like effects, but it has more than survived the years – it's become a New York symbol.

MADISON SQUARE PARK

E 23rd and 26th sts and Madison Ave and Broadway. Subway N, R to 23rd St. MAP P.101, POCKET MAP D10

Perhaps because of the stateliness of its buildings and the park-space in the middle, **Madison Square** possesses a grandiosity that Union Square has long since lost. Next to the Art Deco Metropolitan Life Company's building and clock tower on the eastern side, the Corinthian-columned marble facade of the Appellate Division of the **New York State Supreme Court** is resolutely righteous with its statues of Justice, Wisdom and Peace, though the chamber where arguments are heard (Tues–Thurs 2pm) is well-nigh Rococo in its detail. The grand structure behind that, the 1928 **New York Life Building**, was the work of Cass Gilbert, creator of the Woolworth Building (see p.42).

There are plenty of places to sit and relax in and around the park, including a pedestrianized triangle on its western side. In the southeast corner is the original outpost of Danny Meier's popular *Shake Shack* (see p.105), and at the northwest corner of 23rd and Broadway, the celebrity-chef-owned *Eataly* (see p.104).

THE FLATIRON BUILDING

69TH REGIMENT ARMORY

68 Lexington Ave between 25th and 26th sts. Subway #6 to 23rd or 28th sts Ⓦ www.sixtyninth.net. MAP P.101, POCKET MAP E10.

The lumbering but landmarked **69th Regiment Armory** building, with its mansard roof and arched drill shed, was the site of the famous Armory Show of 1913, which brought modern art to New York; it was also, briefly, a very early home to the Knicks' basketball team. These days it retains its original function as the headquarters of the National Guard's "Fighting Sixth-Ninth", though its drill hall is still used for events and exhibitions.

CHURCH OF THE TRANSFIGURATION

1 E 29th St between Fifth and Madison aves. Subway N, R, #6 to 28th St. MAP P.101, POCKET MAP D10

Made from brown brick and topped with copper roofs, the dinky rusticated Episcopalian **Church of the Transfiguration** was once a station in the Underground Railroad, and has long been a traditional place of worship for showbiz people and other such outcasts. The church remains headquarters to the oldest boys' choir in the city, originally formed in 1881. The chapel itself is an intimate wee building set in a gloriously leafy garden. Its interior is furnished throughout in warm wood, and soft candlelight illuminates the figures of famous actors memorialized in the stained glass.

THE EMPIRE STATE BUILDING

Fifth Ave and 34th St. Subway B, D, F, M, N, Q, R to 34th St Ⓣ 212/736-3100, Ⓦ www.esbnyc.com. Daily 8am–2am, last trip 1.15am. $22, $16 for ages 6 to 12, additional $15 for ticket to 102nd-floor Observatory. MAP P.101, POCKET MAP D10

THE EMPIRE STATE BUILDING

The 1931 **Empire State Building**, easily the city's most evocative symbol, was New York's tallest skyscraper for years until being topped by the original World Trade Center; after 9/11 it was the tallest once more, before being overtaken again by the new One World Trade Center in 2012. It stands at 102 floors and 1454ft – toe to TV mast – but its height is deceptive, rising in stately tiers with steady panache. Standing on Fifth Avenue below, it's easy to walk by without seeing it. From elsewhere, it can seem ubiquitous, especially at night, when it's lit in various colours.

Admire the immaculately restored Art Deco lobby and ceiling before the elevators take you to the main **86th-floor Observatory**. The views from the outside walkways here are as stunning as you'd expect; on a clear day visibility is up to eighty miles. A second set of elevators can take you to the smallish **102nd-floor Observatory**, at the base of the radio and TV antennaes; the price makes it more for completists.

Shops

ABC CARPET AND HOME

888 Broadway at E 19th St. Subway N, R to 23rd St. Mon–Sat 10am–7pm, Sun 11am–6.30pm. MAP P.101, POCKET MAP D11

Six floors of antiques and country furniture, knick-knacks, linens and, of course, carpets. The grandiose, museum-like setup is half the fun.

ACADEMY RECORDS

12 W 18th St between 5th and 6th sts. Subway F, M to 14th St. Mon–Wed & Sun 11am–7pm, Thurs–Sat 11am–8pm. MAP P.101, POCKET MAP D11

Used, rare and hard-to-find music is the focus; this outlet has an exceptional selection for classical music fans.

BOOKS OF WONDER

18 W 18th St between Fifth and Sixth aves. Subway #1 to 18th St; F, M to 14th St; L, N, Q, R, #4, #5, #6 to Union Square. Mon–Sat 10am–7pm, Sun 11am–6pm. MAP P.101, POCKET MAP D11

There's no better place in the city for kids' books; helpful staff, regular story times, frequent author readings and an outlet of the *Cupcake Café* (see p.128) make coming here a pleasure.

EATALY

200 Fifth Ave at W 23rd St. Subway N, R to 23rd St; #6 to Astor Place. Market daily 10am–11pm. MAP P.101, POCKET MAP D10

This vast and wildly popular Mario Batali venture is part Italian café/restaurant complex, part food market. There is an incredible range of delicious wine, cheese, meat, bread and seafood for sale, sourced locally or flown in from Italia, and a wide choice of different places to stop and nibble on the tempting offerings.

KALUSTYAN'S

KALUSTYAN'S

123 Lexington Ave between E 28th and 29th sts. Subway #6 to 28th St. Mon–Sat 10am–8pm, Sun 11am–7pm. MAP P.101, POCKET MAP E10

This heavenly scented store has been selling a variety of Indian food products, spices and hard-to-find ingredients since 1944. Today its selection covers a range of foods from around the globe.

THE OLD PRINT SHOP

150 Lexington Ave between 29th & 30th sts. Subway #6 to 28th St. Sept–May Tues–Fri 9am–5pm, Sat 9am–4pm, June–Aug Mon–Thurs 9am–5pm, Fri 9am–4pm. MAP P.101, POCKET MAP E10

This fascinating and long-established shop is by far the best place to find yourself a great old map of a New York neighbourhood, a rare first-edition art book or a historic print from an old edition of *Harper's Weekly* to hang up and enjoy when you get home.

Cafés and snacks

CITY BAKERY

3 W 18th St between Fifth and Sixth aves. Subway F, M to 14th St. Mon–Fri 7.30am–7pm, Sat 7.30am–6.30pm, Sun 9am–6pm. MAP P.101, POCKET MAP D11

A smart stop for a satisfying lunch or a sweet-tooth craving. The vast array of pastries is head and shoulders above most in the city. Try a cookie or pretzel croissant with a hot chocolate.

EISENBERG'S SANDWICH SHOP

174 Fifth Ave between E 22nd and 23rd sts. Subway N, R to 23rd St. Mon–Fri 6.30am–8pm, Sat 6.30am–6pm, Sun 6.30am–4pm. MAP P.101, POCKET MAP D10

A colourful luncheonette, this slice of NY life serves great tuna sandwiches, matzoh ball soup and old-fashioned fountain sodas.

NO. 7 SUB

1177 Broadway between 28th and 29th sts, in the Ace Hotel. Subway N, R to 28th St ⓣ 212/532-1680. Mon–Fri 8am–10.30am & 11.30am–5pm. MAP P.101, POCKET MAP D10

Part of the dazzling array of foodstuffs associated with the *Ace* hotel, this sandwich vendor deals up esoteric combinations that aren't done justice by their lists of ingredients (sample: broccoli, lychee muchim, ricotta salata, pine nuts). The menu changes, but you should do well whatever you choose (most sandwiches are $9).

ROOMALI

97 Lexington Ave at 27th St. Subway #6 to 28th St. Mon–Sat noon–11pm, Sun 1–11pm. MAP P.101, POCKET MAP E10

There are lots of decent, inexpensive Indian restaurants in the area, but if you're looking for a quick, portable snack (though somewhat desultory service), try one or two of the tasty roti wraps at *Roomali*. There are lots of veggie options, and they're all made with just the right amount of spice.

SHAKE SHACK

Madison Square Park, near Madison Ave and E 23rd St; other locations across the city. Subway N, R, W to 23rd St. Daily 11am–11pm. MAP P.101, POCKET MAP D10

Danny Meyer's leafy food kiosk has become a phenomenon, with a long wait for tables pretty much all day (try to avoid prime lunch and evening hours) and spawning Upper West Side and Soho offshoots, as well as a spot at the Mets' Citi Field. Folks come for perfectly grilled burgers and frozen custard shakes, and everything is under $7.

STUMPTOWN COFFEE ROASTERS

20 W 29th St between Broadway and Fifth Ave, in the Ace Hotel. Subway N, R to 28th St. Daily 6am–8pm. MAP P.101, POCKET MAP D10

One of the country's most renowned coffee roasters brings its brews to a hip hotel; you'll have your latte methodically made by baristas dressed as 1920s dandies.

EISENBERG'S SANDWICH SHOP

Restaurants

15 EAST

15 E 15th St between Fifth Ave and Broadway. Subway L, N, Q, R, #4, #5, #6 to 14th St–Union Square ☎212/647-0015. Mon–Fri noon–1.45pm, Sat 5.30–11pm. MAP P.101, POCKET MAP C17

The attention given to both cooked dishes (slow-poached octopus, sea urchin risotto) and fresh sushi/sashimi (chef's selection $55–60) elevates this stylish Japanese restaurant.

ALDEA

31 W 17th St between Fifth and Sixth aves. Subway F, M to 14th St ☎212/675-7223. Mon 11.30am–2pm & 5.30–10pm, Tues–Thurs 11.30am–2pm & 5.30–11.30pm, Fri 11.30am–2pm & 5.30pm–midnight, Sat 5.30pm–midnight. MAP P.101, POCKET MAP D11

In a cool, relaxed dining room, Portuguese-accented dishes come exquisitely prepared and full of flavour. Prices are eminently reasonable (entrees $21–28), and a $20 three-course prix-fixe at lunch seals the deal.

ARIRANG

32 W 32nd St, between Fifth and Sixth aves. Subway B, D, F, M, N, Q, R to 34th St-Herald Square ☎212/967-5088. Daily 10am–midnight. MAP P.101, POCKET MAP D9

Somewhat hard to find (and up three flights), but worth seeking out for the chicken soups – with handmade dough flakes ($9.45) or ginseng ($17.95) or, if you're with friends, chicken cooked in a casserole ($49.95).

GRAMERCY TAVERN

42 E 20th St between Broadway and Park Ave S. Subway N, R,#6 to 23rd St ☎212/477-0777. Main dining room: Mon–Thurs noon–2pm & 5.30–10pm, Fri noon–2pm & 5.30–11pm, Sat 5.30–11pm, Sun 5.30–10pm; Front tavern: noon–11pm, later on weekends. MAP P.101, POCKET MAP D10

One of NYC's best restaurants; its neo-colonial decor, exquisite New American cuisine and perfect service make for a memorable meal. The seasonal tasting menus are well worth the steep prices ($116), but you can also drop in for a drink or cheaper and more casual meal in the lively front room.

I TRULLI ENOTECA AND RISTORANTE

122 E 27th St between Lexington and Park aves. Subway #6 to 28th St ☎212/481-7372. Mon–Thurs noon–3pm & 5.30–10.30pm, Fri noon–3pm & 5.30–11pm, Sat 5–11pm, Sun 3–10pm; Enoteca Mon–Sat 3–10.30pm (food to take away Mon–Thurs 11am–3pm). MAP P.101, POCKET MAP E10

Choose between the lovely restaurant serving quality southern Italian food and the impressive wine bar next door which has a limited menu.

MAIALINO

Gramercy Park Hotel, 2 Lexington Ave. Subway #6 to 23rd St ☎212/777-2410. Mon–Thurs 7.30–10am, noon–2pm & 5.30–10.30pm, Fri 7.30–10am, noon–2pm & 5.30–11pm, Sat 10am–2pm & 5.30–11pm, Sun 10am–2pm & 5.30–10.30pm. MAP P.101, POCKET MAP E10

If a place can be both rustic and refined, Danny Meier's attractive Roman trattoria, looking out on Gramercy Park, fits the bill. Much of the focus is on the hog (which gives the place its name) – the special is roast suckling pig. Reservations essential.

UNION SQUARE CAFÉ

21 E 16th St between Fifth Ave and Union Square W. Subway L, N, Q, R, T #4, #5, #6 to 14th St ☎212/243-4020. Mon–Thurs noon–9.45pm, Fri noon–10.45pn, Sat 11am–10.45pm, Sun 11am–9.45pm. MAP P.101, POCKET MAP D11

Choice California-style dining with a classy but comfortable downtown atmosphere. Not at all cheap – prices average $100+ for two, without drinks – but the creative menu and great people-watching are a real treat.

Bars

230 FIFTH

230 Fifth Ave. Subway N, R, #6 to 23rd St. Mon–Fri 4pm–4am, Sat & Sun 11am–4am. MAP P.101, POCKET MAP D10

Classy lounge bar with the best views of Midtown and the biggest roof garden in the city – blankets and heaters are provided in winter. Drinks and snacks are reasonably priced for the experience (martinis from $14; no cover). No sneakers/ trainers, and shirts for men.

BIRRERIA

Eataly, 200 Fifth Ave at 23rd St. Subway N, R, #6 to 23rd St ☎212/937-8910. Daily 11.30am–10.30pm (last seating, though bar may remain open later). MAP P.101, POCKET MAP D10

A sprawling rooftop bar, *Birreria* is a modern twist on the beer garden with handcrafted ales and homemade sausages on offer.

MOLLY'S

287 Third Ave between E 22nd and 23rd sts. Subway #6 to 23rd St. Daily 11am–4am. MAP P.101, POCKET MAP E10

While the city trends move toward gastropubs and handcrafted cocktails, the friendly bartenders at *Molly's* pour the best pints of Guinness.

OLD TOWN BAR & RESTAURANT

45 E 18th St between Broadway and Park Ave S. Subway L, N, Q, R,#4, #5, #6 to 14th St–Union Square. Mon–Fri 11.30am–2am, Sat noon–2am, Sun 1pm–2am. MAP P.101, POCKET MAP D11

This atmospheric and spacious bar is popular with publishing types, models and photographers. Great burgers.

PETE'S TAVERN

129 E 18th St at Irving Place. Subway L, N, Q, R, #4, #5, #6 to 14th St–Union Square. Daily 11am–2.30am. MAP P.101, POCKET MAP E11

Former speakeasy that claims to be the oldest bar in New York – it opened in 1864. These days it inevitably trades on its history, though its well-worn counter and outdoor seating are convivial enough.

PETE'S TAVERN

Clubs and live music

BLUE SMOKE: JAZZ STANDARD

116 E 27th St between Park and Lexington aves. Subway #6 to 28th St ☎212/576-2232, Ⓦwww.jazzstandard.com. Sets at 7.30pm and 9.30pm Mon–Thurs & Sun, with an extra set at 11.30pm Fri & Sat. Cover $20–35. MAP P.101, POCKET MAP E10

This gourmet club books all flavours of jazz and serves sublime BBQ, the best in-club grub in town.

IRVING PLAZA

17 Irving Place at 15th St. Subway L, N, Q, R, #4, #5, #6 to 14th St–Union Square ☎212/777-6800. MAP P.101, POCKET MAP E11

Once home to a Broadway musical (thus the dangling chandeliers and blood-red interior), *Irving Plaza* is a small-to-midsize concert hall with a rock-and-roll heart.

Midtown

The largely corporate and commercial area east of Sixth Avenue all the way to the river, from the 40s through the 50s, is known as Midtown. You'll find the city's sniffiest boutiques, best Art Deco facades and exemplary Modernist skyscrapers scattered primarily along E 42nd and E 57th streets and Fifth, Madison and Park avenues. Fifth is the grand sight- and store-studded spine of Manhattan; the sidewalks nearly reach a standstill at Christmas, with shoppers stalled at elaborate window displays. Cornelius Vanderbilt's Beaux-Arts train station, Grand Central Terminal, anchors Park Avenue, while major museums and city symbols such as the Museum of Modern Art, Rockefeller Center and the United Nations dot the rest of the landscape.

THE MORGAN LIBRARY AND MUSEUM

225 Madison Ave between E 36th and 37th sts. Subway #6 to 33rd St ⓣ 212/685-0008, ⓦ www.themorgan.org. Tues–Thurs 10.30am–5pm, Fri 10.30am–9pm, Sat 10am–6pm, Sun 11am–6pm. $15, free Fri 7–9pm. MAP P.109, POCKET MAP D9

The uplifiting **Morgan Library** in Murray Hill was originally built to hold the fruits of financier J.P. Morgan's collecting sprees during frequent trips abroad; he claimed keen interest in "all the beautiful things in the world", in this case, illuminated manuscripts, paintings, prints and furniture. A stunning Renzo Piano-designed gathering space brings together Morgan's library, annex and nineteenth-century brownstone.

The collection of nearly 10,000 drawings and prints, including works by Da Vinci, Degas and Dürer, is augmented by the rare literary manuscripts of Dickens, Jane Austen and

GRAND CENTRAL TERMINAL

Thoreau, as well as handwritten correspondence between Ernest Hemingway and George Plimpton and musical scribblings by everyone from Haydn to Dylan. Morgan's personal library and study, part of the just-restored McKim building at the core of the complex, are also on view.

GRAND CENTRAL TERMINAL

E 42nd St between Lexington and Vanderbilt aves. Subway S, #4, #5, #6, #7 to 42nd St–Grand Central ⓣ 212/935-3960 or ⓣ 212/883-2420 for tours. Ⓦ www.grandcentralterminal.com.

MAP P.109, POCKET MAP E8

Built in 1871 under the direction of Cornelius Vanderbilt, **Grand Central Terminal** was a masterly piece of urban planning in its day. With a basic iron frame and dramatic Beaux-Arts skin, the main train station's concourse is a sight to behold – 470ft long and 150ft high, it boasts a barrel-vaulted ceiling speckled like a Baroque church with a painted representation of the winter night sky. The station's more esoteric reaches include a lower concourse brimming with takeaway options as well as the landmark *Oyster Bar and Restaurant* (see p.120). Wednesday tours (contributions accepted; 90min) of the station begin at 12.30pm from the main information booth; a 12.30pm tour on Fridays (free; 90min) takes in some of the neighbouring area as well and starts across the street in the glass atrium of 120 Park Avenue. You can also embark on an informative, self-guided audio tour (daily 9am–6pm; $7) by picking up a device at one of the windows marked 'GCT Tour ', on the main concourse.

THE CHRYSLER BUILDING

THE CHRYSLER BUILDING

405 Lexington Ave between E 42nd and E 43rd sts. Subway S, #4, #5, #6, #7 to 42nd St–Grand Central. MAP P.109, POCKET MAP E8

One of Manhattan's best-loved structures, the **Chrysler Building** dates from a time (1928–30) when architects married prestige with grace and style. The car-motif friezes, jutting gargoyles and arched stainless-steel pinnacle give the solemn Midtown skyline a welcome whimsical touch. The lobby, once a car showroom, is all you can see of the building's interior – still worth it to get a look at the walls covered in African marble, murals depicting airplanes, machines and the brawny builders who worked on the tower, and showy elevator doors with inlaid wood.

THE UNITED NATIONS

First Ave at E 46th St. Subway S, #4, #5, #6, #7 to 42nd St–Grand Central ⓣ 212/963-8687, ⓦ www.un.org. Guided tours (45min) Mon–Fri 9.30am–4.45pm, Sat & Sun audio tours only 10am–4.15pm. $16, $11 children 5–12. MAP P.109, POCKET MAP F8

A must-visit only for those obsessed by global goings-on, the **United Nations complex** comprises the glass-curtained Secretariat, the curving sweep of the General Assembly and, connecting them, the low-rising Conference Wing. Tours – bring ID for security purposes – take in the UN conference chambers and its constituent parts. Even more revealing than the stately rooms are its thoughtful exhibition spaces and artful country gifts on view.

THE MET LIFE BUILDING

200 Park Ave between E 44th and E 45th sts. Subway S, #4, #5, #6, #7 to 42nd St–Grand Central. MAP P.109, POCKET MAP E8

The unsubtle bulk of the **Met Life Building**, looming over the southern end of Park Avenue before its interruption by Grand Central, steals the thunder of many of the more delicate structures around it. Bauhaus guru Walter Gropius had a hand in the design, and the critical consensus is that he could have done better. As the headquarters of the now-defunct Pan Am airline, the building, in profile, was meant to suggest an aircraft wing. The blue-grey mass certainly adds drama to the cityscape, even as it seals the avenue at 44th Street.

WALDORF ASTORIA HOTEL

301 Park Ave between E 49th and E 50th sts. Subway #6 to 51st St. MAP P.109, POCKET MAP E8

The solid mass of the 1931 **Waldorf Astoria Hotel** helps contribute to the conspicuous wealth of Park Avenue. Even if you're not staying here (lucky you if you are; see p.180 for review), duck inside the block-long lobby to stroll through vintage Deco grandeur, sweeping marble and hushed luxury, which continues

THE UNITED NATIONS

downstairs in the grand circular bar of the *Bull and Bear.*

ST BARTHOLOMEW'S CHURCH

325 Park Ave at E 50th St. Subway #6 to 51st St ⓦ www.stbarts.org. Mon, Tues & Thurs–Sat 9am–6pm, Wed 9am–7pm, Sun 8am–6pm, choir service Sun 11am MAP P.109, POCKET MAP E8

The Episcopalian **St Bartholomew's Church** is a low-slung Romanesque hybrid with portals designed by McKim, Mead and White. Adding immeasurably to the street, it gives the lumbering skyscrapers a much-needed sense of scale. Due to the fact that it's on some of the city's most valuable real estate, the church fought against developers for years and ultimately became a test case for New York City's landmark preservation law.

THE SEAGRAM BUILDING

375 Park Ave between E 52nd and E 53rd sts. Subway E, M, V Lexington Ave/53rd St; #6 to 51st St. MAP P.109, POCKET MAP E7

Designed by Mies van der Rohe with Philip Johnson, the 1958 **Seagram Building** was the seminal curtain-wall skyscraper. Its floors are supported internally, allowing for a skin of smoky glass and whisky-bronze metal. Every interior detail – from the fixtures to the lettering on the mailboxes – was specially designed. The plaza, an open forecourt designed to set the building apart from its neighbours, was such a success that the city revised the zoning laws to encourage other high-rise builders to supply similar public spaces.

More Midtown monuments

The city, especially Midtown, is filled with far too many landmark, innovative or just plain unusual buildings to list in these pages. If you're interested in the subject of architecture, try to catch the following in addition to the ones described in this chapter: the **Ford Foundation Building**, 320 E 43rd St between First and Second aves, whose atrium is one of New York's great indoor/outdoor experiences; Phillip Johnson's **Lipstick Building**, 885 Third Ave between E 53rd and 54th sts, named for its curved, telescoping shape; and the right-angle steel and glass slabs of the **Lever House**, 390 Park Ave, also between E 53rd and 54th sts.

CITIGROUP CENTER

601 Lexington Ave between E 53rd and E 54th sts. Subway #6 to 51st St. MAP P.109, POCKET MAP E7

Opened in 1978, the chisel-topped **Citigroup Center** (formerly the Citicorp Center) is one of Manhattan's most conspicuous landmarks. The slanted roof was designed to house solar panels to provide power for the building, and it adopted the distinctive building-top as a corporate logo. Inside lies small **St Peter's Church**, known as "the Jazz Church" for being the venue of many a jazz musician's funeral.

THE SONY BUILDING

550 Madison Ave between E 55th and E 56th sts. Subway E, M to 5th Ave/53rd St or Lexington Ave/53rd St. MAP P.109, POCKET MAP D9

Philip Johnson's 38-storey **Sony Building** (1978–84) follows the Postmodernist theory of eclectic borrowing from historical styles: a Modernist skyscraper sandwiched between a Chippendale top and a Renaissance base. Even though the first floor is well worth ducking into to soak in the brute grandeur – and, if you've got kids and booked well in advance, to visit the **Sony Technology Wonderlab** (free; ⓣ212/833-8100) – some speculate Johnson should have followed the advice of his teacher, Mies van der Rohe: "It's better to build a good building than an original one."

THE NEW YORK PUBLIC LIBRARY

E 42nd St and Fifth Ave. Subway B, D, F, M, #4, #5, #6 to 42nd St ⓣ212/930-0830, ⓦwww.nypl.org. Mon & Thurs–Sat 10am–6pm, Tues & Wed 10am–8pm, Sun 1–5pm, building tours at 11am & 2pm. MAP P.109, POCKET MAP D8

This monumental Beaux Arts building, faced in brilliant white marble (and recently restored for the library's

NEW YORK PUBLIC LIBRARY

centennial), is the headquarters of the largest public-library system in the world. Plenty of folks meet at the **NYPL**'s steps, framed by two majestic reclining lions, to while away the time; head inside to explore the place on your own or to take a free guided tour. The latter gives a good all-round picture of the building, taking in the **Map Room** and evocative **Periodicals Room**, with its stunning faux-wood ceiling and paintings of old New York. The undisputed highlight, however, is the large, coffered 636-seat **Reading Room** on the third floor. Authors Norman Mailer and E.L. Doctorow worked here, as did Leon Trotsky during his brief sojourn in New York just prior to the 1917 Russian Revolution. It was also here that Chester Carlson came up with the idea for the Xerox copier. Plans are in the works to modernize the system, move many books from the underground stacks and to allow for lending – as of now, any item request works in an archaic system, complete with pneumatic tubes.

BRYANT PARK

Sixth Ave between W 40th and 42nd sts. Subway B, D, F, M to 42nd St
212/768-4242, www.bryantpark.org. MAP P.109, POCKET MAP D8

Right behind the public library, **Bryant Park** is a grassy, square block filled with slender trees, flowerbeds, a small carousel and inviting chairs. The restoration of the park is one of the city's resounding success stories, as it was a seedy eyesore until 1992. It officially became a park in 1847 and, like Greeley Square to the south, is named after a newspaper editor – William Cullen Bryant of the *New York Post*, also famed as a poet and instigator of Central Park. Bryant Park was the site of the first American World's Fair in 1853, with a Crystal Palace, modelled on the famed London Crystal Palace, on its grounds – an edifice that burned in 1858. Summertime brings a lively scene to the park all day long: free jazz and yoga classes, table tennis and free outdoor movies on Monday evenings.

BRYANT PARK

DIAMOND ROW

W 47th St between Fifth and Sixth aves. Subway B, D, F, M to 47–50th St-Rockefeller Center. MAP P.109, POCKET MAP D8

You'll know **Diamond Row** by the diamond-shaped lamps mounted on pylons at either end. This strip, where you can get jewellery fixed at reasonable prices, features wholesale and retail shops chock-full of gems and was first established in the 1920s. These stores are largely managed by Hasidic Jews, and the workaday vibe feels more like the Garment District or the old Lower East Side than a part of tourist Midtown.

ROCKEFELLER CENTER

ROCKEFELLER CENTER

From Fifth to Sixth aves between W 48th and W 51st sts. Subway B, D, F, M to 47–50th St/ Rockefeller Center ☎ 212/332-6868, www.rockefellercenter.com. Tours daily 10am–4pm, $15 (☎ 212/332-6621) MAP P.109, POCKET MAP D8

The heart of Midtown's glamour, **Rockefeller Center** was built between 1932 and 1940 by John D. Rockefeller Jr, son of the oil magnate, and is one of the finest pieces of urban planning anywhere, balancing office space with cafés, underground concourses and rooftop gardens that work together with a rare intelligence and grace. At its centre, the **Lower Plaza** holds a sunken restaurant in the summer months. It's a great place for afternoon cocktails beneath Paul Manship's golden *Prometheus* sculpture. In winter this area becomes an ice rink for skaters to show off their skills to passing shoppers. Each Christmas since 1931, a huge tree is on display above the statue; its lighting, with accompanying musical entertainment, draws throngs in early December.

THE GE BUILDING

30 Rockefeller Plaza between W 49th and W 50th sts. Subway B, D, F, V to 47–50th St/ Rockefeller Center. NBC Studio tours Mon–Sat 8.30am–5.30pm, Sun 9.15am–5.30pm; reservations at the NBC Experience Store Tour Desk ☎ 212/664-7174, www.nbcstudiotour.com. $24, children 6–18 $21; free ticket for a show recording from the mezzanine lobby or out on the street. MAP P.109, POCKET MAP D8

Perhaps the apogee of Art Deco styling, the **GE Building** (or **30 Rock**) rises 850ft, its symmetrical monumental lines matching the scale of Manhattan itself. In the GE lobby, José Maria Sert's murals, *American Progress* and *Time*, are in tune with the 1930s Art Deco ambience – though paintings by Diego Rivera were scrapped after the artist refused to remove an image glorifying Lenin. Among the building's many offices are the **NBC Studios**, which produce the long-running comedy hit *Saturday Night Live*. Curiosity-satisfying hour-long tours behind the scenes of select shows leave every thirty minutes Mon–Fri, and every fifteen minutes on weekends.

City views

Top of the Rock and the Empire State Building are the obvious places to go for panoramic views of New York, but you can save a bit of money and find unique angles on the city at any of the following:

The mid-point of **Brooklyn Bridge** (p.42), to see the Financial District.

The **High Line** (p.92), for a look up Tenth Avenue.

General Worth Square next to Madison Square Park (p.102), for a look at the Flatiron, Metlife tower, the park and a lot of whizzing traffic.

The Cantor Rooftop Garden at the Met (p.145), for views of Central Park.

Empire–Fulton Ferry Park in Dumbo (p.163), for glimpses of the Brooklyn and Manhattan bridges.

TOP OF THE ROCK OBSERVATION DECK

30 Rockefeller Plaza at W 50th St. Subway B, D, F, M to 47–50th St–Rockefeller Center ⓣ212/698-2000, ⓦwww.topoftherocknyc.com. Daily 8am–midnight, last elevator at 11pm. $25, children 6–12 $16. MAP P.109, POCKET MAP D8

It's a lot to pay for a view, but what a view. Arguably as grand as that from the Empire State Building (with the added bonus of being to able to see the Empire State), the panorama from the top of the **GE Building** lets you examine the layout of Central Park and how built-up downtown is compared to uptown, offers a vertiginous look at St Patrick's Cathedral and looks out to the George Washington Bridge and beyond. The film that introduces a bit of history on Rockefeller Center is missable; just head to the elevator that whisks you up to floor 67, with additional decks on floors 69 and 70 accessible by stairs.

RADIO CITY MUSIC HALL

1260 Sixth Ave at W 50th St. Subway B, D, F, M to 47–50th St/Rockefeller Center. Tickets ⓣ1-866/858-0008, tours ⓣ212/247-4777, ⓦwww.radiocity.com. Daily 11.30am–3pm. Tour $19.25, children 12 and under $12.50, ticket prices for concerts vary. MAP P.109, POCKET MAP D8

Heralded by one of the most familiar marquees in New York, the world-famous concert hall **Radio City** is the last word in 1930s luxury. If you're not taking in a show – greats such as Sinatra used to grace the stage here, but these days it's better-known for its "Christmas Spectacular" than for any major bookings – you'll need to join one of the hour-long "Stage Door" behind-the-scenes walking tours to see it. The staircase is resplendent, with the world's largest chandeliers, while the huge auditorium looks like an extravagant scalloped shell. The movable parts of the stage hold some fascination, and there's a brief meeting with a Rockette too.

RADIO CITY MUSIC HALL

ST PATRICK'S CATHEDRAL

50th St and Fifth Ave. Subway B, D, F, M to 47–50th St–Rockefeller Center 212/753-2261, www.saintpatrickscathedral.org. Daily 7am–8.30pm, services throughout the day. MAP P.109, POCKET MAP D8

Designed by James Renwick and completed in 1888, **St Patrick's Cathedral** is the result of a painstaking academic tour of the Gothic cathedrals of Europe – perfect in detail, yet rather lifeless in spirit, with a sterility made all the more striking by the glass-black **Olympic Tower** next door, an exclusive apartment block where Jackie Kennedy Onassis once lived.

PALEY CENTER FOR MEDIA

25 W 52nd St between Fifth and Sixth aves. Subway B, D, F, M to 47–50th St–Rockefeller Center; E, M to Fifth Ave/53rd St 212/621-6800, www.mtr.org. Wed–Sun noon–6pm, Thurs noon–8pm. $10, under 14 $5. MAP P.109, POCKET MAP D7

The former Museum of Television and Radio still largely centres on its extensive archive of American TV and radio broadcasts, so if you want to view episodes of beloved but short-lived series like *Freaks and Geeks* or old classics like *Dragnet* or the *Honeymooners*, this is the place. An excellent computerized reference system lets you have a show at your fingertips in no time.

THE MUSEUM OF MODERN ART

11 W 53rd St between Fifth and Sixth aves. Subway B, D, F, M to 47–50th St–Rockefeller Center; E, M to Fifth St/53rd St 212/708-9400, www.moma.org. Mon, Wed, Thurs, Sat & Sun 10.30am–5.30pm, Fri 10.30am–8pm. $25, children 16 and under free, free Fri 4–8pm. MAP P.109, POCKET MAP D7

The Museum of Modern Art – **MoMA** to its friends – offers the finest and most complete account of late nineteenth- and twentieth-century art you're likely to find in the world. More than 100,000 paintings, sculptures, drawings, prints, photographs, architectural models and design objects make up the collection, along with a world-class film archive. After undergoing its latest expansion, completed in 2004 and doubling the exhibition space, another is already in the works – gallery space in a soaring Jean Nouvel-designed skyscraper next door that will be one of the city's tallest buildings.

MoMA

The core is the **Paintings and Sculpture galleries**, and if this is your priority, head straight for the fifth floor – to Painting and Sculpture 1, which starts with Cézanne, Gauguin and the Post-Impressionists of the late nineteenth century, takes in Picasso, Braque and Matisse (who has his own dedicated room, highlighted by the self-referential *Red Studio* and odd perspective of *The Dance*), moves through De Chirico, Duchamp and Mondrian, and finishes up with the surrealists Miró, Magritte and Dalí.

Painting and Sculpture 2, on the fourth floor, displays work from the 1940s to 1980s and inevitably has a more American feel, with works by Abstract Expressionists Pollock, Rothko and Barnett Newman, as well as lots of familiar work from the modern canon – Jasper Johns' *Flag*, Robert Rauschenberg's mixed media paintings, Warhol's soup cans and Roy Lichtenstein's cartoons.

The third-floor **Photography galleries** rotate frequently, but holdings include photos of Paris by Cartier-Bresson and Richard Avedon's penetrating portraits of cultural icons. **Architecture and Design**, on the same floor, hosts revolving exhibits showcasing every aspect of design from mid-nineteenth century on. **The Drawing galleries**, also on this floor, feature a glittering array of twentieth-century artists – Lucien Freud, Robert Rauschenberg and his old roommate Willem de Kooning, among many others. Finally, the spacious second-floor galleries give MoMA the chance to feature contemporary art (1980s to present) in all media.

TRUMP TOWER

If you need to refuel, the second-floor café, *Café 2*, serves very good, slickly presented Italian-style food. *Terrace 5*, on the fifth floor, is a more formal option, and provides nice views of the ground-level sculpture garden. A very swanky restaurant, *The Modern*, sits on the first floor.

TRUMP TOWER

725 Fifth Ave between 56th and 57th sts. Subway F to 57th St. MAP P.109, POCKET MAP D7

New York real-estate developer Donald Trump's outrageously overdone high-rise and atrium, **Trump Tower**, is just short of repellent to many – though perhaps not to those who frequent the boutiques on the lower floors. Perfumed air, polished marble panelling and a five-storey waterfall are calculated to knock you senseless. The building is clever, a neat little outdoor garden is squeezed high in a corner, and each of the 230 apartments above the atrium provides views in three directions.

Shops

APPLE STORE

767 Fifth Ave between 58th and 59th sts; other locations. Subway N, R to 5th Ave/59th St. Daily 24hr. MAP P.109, POCKET MAP D7

There are now five Apple stores in town, though this is the most striking – and purportedly the biggest moneymaking retail outfit on Fifth Avenue. A giant glass cube rises from the sidewalk to herald the entrance; descend the spiral staircase within to see the latest in gadgets and techno-gear.

BERGDORF GOODMAN

754 and 745 Fifth Ave at 58th St. Subway F to 57th St; N, R to Fifth Ave/59th St. Mon–Fri 10am–8pm, Sat 10am–7pm, Sun noon–6pm. MAP P.109, POCKET MAP D7

This venerable department store caters to the city's wealthiest shoppers and, in an unusual setup, flanks Fifth Avenue. Haute couture designers fill both buildings, one for men, one for women.

BLOOMINGDALE'S

1000 Third Ave at E 59th St. Subway N, R, #4, #5, #6 to 59th St. Mon, Tues & Wed 10am–8.30pm, Thurs–Sat 10am–10pm, Sun 10am–9pm. MAP P.109, POCKET MAP E7

One of Manhattan's most famous department stores, packed with designer clothiers, perfume concessions and housewares.

THE COMPLETE TRAVELLER

199 Madison Ave at E 35th St. Subway #6 to 33rd St. Mon–Fri 9.30am–6.30pm, Sat 10am–6pm, Sun noon–5pm. MAP P.109, POCKET MAP D9

Manhattan's premier travel bookshop, stocked with new and secondhand titles, including a huge collection of *Baedekers*.

TIFFANY'S

SAKS FIFTH AVENUE

611 Fifth Ave at 50th St. Subway E, M to 53rd St; B, D, F, M to 47–50th St–Rockefeller Center. Mon–Sat 10am–8pm, Sun 11am–7pm. MAP P.109, POCKET MAP D8

Every bit as glamorous as it was when it opened in 1922, Saks remains virtually synonymous with style and quality.

TANNEN'S MAGIC

45 W 34th St, Suite 608, between Fifth and Sixth aves. Subway B, D, F, M, N, Q, R to 34th St-Herald Square. Mon–Fri 11am–6pm, Sat & Sun 10am–4pm. MAP P.109, POCKET MAP D9

Your kids will never forget a visit to the largest magic shop in the world, full of props, tricks and magic sets. The staff is made up of magicians too.

TIFFANY & CO.

727 Fifth Ave at E 57th St. Subway N, R, W to Fifth Ave/59th St. Mon–Sat 10am–7pm, Sun noon–6pm. MAP P.109, POCKET MAP D7

Tiffany's soothing green marble and weathered wood interior is perhaps best described by Truman Capote's fictional Holly Golightly: "It calms me down right away . . . nothing very bad could happen to you there."

Cafés and snacks

FRANÇOIS CHOCOLATE BAR

1 W 58th St at The Plaza. Subway N, Q, R to Fifth Ave-59th St. Mon–Sat 9.30am–6.30pm, Sun 10.30am–5.30pm.
MAP P.109, POCKET MAP D7

The macaroons, mousse and hot chocolate here are made to the exacting standards of the finest Parisian patisseries – real French chocolate is on offer as well as delicious buttery pastry.

Restaurants

AI FIORI

400 Fifth Ave, between 36th and 37th sts in the Setai hotel. Subway B, D, F, M, N, Q, R to 34th St-Herald Square; #6 to 33rd St ☎212/613-8660. Mon–Thurs 7–10.30am, 11.45am–2.30pm & 5.30–9.30pm, Fri 7–10.30am, 11.45am–2.30pm & 5.30–10.30pm, Sat 8–10.30am, 11.45am–2.30pm & 5.30–10.30pm, Sun 8–10.30am, 11.45am–2.30pm & 5.30–9.30pm.
MAP P.109, POCKET MAP D9

The decor and atmosphere are unmemorable, but the elegant French-Italian dishes are anything but. Splurge on the four-course prix-fixe menu ($89), which allows you to choose your dishes (butter-poached lobster, for example) from the outstanding regular menu.

AQUAVIT

AQUAVIT

65 E 55th St between Madison and Park aves. Subway #6 to 51st St ☎212/307-7311. Mon–Fri 11.45am–2.30pm & 5.30–10.30pm, Sat 5.30–10.30pm.
MAP P.109, POCKET MAP D7

Go for a blowout in the main dining room or a more casual, and much less expensive, meal in the café. Either way, you'll sample Scandinavian food at its finest: silky gravlax, herring every which way, smoked Arctic char, Swedish meatballs and much more.

CHO DANG GOL

55 W 35th St between Fifth and Sixth aves. Subway B, D, F, M, N, Q, Rto 34th St ☎212/695-8222. Daily 11.30am–10.30pm.
MAP P.109, POCKET MAP D9

Korean restaurants proliferate on 32nd Street between Fifth and Sixth; this one, a little off the path, specializes in home-made tofu every which way. There's more, though, like simmered pork belly served as part of a spicy lettuce wrap.

EMPORIUM BRASIL

15 W 46th St between Fifth and Sixth aves. Subway B, D, F, M, V to 47-50th St-Rockefeller Center ☎212/764-4646. Mon–Wed 11.30am–10pm, Thurs–Sat 11.30am–11pm, Sun noon–9.30pm.
MAP P.109, POCKET MAP D8

Check out the authentic Brazilian food and atmosphere, enhanced by (relatively) reasonable prices for midtown. On Saturday afternoons, Brazil's national dish, the tasty *feijoada* (a stew of meaty pork and black beans, with rice) takes centre stage.

OYSTER BAR

HATSUHANA

17 E 48th St between Fifth and Madison aves. Subway #6 to 51st St ☎ 212/355-3345; another branch at 237 Park Ave. Mon–Fri 11.45am–2.45pm & 5.30–10pm, Sat 5–10pm. MAP P.109, POCKET MAP D8

A longtime favourite of local sushi lovers, this place is not cheap but won't break the bank – and the freshness of the fish compensates in any case.

KEENS STEAKHOUSE

72 W 36th St, between Fifth and Sixth aves. Subway B, D, F, M, N, Q, R to 34th St-Herald Square ☎ 212/947-3636.Mon–Fri 11.45am–10.30pm, Sat 5–10.30pm, Sun 5–9pm. MAP P.109, POCKET MAP D9

This 130-year-old chophouse is a classic; the bustling pub makes a great place for a martini and junior-sized mutton chop, or you can go all out on the larger cuts served in the rambling dining room.

LA GRENOUILLE

3 E 52nd St between Fifth and Madison aves. Subway E, M to Fifth Ave–53rd St ☎ 212/752-1495. Tues–Fri noon–2.30pm & 5–10.30pm, Sat 5–10.30pm. MAP P.109, POCKET MAP D7

The haute French cuisine here has melted hearts and tantalized palates since 1962. All the classics are done to perfection, and the service is gracious. Its prix-fixe lunch is $38–52, and dinner is $78–95 per person.

MENCHANKO TEI

131 E 45th St between Lexington and Third aves, another branch on 55th St. Subway #6 to 42nd St ☎ 212/986-6805. Mon–Thurs 11.30am–11.30pm, Fri 11.30am–midnight, Sat 11.30am–11pm, Sun 11.30am–10.30pm. MAP P.109, POCKET MAP E8

One of the better ramen options outside the East Village. Slurp up a steaming cauldron of soy-flavoured broth, chewy noodles, simmered pork and head-on shrimp.

THE MODERN

9 W 53rd St. Subway E, M to Fifth Ave-53rd St. Subway E, M to Fifth Ave-53rd St ☎ 212/333-1220. Mon–Thurs noon–2pm & 5–9.30pm, Fri noon–2pm & 5.30–10.30pm, Sat 5.30–10.30pm, Bar Room only on Sun 11.30am–9.30pm. MAP P.109, POCKET MAP D7

MoMA's fine dining offering is elegant without trying too hard. Seasonal ingredients are artfully combined to yield unexpected dishes: say, chorizo-crusted codfish with white cocoa-bean purée. Four-course set meals cost from $98. The *Bar Room at the Modern* offers more casual dining.

OYSTER BAR

Lower level, Grand Central Terminal at 42nd St and Park Ave. Subway S, #4, #5, #6, #7 to 42nd St–Grand Central ☎ 212/490-6650. Mon–Fri 11.30am–9.30pm, Sat noon–9.30pm. MAP P.109, POCKET MAP E8

Down in the vaulted cellars of Grand Central, the fabled *Oyster Bar* draws midtown office workers for lunch and seafood-lovers for dinner, who choose from a staggering list of daily catches including barramundi and steamed Maine lobster. Prices are moderate to expensive, but you can always just have a chowder or something from the counter.

Bars

CAMPBELL APARTMENT

Grand Central Terminal, southwest balcony, E 42nd St. Subway S, #7, #4, #5, #6 to 42nd St–Grand Central ☎212/953-0409. Mon–Thurs noon–1am, Fri noon–2am, Sat 2pm–2am, Sun 2pm–midnight. MAP P.109, POCKET MAP E8

Once home of businessman John W. Campbell, who oversaw the construction of Grand Central, this majestic space – built to look like a thirteenth-century Florentine palace – was sealed up for years. Now, it's one of New York's most distinctive bars. Go early and don't wear sneakers or a T-shirt.

KING COLE BAR

2 E 55th St between Fifth and Madison aves, in the St Regis Hotel. Subway E, M to Fifth Ave/53rd St; F to 57th St. Mon–Thurs 11.30am–midnight, Fri & Sat 11.30am–1am, Sun noon–midnight. MAP P.109, POCKET MAP D7

You'll need to dress smart and be prepared to spend at the reputed home of the Bloody Mary, but sipping a cocktail at a table or under the Maxfield Parrish mural at the bar, you'll surely feel like a million bucks.

PJ CLARKE'S

915 Third Ave at E 55th St. Subway #6 to 51st St; E, M to Lexington Ave/53rd St ☎212/317-1616. Daily 11.30am–4am. MAP P.109, POCKET MAP E7

One of the city's most famous watering holes, *PJ Clarke's* alehouse serves good beers, but only Guinness comes in a pint serving. Tables with red-and-white checked cloths await diners in the back, where you can choose from a classic American menu. You may recognize it as the setting of the film *The Lost Weekend*.

CAMPBELL APARTMENT

Times Square and the Theater District

The towering signs and flashing lights of Times Square, the blocks just north of 42nd Street where Seventh Avenue intersects with Broadway, bring a whole new meaning to the term "sensory overload". More than 270,000 workers alone pass through daily and, on New Year's Eve, hundreds of thousands more come to watch the apple drop at midnight. The seedy days are gone, but ostentatious displays of media and commercialism still reign. The adjoining Theater District and its million-dollar Broadway productions draw crowds, while Hell's Kitchen to the west offers innumerable restaurants as well as some gritty nightlife. You may wind up spending a decent amount of time here – it's a major hotel base and you'll probably want to take in a show or two – but there are few, if any, must-see sights (other than the sheer spectacle).

TIMES SQUARE

Broadway, Seventh Ave and 42nd St. Visitor Center at 1560 Broadway. Subway N, Q, R, #1, #2, #3 to Times Square-42nd St www.timessquarenyc.org. MAP P.123, POCKET MAP D8

If not always so in the public imagination, **Times Square** is now a largely sanitized universe of popular consumption. It takes its name from the *New York Times* offices built in 1904 (the current *Times* building, a Renzo Piano creation, is at Eighth Avenue between 40th and 41st streets); publisher Adolph Ochs staged a New Year's celebration here in honour of their opening. This

TIMES SQUARE

tradition continues today: hundreds of thousands arrive early to pack the streets, party (as best they can without being able to purchase or publicly consume alcohol) and watch the giant Waterford Crystal Ball drop on One Times Square. The neon, so much a signature of the square, was initially confined to the theatres and spawned the term "the Great White Way", but myriad ads for hundreds of products now form one of the world's most garish nocturnal displays.

HELL'S KITCHEN

MAP P.123, POCKET MAP C8

Between 34th and 59th streets west of Eighth Avenue, **Hell's Kitchen** mostly centres on the engaging slash of restaurants, bars, ethnic delis and food shops of Ninth Avenue – the staging set for the excellent **Ninth Avenue International Food Festival** (ⓦninthavenuefoodfestival.com) each May. Once one of New York's most violent and lurid neighbourhoods, it was first populated by Irish and Eastern European immigrants, who were soon joined by Greeks, Puerto Ricans and blacks. The rough-and-tumble area was popularized in the 1957 musical *West Side Story*. But things have changed quite a bit: the odd tatty block is now countered by trim residential streets, and construction and renovation of luxury apartments and hotels occurs at sometimes breakneck speed. Along with other gentrifiers, there's now a substantial gay community, with nearly as many gay bars and nightspots as in Chelsea or the East Village.

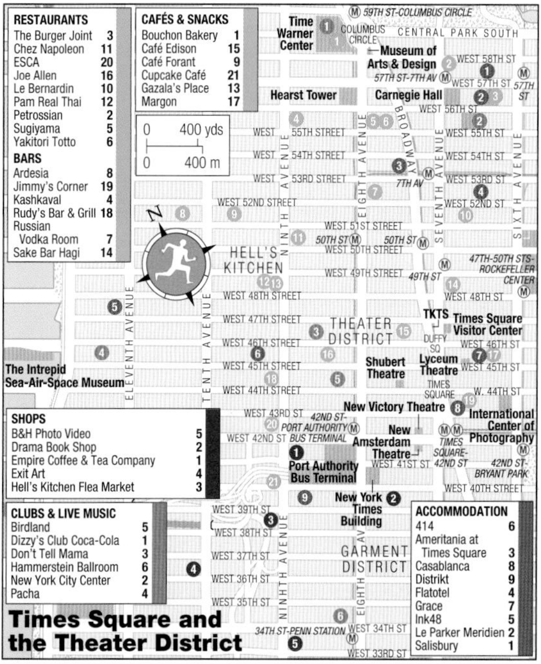

The Theater District

West of Broadway and north of 42nd Street, the Theater District helps light up Times Square. Of the great old palaces still in existence, the **New Amsterdam**, at 214 W 42nd St, and family-oriented **New Victory**, at 209 W 42nd St, have been refurbished to their original splendour. **The Lyceum**, at 149 W 45th St, has its original facade, while the **Shubert Theater**, at 225 W 44th St, has a magnificent landmark interior that belies its simple outward appearance.

If you want to see a **show**, check out the TKTS booth at 47th Street in Times Square (there are other booths at the South Street Seaport and 1 Metro Center), which sells half-price, same-day tickets for Broadway shows (Mon & Wed–Sat 3–8pm, Tues 2–8pm for evening shows, also Wed & Sat 10am–2pm, Sun 11am–3pm for matinees). The booth has available at least one pair of tickets for each performance of every Broadway and off-Broadway show, at 20 to 50 percent off (plus a $4 per ticket service charge). Also, many theatre box offices sell greatly reduced "standing room only" tickets the day of the show.

THE INTREPID SEA-AIR-SPACE MUSEUM

Pier 86 at W 46th St and Twelfth Ave. Subway A, C, E to 42nd St; C, E to 50th St
212/245-0072, www.intrepidmuseum.org. April–Sept Mon–Fri 10am–5pm, Sat & Sun 10am–6pm; Oct–March Tues–Sun 10am–5pm. $22, ages 3–17 $17. MAP P.123, POCKET MAP B8

This impressive, 900ft-long old aircraft carrier has picked up capsules from the Mercury and Gemini space missions and made several trips to Vietnam. It holds an array of modern and vintage air- and seacraft, including the A-12 Blackbird, the world's fastest spy plane, and the USS *Growler*, the only guided missile submarine open to the public. Interactive exhibits dominate the interior hangar, but make sure to explore further into the bowels of the carrier, where you can see the crew's dining and sleeping quarters, the anchor room and lots of navigational gadgets. The museum is also home to the retired *Concorde*, as well as the space shuttle *Enterprise* (just a test vehicle – it never made it to outer space).

INTREPID SEA-AIR-SPACE MUSEUM

CARNEGIE HALL

INTERNATIONAL CENTER OF PHOTOGRAPHY

1133 Sixth Ave at 43rd St. Subway B, D, F, V to 42nd St ☎212/857-0000, ©www.icp.org. Tues & Wed 10am–6pm, Thurs & Fri 10am–8pm, Sat & Sun 10am–6pm. $12. MAP P.123, POCKET MAP D8

Founded in 1974 by Cornell Capa (brother of war photographer Robert Capa), this exceptional museum and school sponsors around twenty exhibits a year dedicated to "concerned photography", avant-garde and experimental works, and retrospectives of modern masters. Many shows focus on works from their own extensive permanent collection, which holds basically all of Robert Capa's photography, as well as that of New York sensationalist Weegee.

CARNEGIE HALL

154 W 57th St at Seventh Ave. Subway N, Q, R to 57th St ☎212/903-9765, tickets ☎212/247-7800, ©www.carnegiehall.org. Tours late Sept–June usually Mon–Fri 11.30am, 12.30pm, 2pm & 3pm, Sat 11.30am & 12.30pm, Sun 12.30pm. $10. MAP P.123, POCKET MAP D7

One of the world's great concert venues, stately Renaissance-inspired **Carnegie Hall** was built by steel magnate Andrew Carnegie for $1 million in 1891. Tchaikovsky conducted on opening night and Mahler, Rachmaninov, Toscanini, Frank Sinatra, Duke Ellington and Judy Garland have all played here. The superb acoustics help to ensure full houses most of the year; those craving a behind-the-scenes glimpse should take the excellent tours.

COLUMBUS CIRCLE

Intersection of Broadway, Central Park West and 59th St. Subway A, B, C, D, #1 to 59th St–Columbus Circle. MAP P.123, POCKET MAP C7

A rare Manhattan roundabout that separates Midtown from the Upper West Side, **Columbus Circle** is best experienced from its centre island underneath the statue of Columbus himself, who stands uncomfortably atop a lone column. From there you can look out at at the horse and carriages off Central Park and some striking buildings, like the Hearst Tower, Time Warner Center and Two Columbus Circle. Off the circle at the Central Park entrance is the **USS Maine Monument**, a large stone column with the prow of a ship jutting out from its base; a dazzlingly bright gilded statue of Columbia Triumphant tops it off. The monument is dedicated to the 260 seamen who died in an explosion that helped propel the Spanish–American War.

HEARST TOWER

300 W 57th St at Eighth Ave. Subway A, B, C, D, #1 to 59th St–Columbus Circle. MAP P.123, POCKET MAP C7

The limestone base of the **Hearst Tower** waited for a skyscraper to top it since the Great Depression. Finally completed in 2006, the glass-and- steel geometry of the Hearst Tower sits ingeniously – and somewhat incongruously – inside the shell of that base. It's certified as one of the most environmentally friendly high-rises ever constructed and was the first skyscraper to begin construction post 9/11.

MUSEUM OF ARTS AND DESIGN

2 Columbus Circle. Subway A, B, C, D, #1 to 59th St–Columbus Circle ☎ 212/299-7777, www.madmuseum.org. Tues–Sun 11am–6pm, Thurs & Fri until 9pm. $15, Thurs & Fri 6–9pm pay what you wish. MAP P.123, POCKET MAP C7

The story of the building that arcs along the south side of Columbus Circle is as interesting as the holdings of the **Museum of Arts and Design** that occupy it. Built in the 1960s to house the Gallery of Modern Art, Two Columbus Circle was regarded as an architectural folly (and a failure as a museum), yet after years of abandonment and disrepair, the building became the subject of an epic battle over its significance and status. Noted architects like Robert A.M. Stern fought for its preservation but eventually failed, and the Museum of Arts and Design (the former American Crafts Museum) had the building totally redesigned. Gone are the portholes and white marble; in their place, slots, ceramic and glass that seem to form letter shapes on the facade. The eclectic collection inside features everything from blown-glass objets d'art to contemporary jewellery; the temporary exhibits frequently take centre stage.

TIME WARNER CENTER

10 Columbus Circle. Subway A, B, C, D, #1 to 59th St–Columbus Circle. MAP P.123, POCKET MAP C7

The glassy, curving **Time Warner Center**, a massive, $1.7 billion home for companies like CNN and Warner Books, with a shopping complex on its lower levels, opened in 2004. The timing and design make it hard not to think of it as a more modern, less-loved variation of the Twin Towers. None of the shops merits any particular interest, though some of the city's priciest restaurants (*Per Se*, *Masa*) dish it out here.

TIME WARNER CENTER

Shops and galleries

B&H PHOTO VIDEO

420 Ninth Ave at 34th St. Subway A, C, E to 34th St. Mon–Thurs 9am–7pm, Fri 9am–1pm, Sun 10am–6pm. MAP P.123, POCKET MAP C9

You'll find a staggering array of cameras, camcorders, blu-ray players and every other kind of home electronic you might want or need; there's a used-goods section upstairs. Closed on Saturdays and Jewish holidays.

DRAMA BOOK SHOP

250 W 40th St between Seventh and Eighth aves. Subway A, C, E, N, Q, R, #1, #2, #3, #7 to 42nd St. Mon–Sat 11am–7pm, Thurs until 8pm. MAP P.123, POCKET MAP C9

A long-running shop that stocks theatre books, scripts and publications on all manner of drama-related subjects.

EMPIRE COFFEE AND TEA COMPANY

568 Ninth Ave between 41st and 42nd aves. Subway A, C, E to 42nd St. Mon–Fri 7.30am–7pm, Sat 9am–6.30pm, Sun 10am–6pm. MAP P.123, POCKET MAP C8

One-hundred-year-old coffee roaster that looks and smells authentic. There are lots of exotic teas, too.

EXIT ART

475 Tenth Ave between 36th and 37th aves. Subway A, C, E to 34th St. Mon–Fri 10am–6pm, Sat noon–6pm. MAP P.123, POCKET MAP B9

An alternative space, this bi-level gallery draws a hip crowd for its big installations and its focus on edgy cultural and political subjects; usually five or six major exhibitions a year.

HELL'S KITCHEN FLEA MARKET

HELL'S KITCHEN FLEA MARKET

W 39th St between Ninth and Tenth aves. Subway A, C, E to 42nd St. Sat & Sun 9am–6pm. MAP P.123, POCKET MAP C9

While there's still an indoor flea market in Chelsea, the outdoor version relocated to Hell's Kitchen; you'll find a mishmash of home decorations, antique jewellery, electronics and other odds and ends..

Cafés and snacks

BOUCHON BAKERY

Ten Columbus Circle, Third Floor, Time Warner Center; another location in Rockefeller Center. Subway A, B, C, D, #1 to 59th St–Columbus Circle. Mon–Sat 8am–9pm, Sun 8am–7pm (café menu daily 11.30am–6pm). MAP P.123, POCKET MAP C7

At this Thomas Keller establishment you can get something to go from the counter or sit at a table and take some time to gaze through the windows onto the corner of leafy Central Park, grazing on a ham-and-cheese sandwich, croissant or a decadent pastry.

CAFÉ EDISON

228 W 47th St between Broadway and Eighth Ave, in the Hotel Edison. Subway C, E, #1 to 50th St ☎ 212/840-5000. Mon–Sat 6am–9.30pm, Sun 6am–7.30pm. MAP P.123, POCKET MAP C8

This old-style coffeeshop might give a little attitude with the service, but that's just part of the gruff charm. It manages to be a favourite with theatre-types in any case. And the tasty matzoh ball soup and brisket sandwiches more than compensate.

CAFÉ FORANT

449 W 51st St between Ninth and Tenth aves. Subway C, E to 50th St. Tues–Fri 10am–10pm, Sat & Sun 10am–5pm. MAP P.123, POCKET MAP C7

Cafés don't come friendlier than this quiet neighbourhood spot, tucked down a quiet street in Hell's Kitchen. The brunch food is stellar, sandwiches and salads are fresh, the coffee is strong and the price is right. Cash only.

CUPCAKE CAFÉ

545 Ninth Ave St between 40th and 41st sts. Subway A, C, E to 42nd St. Mon–Sat 8am–7pm, Sun 9am–7pm. MAP P.123, POCKET MAP C9

The coffee and cupcakes are impeccable at this shabby chic café; there's another location within Books of Wonder (see p.104).

GAZALA'S PLACE

709 Ninth Ave, between 48th and 49th sts. Subway C, E to 50th St. Daily 11am–10.30pm. MAP P.123, POCKET MAP C8

Supposedly the only Druze (a Middle Eastern sect) restaurant in the States – besides the outpost at 380 Columbus Ave on the UWS – *Gazala's* serves a full lunch and dinner menu, but is best-known for its flaky *bourekas* ($8), giant savoury pastries stuffed with cheese and other items.

MARGON

136 W 46th St, between Sixth and Seventh aves. Subway B, D, F, M to 47–50th sts-Rockefeller Center, N, Q, R to 49th St ☎ 212/354-5013. Mon–Fri 6am–5pm, Sat 7am–3pm. MAP P.123, POCKET MAP D8

This narrow Cuban lunch counter is nearly always packed, but the jostling is worth it; savoury Cuban sandwiches ($9 with rice and beans), garlicky *pernil* (roast pork; Wed special, $8.75) and, best of all, brightly seasoned octopus salad ($11) top the choices.

Restaurants

THE BURGER JOINT

119 W 56th St between Sixth and Seventh aves, in Le Parker Meridien. Subway F, N, Q, R to 57th St. Mon–Thurs & Sun 11am–11.30pm, Fri & Sat 11am to midnight. MAP P.123, POCKET MAP D7

The secret has long been out on the retro hamburger stand incongruously located in a swish Midtown hotel. Good for late-night eating; you might have to wait for a table, though.

CHEZ NAPOLEON

365 W 50th St between Eighth and Ninth aves. Subway C, E to 50th St ☎ 212/265-6980. Mon–Fri noon–2pm & 5–9.30/10pm, Sat 4.30–9.30/10pm. MAP P.123, POCKET MAP C8

One of several highly authentic Gallic eateries that sprung up around here in the 1940s and 1950s, *Chez Napoleon*, a friendly, family-run bistro, is kind of stuck in a time warp – in a good way. There's a good-value prix-fixe, and the wines are well priced.

ESCA

402 W 43rd St at Ninth Ave. Subway A, C, E to 42nd St-Port Authority. Mon noon–2.30pm

& 5–10.30pm, Tues–Sat noon–2.30pm & 5–11.30pm, Sun 4.30–10.30pm. 212/564-7272, www.esca-nyc.com. MAP P.123, POCKET MAP C9

Co-owned by Mario Batali, but more the baby of chef and co-owner Dave Pasternack, whose passion for fresh fish is evident. Lots of crudo ($18–20) and whole fish grilled or salt-baked (entrees $30–37).

JOE ALLEN

326 W 46th St between Eighth and Ninth aves. Subway A, C, E to 42nd St 212/581-6464. Mon, Tues & Thurs noon–11.45pm, Wed & Sun 11.30am–11.45pm, Fri noon–midnight, Sat 11.30am–midnight. MAP P.123, POCKET MAP C8

The tried-and-true formula of checked tablecloths, old-fashioned bar-room feel, and reliable American food at moderate prices works well at this popular pre-theatre spot. Make a reservation.

LE BERNARDIN

155 W 51st St between Sixth and Seventh aves. Subway B, D, F, M to 47-50th St-Rockefeller Center or #1 to 50th St 212/554-1515. Mon–Thurs noon–2.30pm & 5.15–10.30pm, Fri noon–2.30pm & 5.30–11pm, Sat 5.30–11pm. MAP P.123, POCKET MAP D7

One of the finest and priciest French restaurants in the city; the award-winning chef, Eric Ripert, offers inventive takes on every kind of fish and seafood imaginable. His sauces are not to be believed.

PAM REAL THAI

404 W 49th St, between Ninth and Tenth aves. Subway C, E to 50th St. Mon–Thurs & Sun 11.30am–11pm, Fri & Sat 11.30am–11.30pm 212/333-7500, www.pamrealthaifood.com. MAP P.123, POCKET MAP C8

Pam has won a following for its spicy food and some slightly unusual dishes (fermented fish kidneys, $10.95); it's better to stick with a *larb* (salad with minced meat, $5.95) and one of the curries ($8–13). Cash only.

LE BERNARDIN

PETROSSIAN

182 W 58th St at Seventh Ave. Subway A, B, C, D, #1 to 59th St/Columbus Circle 212/245-2214. Mon–Thurs & Sun 11am–3.30pm & 5–11pm, Fri & Sat 11.30am–3pm & 5.30–11pm. MAP P.123, POCKET MAP D7

Ink granite and etched mirrors set the mood at this Art Deco temple to decadence, where champagne and caviar are tops. More affordable options include a $38 prix-fixe dinner.

SUGIYAMA

251 W 55th St between Broadway and Eighth Ave. Subway B, D, E to Seventh Ave, N, Q, R to 57th St-Seventh Ave 212/956-0670. Tues–Sat 5.30–11.45pm (last seating 10.15pm). MAP P.123, POCKET MAP C7

You may want to take out a loan before dining at this superb Japanese restaurant, where you're guaranteed an exquisite experience, from its enchanting *kaiseki* (chef's choice) dinners to its regal service. Reservations recommended.

YAKITORI TOTTO

251 W 55th St between Broadway and Eighth Ave. Subway A, B, C, D, #1 to 59th St–Columbus Circle; N, Q, R to 57th St; B, D, E to Seventh Ave ☎212/245-4555. Mon–Thurs 11.30am–2pm & 5.30pm–midnight, Fri 11.30am–2pm & 5.30pm–1am, Sat 5.30pm–1am, Sun 5.30–11pm. MAP P.123, POCKET MAP C7

Just upstairs from *Sugiyama* (see p.129), this popular hideaway is perfect for late-night snacking – though you may miss out on some of the more esoteric grilled skewers (soft knee bone served rare, anyone?), which can be gone by then. Chicken heart, skirt steak and chicken thigh with scallion all burst with flavour.

Bars

ARDESIA

510 W 52nd St between Tenth and Eleventh aves. Subway C, E to 50th St. Mon–Wed 5pm–midnight, Thurs–Sat 5pm–2am, Sun 5pm–11pm ☎212/247-9191, www.ardesia-ny.com. MAP P.123, POCKET MAP B7

A sleek but comfortable wine bar with a bold snack menu (home-made pretzels, quail-egg toast, home-cured meats) and a diverse selection of vintages, thirty of which are available by the glass ($8–14).

JIMMY'S CORNER

JIMMY'S CORNER

140 W 44th St between Broadway and Sixth Ave. Subway B, D, F, M, N, Q, R, V, W, #1, #2, #3 to 42nd St. Mon–Sat 10am–4am, Sun 1pm–4am. MAP P.123, POCKET MAP D8

The walls of this long, narrow corridor of a bar, owned by an ex-fighter/trainer, comprise a virtual Boxing Hall of Fame. You'd be hard pressed to find a more characterful dive anywhere in the city – or a better jazz/r&b jukebox.

KASHKAVAL

856 Ninth Ave between 55th and 56th sts. Subway A, B, C, D, #1 to 59th St/Columbus Circle. Daily 11am–midnight. MAP P.123, POCKET MAP C7

Tucked in the back of a cheese shop, this cosy wine bar serves up tasty bites, including excellent cheese and meat plates, cold meze (beetroot *skordalia* is a must) and an array of fondues.

RUDY'S BAR & GRILL

627 Ninth Ave between W 44th and 45th sts. Subway A, C, E to 42nd St–Port Authority. Daily 8am–4am. MAP P.123, POCKET MAP C8

One of New York's cheapest, friendliest and liveliest dive bars, a favourite with local actors and musicians. Rudy's offers free hot dogs and a great backyard.

RUSSIAN VODKA ROOM

265 W 52nd St between Broadway and Eighth Ave. Subway C, E, #1 to 50th St. Mon–Wed & Sun 4pm–2am, Thurs–Sat 4pm–4am MAP P.123, POCKET MAP C7

They serve more than fifty types of vodka here, including their own fruit-flavoured and sublime garlic-infused concoctions; there's also caviar and plenty of small plates. Under the dim lighting, office workers mingle with Russian and Eastern European expats; whatever you do, don't ask for a mixer with your shot.

SAKE BAR HAGI

152 W 49th St between Sixth and Seventh aves. Subway B, D, M, Q to 47–50th St-Rockefeller Center, N, R to 49th St, #1 to 50th St ⓣ 212/764-8549. Daily 5.30pm–3.30am. MAP P.123, POCKET MAP D8

Bustling izakaya (snack) bar, with cheap sakes and beer, plus a fine array of accompaniments like grilled fatty pork, yellowtail collar and yakitori.

Clubs and live music

BIRDLAND

315 W 44th St between Eighth and Ninth aves Subway A, C, E to 42nd St–Port Authority. ⓣ 212/581-3080, ⓦ www.birdlandjazz.com. Cover $20–50, $10 food/drink minimum. MAP P.123, POCKET MAP C8

Celebrated alto saxophonist Charlie "Bird" Parker has served as the inspiration for this jazz venue, which has existed in some incarnation for sixty years – while not the original, they still put on good shows. Sets are at 8.30pm and 11pm nightly.

DIZZY'S CLUB COCA-COLA

Time Warner Center, Broadway at W 60th St, 5th floor. Subway A, B, C, D, #1 to 59th St-Columbus Circle ⓣ 212/258-9595, ⓦ www.jalc.org. Shows at 7.30 & 9.30pm. $20–35 cover, $10 minimum at tables. MAP P.123, POCKET MAP C7

Part of Jazz at Lincoln Center's home within the Time Warner Center, this room named in honour of Dizzy Gillespie is the only great jazz venue in town with a view – that of Central Park. Book a table for dinner or just drinks and enjoy hot acts.

DON'T TELL MAMA

343 W 46th St between Eighth and Ninth aves. Subway A, C, E to 42nd St–Port Authority or 50th St ⓣ 212/757-0788, ⓦ www.donttellmamanyc.com. Cover $10–25. MAP P.123, POCKET MAP C8

HAMMERSTEIN BALLROOM

The lively, convivial piano bar and cabaret features rising stars. Two-drink minimum in cabaret rooms; showtimes vary.

HAMMERSTEIN BALLROOM

311 W 34th St between Eighth and Ninth aves. Subway A, C, E, #1, #2, #3 to 34th St-Penn Station ⓣ 212/564-4882, ⓦ www.mcstudios.com. MAP P.123, POCKET MAP C9

A grand 1906 building that has seen incarnations as an opera house, vaudeville hall and Masonic temple, the *Hammerstein* is now a prime rock space; a second venue, the *Grand*, hosts shows too.

NEW YORK CITY CENTER

131 W 55th St at Seventh Ave. Subway B, D, E to Seventh Ave; F to 57th St; N, Q, R to 57th St–Seventh Ave ⓣ 212/581-1212, ⓦ www.citycenter.org. MAP P.123, POCKET MAP D7

This large, restored venue – once a temple – revives long-forgotten musicals; plays host to the Manhattan Theatre Club; and is a major dance site.

PACHA

618 W 46th St between Eleventh and Twelfth aves. Subway C, E to 50th St. $20–40 cover. MAP P.123, POCKET MAP B8

A sprawling dance spot that plays host to giant crowds, this is the New York outpost of the chain of Ibiza superclubs.

Central Park

"All radiant in the magic atmosphere of art and taste", enthused *Harper's* magazine upon the opening in 1876 of Central Park, the first landscaped park in the US. Today, few New Yorkers could imagine life without it. Set smack in the middle of Manhattan, extending from 59th to 110th streets, it provides residents (and street-weary tourists) with a much-needed refuge from the arduousness of big-city life. The two architects commissioned to transform 843 swampy acres, Frederick Law Olmsted and Calvert Vaux, were inspired by classic English landscape gardening. They designed 36 elegant bridges, each unique, and planned a revolutionary system of four sunken transverse roads to keep traffic out of sight. Although some of the open space has been turned into asphalted playgrounds, the intended sense of captured nature largely survives.

WOLLMAN MEMORIAL ICE SKATING RINK

830 Fifth Ave at E 63rd St. Subway N, R to Fifth Ave–59th St 212/439-6900, www.wollmanskatingrink.com. Oct–April Mon & Tues 10am–2.30pm, Wed & Thurs 10am–10pm, Fri & Sat 10am–11pm, Sun 10am–9pm. Mon–Fri $10.75, Sat & Sun $16, children $6. MAP P.133, POCKET MAP D6

Get in the rink for some of the city's most atmospheric ice skating; you're surrounded by onlookers, trees and, beyond that, a brilliant view of Central Park South's skyline. In summers, **Wollman Rink** becomes **Victorian Gardens**, a small amusement park.

CENTRAL PARK

CENTRAL PARK ZOO

Enter at Fifth Ave and E 64th St. Subway N, R to Fifth Ave–59th St 212/439-6500, www.centralparkzoo.com. April–Oct Mon–Fri 10am–5pm, Sat & Sun 10am–5.30pm, Nov–March daily 10am–4.30pm. $12, ages 3–12 $7. MAP P.133, POCKET MAP D6

This small zoo contains over a hundred species in largely natural-looking homes with the animals as close to the viewer as possible: the penguins, for example, swim around at eye level in Plexiglas pools. Other highlights include giant polar bears and a humid tropical zone filled with exotic birds. The complex also features the **Tisch Children's Zoo**, with a petting zoo and interactive displays.

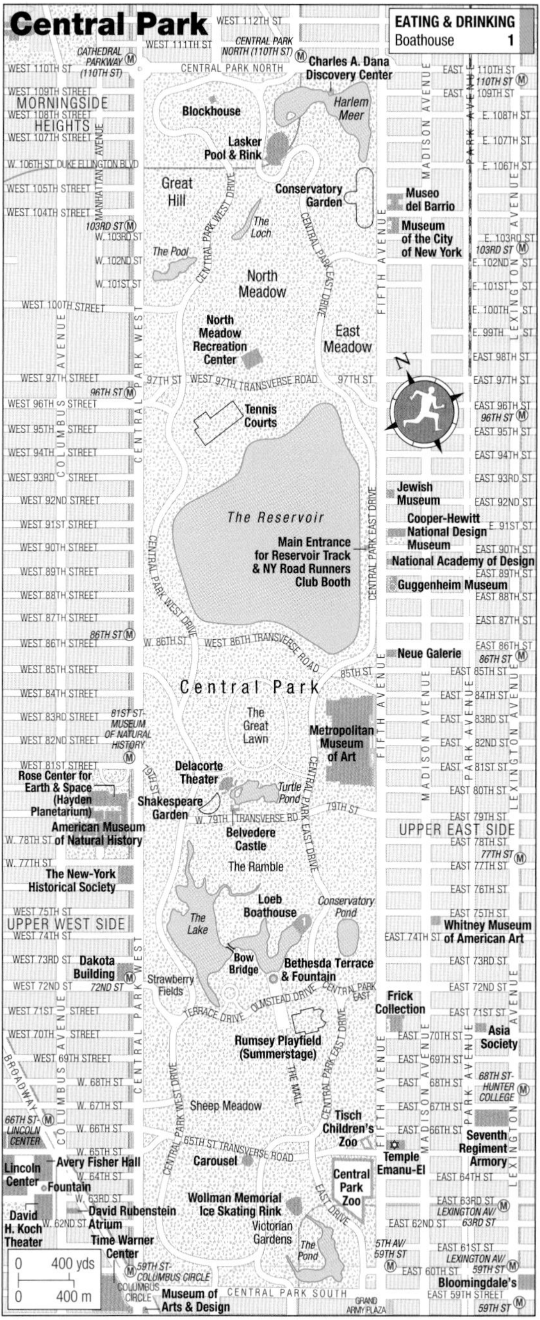
Central Park
EATING & DRINKING
Boathouse 1
WEST 112TH ST
WEST 111TH ST
CENTRAL PARK NORTH (110TH ST)
CATHEDRAL PARKWAY (110TH ST)
WEST 110TH ST
CENTRAL PARK NORTH
Charles A. Dana Discovery Center
Harlem Meer
EAST 110TH ST
110TH ST
EAST 109TH ST
WEST 109TH STREET
MORNINGSIDE HEIGHTS
WEST 108TH STREET
WEST 107TH STREET
Blockhouse
Lasker Pool & Rink
E. 108TH ST
E. 107TH ST
E. 106TH ST
W. 106TH ST DUKE ELLINGTON BLVD
MANHATTAN AVENUE
MADISON AVENUE
PARK AVENUE
WEST 105TH STREET
WEST 104TH STREET
Great Hill
Conservatory Garden
Museo del Barrio
103RD ST
W. 103RD ST
The Loch
Museum of the City of New York
E. 103RD ST
103RD ST
LEXINGTON AVENUE
W. 102ND ST
The Pool
CENTRAL PARK WEST DRIVE
CENTRAL PARK EAST DRIVE
E. 102ND ST
W. 101ST ST
North Meadow
E. 101ST ST
WEST 100TH STREET
E. 100TH ST
North Meadow Recreation Center
East Meadow
E. 99TH ST
FIFTH AVENUE
COLUMBUS AVENUE
CENTRAL PARK WEST
EAST 98TH ST
WEST 97TH STREET
97TH ST
WEST 97TH TRANSVERSE ROAD
97TH ST
EAST 97TH ST
96TH ST
WEST 96TH STREET
Tennis Courts
EAST 96TH ST
96TH ST
WEST 95TH STREET
EAST 95TH ST
WEST 94TH STREET
EAST 94TH ST
WEST 93RD STREET
EAST 93RD ST
Jewish Museum
WEST 92ND STREET
EAST 92ND ST
The Reservoir
Cooper-Hewitt National Design Museum
WEST 91ST STREET
E. 91ST ST
WEST 90TH STREET
Main Entrance for Reservoir Track & NY Road Runners Club Booth
EAST 90TH ST
National Academy of Design
WEST 89TH STREET
EAST 89TH ST
Guggenheim Museum
WEST 88TH STREET
EAST 88TH ST
WEST 87TH STREET
EAST 87TH ST
86TH ST
WEST 86TH STREET
W. 86TH ST
WEST 86TH TRANSVERSE ROAD
Neue Galerie
EAST 86TH ST
86TH ST
WEST 85TH STREET
85TH ST
EAST 85TH ST
Central Park
WEST 84TH STREET
EAST 84TH ST
WEST 83RD STREET
81ST ST-MUSEUM OF NATURAL HISTORY
The Great Lawn
Metropolitan Museum of Art
EAST 83RD ST
WEST 82ND STREET
EAST 82ND ST
WEST 81ST STREET
Delacorte Theater
EAST 81ST ST
Rose Center for Earth & Space (Hayden Planetarium)
79TH ST
Turtle Pond
EAST 80TH ST
Shakespeare Garden
79TH ST
W. 79TH TRANSVERSE RD
EAST 79TH ST
American Museum of Natural History
Belvedere Castle
UPPER EAST SIDE
W. 78TH ST
EAST 78TH ST
77TH ST
W. 77TH ST
The Ramble
EAST 77TH ST
The New-York Historical Society
EAST 76TH ST
Loeb Boathouse
Conservatory Pond
WEST 75TH ST
EAST 75TH ST
UPPER WEST SIDE
The Lake
Whitney Museum of American Art
WEST 74TH ST
EAST 74TH ST
WEST 73RD ST
Dakota Building
Bow Bridge
Bethesda Terrace & Fountain
EAST 73RD ST
WEST 72ND ST
72ND ST
Strawberry Fields
CENTRAL PARK EAST
EAST 72ND ST
Frick Collection
OLMSTEAD DRIVE
TERRACE DRIVE
WEST 71ST STREET
EAST 71ST ST
Asia Society
WEST 70TH STREET
EAST 70TH ST
Rumsey Playfield (Summerstage)
BROADWAY
WEST 69TH STREET
EAST 69TH ST
W. 68TH ST
THE MALL
EAST 68TH ST
68TH ST-HUNTER COLLEGE
W. 67TH ST
Sheep Meadow
EAST 67TH ST
66TH ST-LINCOLN CENTER
W. 66TH ST
Tisch Children's Zoo
EAST 66TH ST
Seventh Regiment Armory
65TH ST TRANSVERSE ROAD
W. 65TH ST
Temple Emanu-El
Lincoln Center
Avery Fisher Hall
Carousel
Central Park Zoo
EAST 64TH ST
W. 64TH ST
Fountain
W. 63RD ST
Wollman Memorial Ice Skating Rink
EAST DRIVE
EAST 63RD ST
LEXINGTON AV/63RD ST
David H. Koch Theater
David Rubenstein Atrium
W. 62ND ST
Victorian Gardens
EAST 62ND ST
Time Warner Center
The Pond
5TH AV/59TH ST
EAST 61ST ST
LEXINGTON AV/59TH ST
0 400 yds
0 400 m
59TH ST-COLUMBUS CIRCLE
COLUMBUS CIRCLE
EAST 60TH ST
Bloomingdale's
Museum of Arts & Design
CENTRAL PARK SOUTH
GRAND ARMY PLAZA
EAST 59TH STREET
59TH ST

THE CAROUSEL

Mid-park at 64th St. Subway A, B, C, D, #1, to 59th St–Columbus Circle ☎ 212/439-6900. Daily: April–Oct 10am–6pm; Nov–March roughly same hours weather permitting. $2.50. MAP P.133, POCKET MAP D6

Built in 1908 and moved to the park from Coney Island in 1951, this hand-carved, wooden **carousel** is one of around 150 such specimens left in the country.

THE MALL

Roughly mid-park from 66th to 72nd sts. Subway #6 to 68th St; B, C to 72nd St. MAP P.133, POCKET MAP D6

If the weather's nice head straight to the **Mall**, where you'll find every manner of street performer. Flanked by statues of Robert Burns and a pensive Sir Walter Scott, with Shakespeare nearby (all part of the so-called literary walk), the Mall is the park's most formal, but by no means quiet, stretch.

THE SHEEP MEADOW

Between 66th and 69th sts on the western side. Subway #1 to 66th St-Lincoln Center. Mid-April to mid-Oct dawn to dusk. MAP P.133, POCKET MAP C6

This swathe of green, named after the fifteen acres of commons where sheep grazed until 1934, is crowded in the summer with picnic blankets.

Two grass courts used for lawn bowling and croquet are found on a hill near the meadow's northwest corner; to the southeast lie volleyball courts. On warm weekends, the area between the **Sheep Meadow** and the north end of the Mall is filled with colourfully attired rollerbladers.

STRAWBERRY FIELDS

W 72nd St and Central Park W. Subway B, C to 72nd St. MAP P.133, POCKET MAP C5

This peaceful pocket of the park is dedicated to the memory of John Lennon, who was murdered in 1980 in front of his home, the **Dakota Building** (see p.148). The tragic event is memorialized with a round Italian mosaic with the word "Imagine" at its centre, donated by Lennon's widow, Yoko Ono.

BETHESDA TERRACE AND FOUNTAIN

Roughly mid-park at 72nd St. Subway B, C to 72nd St. MAP P.133, POCKET MAP D5

The only formal element of the original Olmsted and Vaux plan, the **Bethesda Terrace** overlooks the lake; beneath the terrace is an elaborate arcade with tiled floors. The crowning centrepiece of the **Bethesda Fountain** is the *Angel of the Waters* sculpture.

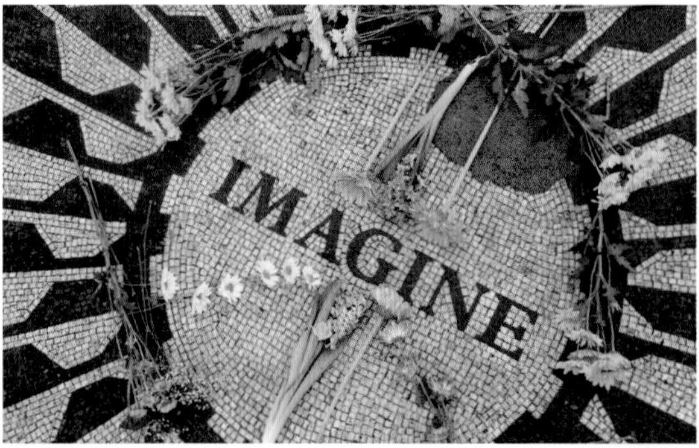

STRAWBERRY FIELDS

ROWING IN CENTRAL PARK

LOEB BOATHOUSE

Mid-park near 74th st. Subway B, C to 72nd St ☎212/517-2233. April–Oct Mon–Fri 10am–6pm, Sat & Sun 9am–6pm, weather permitting $12 for the first hour, and $2.50 per 15min after, $20 deposit required. MAP P.133, POCKET MAP D5

You can go for a Venetian-style gondola ride or rent a rowing boat from the **Loeb Boathouse** on the lake's eastern bank. Bicycles are also available ($9–15/hr or $45–50/day; $200 deposit and ID required).

THE GREAT LAWN

Mid-park from 79th to 85th sts. Subway B, C to 81st or 86th sts. MAP P.133, POCKET MAP D4

The **Great Lawn** hosts free New York Philharmonic and Metropolitan Opera summertime concerts, holds eight softball fields, basketball and volleyball courts, and a running track. At the southern end, **Turtle Pond** is a fine place to view turtles and birds.

BELVEDERE CASTLE

Mid-park at 79th St ☎212/772-0210. Visitor Center April–Oct Tues–Sun 10am–5pm; Nov–March Wed–Sun 10am–5pm. Regular walking tours, birdwatching excursions and educational programmes on offer. MAP P.133, POCKET MAP D5

The highest point in the park (and a splendid viewpoint), **Belvedere Castle**, designed by park architect Vaux and his longtime assistant, Jacob Wrey Mould, houses the New York Meteorological Observatory's **weather centre** and the **Henry Luce Nature Observatory**.

DELACORTE THEATER

Mid-park at 80th St. Subway B, C to 81st St ☎212/539-8750, www.publictheater.org. MAP P.133, POCKET MAP D5

This performance space is most notably home to **Shakespeare in the Park** in the summer. Tickets are free but go quickly; visit the website for details.

CONSERVATORY GARDEN

East side from 104th to 106th sts, entrance at Fifth Ave and 105th St. Subway #6 to 103rd St. MAP P.133, POCKET MAP D2

If you see nothing else above 86th Street in the park, don't miss the **Conservatory Garden**, the park's only formal garden, featuring English, Italian and French styles.

Eating and drinking

You won't have a problem finding vendors for water, ice cream or hot dogs throughout the park, but there's only one true eating destination, the *Boathouse* at Central Park Rowboat Lake, E 72nd St entrance (☎212/517-2233). The main dining spot is a peaceful, romantic setting for a surprisingly good meal, with casual, cheaper bar/grill and café options on site too.

The Upper East Side

The defining characteristic of Manhattan's Upper East Side is wealth. While other neighbourhoods were penetrated by immigrant groups and artistic trends, the area has remained primarily a privileged enclave of the well off, with high-end shops, clean and relatively safe streets, well-preserved buildings and landmarks, most of the city's finest museums, and some of its most famous boulevards: Fifth, Madison and Park avenues. Madison Avenue is lined with designer clothes stores, while primarily residential Park Avenue is stolidly comfortable and often elegant, sweeping down the spine of upper Manhattan. It has awe-inspiring views south, as the avenue coasts down to Grand Central and the Met Life Building. Things are changing, however: in recent years rents have lowered considerably, and the streets a few blocks back from Central Park are beginning to lose their air of exclusivity.

FIFTH AVENUE

Subway F to Lexington Ave/63rd St; N, R to Lexington Ave/59th St; #4, #5, #6 to 59th St; #6 to 68th St, 77th St, 86th St or 96th St. MAP P.137, POCKET MAP D3–D7

The haughty patrician face of Manhattan since the 1876 opening of Central Park along which it runs, **Fifth Avenue** lured the Carnegies, Astors, Vanderbilts, Whitneys and others north to build their fashionable Neoclassical residences. In the late nineteenth century, fanciful mansions were built at vast expense, but lasted only ten or fifteen years before being demolished for even wilder extravagances or, more commonly, grand apartment buildings. As Fifth Avenue progresses north, it turns into the **Museum Mile**.

CARTIER, FIFTH AVENUE

TEMPLE EMANU-EL

1 E 65th St at Fifth Ave. Subway F to Lexington Ave/63rd St; #6 to 68th St ☎ 212/744-1400, www.emanuelnyc.org. Synagogue and museum Sun–Thurs 10am–4.30pm. Free. MAP P.137, POCKET MAP D6

America's largest reform synagogue, the **Temple Emanu-El**, is a brooding, Romanesque–Byzantine cavern. The on-site museum houses a fascinating collection of Judaica.

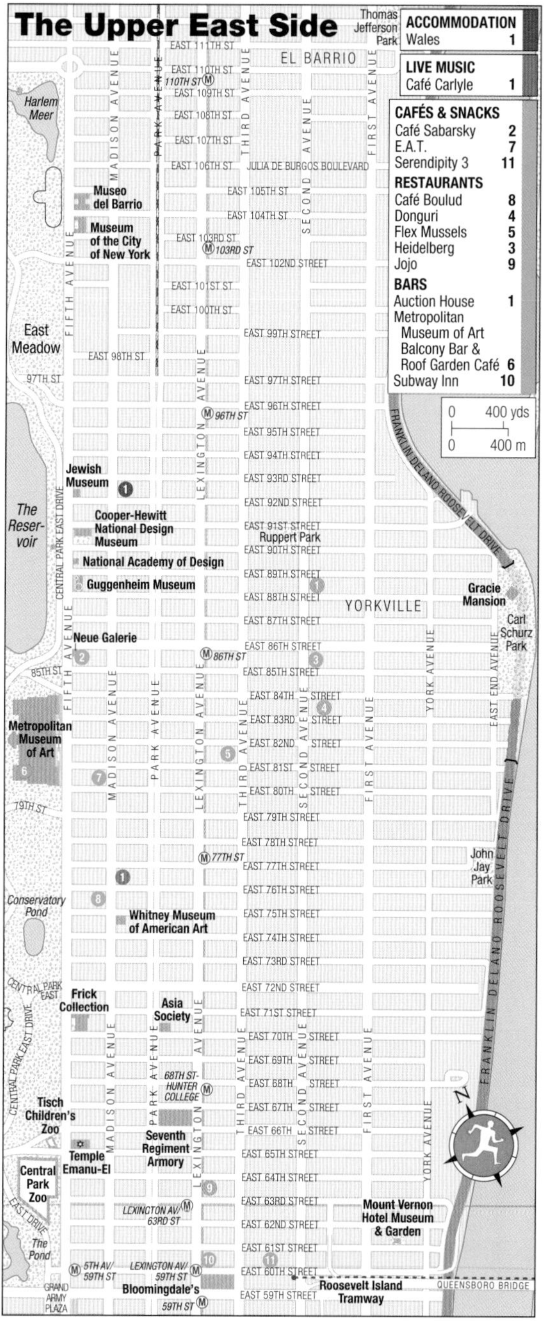

The Upper East Side
ACCOMMODATION
Wales 1
LIVE MUSIC
Café Carlyle 1
CAFÉS & SNACKS
Café Sabarsky 2
E.A.T. 7
Serendipity 3 11
RESTAURANTS
Café Boulud 8
Donguri 4
Flex Mussels 5
Heidelberg 3
Jojo 9
BARS
Auction House 1
Metropolitan Museum of Art Balcony Bar & Roof Garden Café 6
Subway Inn 10
0 400 yds
0 400 m
Thomas Jefferson Park
EL BARRIO
YORKVILLE
Harlem Meer
East Meadow
The Reservoir
Conservatory Pond
The Pond
Museo del Barrio
Museum of the City of New York
Jewish Museum
Cooper-Hewitt National Design Museum
National Academy of Design
Guggenheim Museum
Neue Galerie
Metropolitan Museum of Art
Whitney Museum of American Art
Frick Collection
Asia Society
Tisch Children's Zoo
Central Park Zoo
Temple Emanu-El
Seventh Regiment Armory
Bloomingdale's
Mount Vernon Hotel Museum & Garden
Roosevelt Island Tramway
Gracie Mansion
Carl Schurz Park
John Jay Park
Ruppert Park
GRAND ARMY PLAZA
QUEENSBORO BRIDGE
FRANKLIN DELANO ROOSEVELT DRIVE
CENTRAL PARK EAST DRIVE
FIFTH AVENUE
MADISON AVENUE
PARK AVENUE
LEXINGTON AVENUE
THIRD AVENUE
SECOND AVENUE
FIRST AVENUE
YORK AVENUE
EAST END AVENUE
JULIA DE BURGOS BOULEVARD
EAST 111TH ST
EAST 110TH ST
EAST 109TH ST
EAST 108TH ST
EAST 107TH ST
EAST 106TH ST
EAST 105TH ST
EAST 104TH ST
EAST 103RD ST
EAST 102ND STREET
EAST 101ST ST
EAST 100TH ST
EAST 99TH STREET
EAST 98TH ST
97TH ST
EAST 97TH STREET
EAST 96TH STREET
EAST 95TH STREET
EAST 94TH STREET
EAST 93RD STREET
EAST 92ND STREET
EAST 91ST STREET
EAST 90TH STREET
EAST 89TH STREET
EAST 88TH STREET
EAST 87TH STREET
EAST 86TH STREET
85TH ST
EAST 85TH STREET
EAST 84TH STREET
EAST 83RD STREET
EAST 82ND STREET
EAST 81ST STREET
EAST 80TH STREET
79TH ST
EAST 79TH STREET
EAST 78TH STREET
EAST 77TH STREET
EAST 76TH STREET
EAST 75TH STREET
EAST 74TH STREET
EAST 73RD STREET
EAST 72ND STREET
EAST 71ST STREET
EAST 70TH STREET
EAST 69TH STREET
EAST 68TH STREET
EAST 67TH STREET
EAST 66TH STREET
EAST 65TH STREET
EAST 64TH STREET
EAST 63RD STREET
EAST 62ND STREET
EAST 61ST STREET
EAST 60TH STREET
EAST 59TH STREET
110TH ST
103RD ST
96TH ST
86TH ST
77TH ST
68TH ST-HUNTER COLLEGE
LEXINGTON AV/63RD ST
5TH AV/59TH ST
LEXINGTON AV/59TH ST
59TH ST

FRICK COLLECTION

1 E 70th St at Fifth Ave. Subway #6 to 68th St ☎ 212/288-0700, 🌐 www.frick.org. Tues–Sat 10am–6pm, Sun 11am–5pm. $18; pay what you wish Sun 11am–1pm. MAP P.137, POCKET MAP D6

Built in 1914 for Henry Clay Frick, probably the most ruthless of New York's robber barons, this handsome pile is now the tranquil home of the **Frick Collection**, displaying artwork from the Middle Ages to the nineteenth century. Opened in 1935, the museum has been largely kept as it looked when the Fricks lived there. Much of the furniture is heavy eighteenth-century French, but what sets it apart from most galleries – and the reason many rate the Frick so highly – is that it strives hard to be as unlike a museum as possible. There is no wall text describing the pictures, though you can dial up info on each work using hand-held guides.

This legacy of Frick's self-aggrandizement affords a revealing glimpse into the sumptuous life enjoyed by the city's big industrialists, while the collection includes paintings by Constable, Reynolds, Hogarth, Gainsborough, Goya, Bellini, El Greco, Titian and Vermeer. The **West Gallery** holds Frick's greatest prizes: two Turners, views of Cologne and Dieppe; and a set of piercing self-portraits by Rembrandt, along with his enigmatic *Polish Rider*. Also unmissable are Holbein's famous portraits of Thomas More and Thomas Cromwell in the **Living Hall**, and Vermeer's stunning *Officer and a Laughing Girl*.

At the far end of the West Gallery you will find a tiny chamber called the **Enamel Room**, named after the exquisite set of mostly sixteenth-century Limoges enamels on display.

METROPOLITAN MUSEUM OF ART

1000 Fifth Ave at E 82nd St. Subway #4, #5, #6 to 86th St ☎ 212/535-7710, 🌐 www.metmuseum.org. Tues–Thurs & Sun 9.30am–5.30pm, Fri & Sat 9.30am–9pm. Suggested donation $25. MAP P.137, POCKET MAP D5

The foremost art museum in America, the **Metropolitan Museum of Art** (or the Met) takes in over two million works and spans the cultures of America, Europe, Africa, the Far East, and the classical and Egyptian worlds.

You enter at the **Great Hall**, where you can consult floor plans and check tour times. From here the Grand Staircase

THE FRICK

METROPOLITAN MUSEUM OF ART

leads to the museum's greatest attraction – the **European Painting galleries**. Dutch painting is particularly strong, embracing an impressive range of Rembrandts, Hals and Vermeers – his *Young Woman with a Water Jug* is a perfect example of his skill in composition and tonal gradation, combined with an uncannily naturalistic sense of lighting; you'll also find such masters as Goya, Velázquez, and a room of freaky, dazzling canvases by El Greco, each of which underscores the jarring modernism of his approach.

Highlights of the popular **Nineteenth-Century galleries** include stunning Rodin sculptures and a lauded collection of Impressionists; Manet, Monet, Cézanne and Renoir are all well represented, and there are mesmerizing works by Van Gogh and Gauguin nearby.

The Museum's Asian art section is justly celebrated for its Japanese screens and Buddhist statues, and the Chinese Garden Court, a serene, minimalist retreat; a pagoda, small waterfall and stocked goldfish pond landscaped with limestone rocks, trees and shrubs create a sense of peace.

Close to being a museum in its own right, the **American Wing** is a thorough introduction to the development of fine art in America, with a vast collection of paintings, period furniture, glass, silverware and ceramics. The undeniable standout of the Egyptian collection is the **Temple of Dendur**, built by the emperor Augustus in 15 BC and moved here en masse as a gift of the Egyptian government during the construction of the Aswan High Dam in 1965.

Thanks to a magnificent renovation completed in 2007, one of the largest collections of Roman and Greek art in the world occupies some of the most attractive wings of the museum; check out the wonderfully bright **Greek Sculpture Court**, a fittingly elegant setting for sixth- to fourth-century BC marble sculptures.

Whatever you do choose to see, between May and October be sure to ascend to the **Cantor Roof Garden** (see p.145) for incredible views and changing contemporary sculpture exhibits.

NEUE GALERIE

1048 Fifth Ave at E 86th St. Subway #4, #5, #6 to 86th St ☎ 212/628-6200, Ⓦ www.neuegalerie.org. Thurs–Mon 11am–6pm. $20.
MAP P.137, POCKET MAP D4

Dedicated to early twentieth-century art from Austria and Germany, the **Neue Galerie** occupies an ornate Beaux-Arts mansion built in 1914. It's a relatively small space and the exhibits tend to rotate, but the collection contains some real gems.

The galleries begin on the second floor, where the undoubted star is Gustav Klimt's *Portrait of Adele Bloch-Bauer I* (1907), a resplendent gold portrait from Klimt's "Golden Period". The Bloch-Bauers were one of Vienna's richest Jewish families; the painting was looted by the Nazis in 1938, but descendants sued the Austrian government and had the painting returned in 2006 – the gallery is said to have paid $135 million for it soon after. On this floor you'll also find exceptional work by Egon Schiele and Max Oppenheimer, while the third floor is usually reserved for rotating work of German Expressionism: look out for Paul Klee, Ernst Ludwig Kirchner and Otto Dix.

NEUE GALERIE

GUGGENHEIM MUSEUM

1071 Fifth Ave at E 89th St. Subway #4, #5, #6 to 86th St ☎ 212/423-3500, Ⓦ www.guggenheim.org. Sun–Wed & Fri 10am–5.45pm, Sat 10am–7.45pm. $18; pay what you wish Sat 5.45–7.45pm.
MAP P.137, POCKET MAP D4

Designed by Frank Lloyd Wright, the 1959 **Guggenheim Museum** is better known for the building in which it's housed than its collection. Its centripetal spiral ramp, which winds all the way to its top floor, is an exhilarating space, and some still favour Wright's talents over those of the artists exhibited. Nevertheless, the museum boasts an awe-inspiring ensemble of art, not least its fabulous stash of Kandinsky paintings gathered by Solomon Guggenheim (1861–1949), the mining millionaire who laid the foundations for the museum.

Temporary exhibits, often linked to pieces in the permanent collection, take up most of the galleries, but you'll always see plenty of Kandinsky's exuberant work: look out particularly for the jarring *Komposition 8*, and the abstract *Blue Mountain*.

The Level 2 and 3 annexes also contain permanent displays: highlights include Picasso's haunting *Woman Ironing*, Van Gogh's vivid *Roadway with Underpass*, Cézanne's magnificent *Man with Crossed Arms* and *Dancers in Green and Yellow* by Degas. The museum also owns notable paintings by Chagall, Gauguin, Kirchner, Matisse and Monet, as well as contemporary work by artists such as Roni Horn.

THE GUGGENHEIM MUSEUM

NATIONAL ACADEMY OF DESIGN

1083 Fifth Ave between E 89th and E 90th sts. Subway #4, #5, #6 to 86th St ☎ 212/369-4880, www.nationalacademy.org. Wed–Sun 11am–6pm. $12. MAP P.137, POCKET MAP D4

A trip to the **National Academy of Design**, founded in 1825 along the lines of London's Royal Academy, is more like a visit to a favourite relative's house than to a museum. The building is an imposing Beaux-Arts townhouse, complete with carpeted rooms, a twisting staircase and a fine collection of nineteenth- through to twenty-first-century painting; the landscapes of the Hudson River School are highlights. Anna Huntington's spiralling sculpture *Diana of the Chase* gets pride of place below the cheerful rotunda, one of several naturalistic bronze castings of the Greek goddess Huntington completed in 1922.

COOPER-HEWITT NATIONAL DESIGN MUSEUM

2 E 91st St at Fifth Ave. Subway #4, #5, #6 to 86th St ☎ 212/849-8400, cooperhewitt.org. Mon–Fri 10am–5pm, Sat 10am–6pm, Sun noon–6pm. $15. MAP P.137, POCKET MAP D4

This museum is housed in a mansion completed for the industrialist Andrew Carnegie in 1902 – the handsome interior is as much a draw as the exhibits. An ambitious redevelopment project ("Re:Design") will see the property restored and expanded to house a permanent exhibition dubbed "What is Design?" on the first floor, drawing on the museum's collection of 200,000 items, and two higher floors of temporary exhibits. The museum will be closed until 2013 while the main work is completed.

JEWISH MUSEUM

1109 Fifth Ave at E 92nd St. Subway #6 to 96th St ☎ 212/423-3200, www.thejewishmuseum.org. Mon, Tues, Sat & Sun 11am–5.45pm, Thurs 11am–8pm, Fri 11am–4pm. $12, Sat free. MAP P.137, POCKET MAP D4

With over 28,000 items, this is the largest museum of Judaica outside Israel. Highlights of the permanent exhibition, "Culture and Continuity: The Jewish Journey", include a large and rare collection of Hanukkah lamps, the oldest dating from eighteenth-century Eastern Europe and Germany; you'll also find absorbing temporary displays of works by major international Jewish artists, such as Chagall and Man Ray.

MUSEUM OF THE CITY OF NEW YORK

1220 Fifth Ave at E 103rd St. Subway #6 to 103rd St ⓣ 212/534-1672, ⓦ www.mcny.org. Mon–Fri & Sun 10am–6pm, Sat 10am–8.30pm. $10. MAP P.137, POCKET MAP D2

Spaciously housed in neo-Georgian premises built in 1930, this museum displays an eclectic mix of temporary exhibits highlighting aspects of the city and its history. Only the audiovisual presentation (25min; every 30min) on the second floor, narrated by Stanley Tucci, tackles the history of the city in a conventional way, from the Lenape Indians to the 9/11 attacks. There are three main permanent collections: New York Toy Stories, which includes motion toys, board games, sports equipment, and dollhouses from the 1800s; Trade, which focuses on New York's role as a port from the 1600s to the 1970s; and New York Interiors, with six ornately furnished period rooms behind glass. The galleries will remain open while the museum completes a major multi-year $100 million renovation.

MUSEO DEL BARRIO

1230 Fifth Ave at E 104th St. Subway #6 to 103rd St ⓣ 212/831-7272, ⓦ www.elmuseo.org. Tues–Sat 11am–6pm, Sun 1–5pm. Suggested donation $9 (free every 3rd Sat of month). MAP P.137, POCKET MAP D2

Literally translated as "the neighbourhood museum", **Museo del Barrio** has largely a Puerto Rican emphasis in its traditional and contemporary collections, but the museum embraces the whole of Latin American and Caribbean cultures; its location places it on the edge of East Harlem, also known as "*El Barrio*" or Spanish Harlem. The Pre-Columbian collection includes intricately carved vomiting sticks (used to purify the body with the hallucinogen cohoba before sacred rites).

THE WHITNEY MUSEUM OF AMERICAN ART

945 Madison Ave at E 75th St. Subway #6 to 77th St ⓣ 212/570-3600, ⓦ www.whitney.org. Wed–Thurs, Sat & Sun 11am–6pm, Fri 1–9pm. $18; pay what you wish Fri 6–9pm. MAP P.137, POCKET MAP D5

Boasting some of the best gallery space in the city, the **Whitney** is the perfect forum for one of the pre-eminent collections of twentieth- and twenty-first-century American art. Most of the exhibitions are temporary, including the **Whitney Biennial** (held in even years between March and June), which traditionally gives a provocative overview of contemporary American art. The collection is particularly strong on Marsden Hartley, Georgia O'Keeffe, and such Abstract Expressionists as Jackson Pollock, Willem de Kooning and Mark Rothko; you'll usually find the most noted pieces on permanent display on the fifth floor.

THE WHITNEY MUSEUM

GRACIE MANSION

THE ASIA SOCIETY MUSEUM

725 Park Ave at E 70th St. Subway #6 to 68th St ☎ 212/288-6400, Ⓦ www.asiasociety.org. Tues–Sun 11am–6pm, Fri until 9pm (Sept–June only). $10, free Fri 6–9pm (Sept–June only). MAP P.137, POCKET MAP E6

A prominent educational resource on Asia founded by John D. Rockefeller 3rd, the **Asia Society** offers an exhibition space dedicated to both traditional and contemporary art from all over Asia. Exhibits are revolving, but often draw from the society's extensive permanent collection; recent exhibitions have included the arts of ancient Vietnam and South Indian Chola bronze sculptures. Intriguing performances, political roundtables, lectures, films and free events are frequently held.

MOUNT VERNON HOTEL MUSEUM & GARDEN

421 E 61st St between First and York aves. Subway F to Lexington Ave/63rd St; N, R to Lexington Ave/59th St; #4, #5, #6 to 59th St ☎ 212/838-6878, Ⓦ www.mvhm.org. Tues–Sun 11am–4pm, closed in August. $8. MAP P.137, POCKET MAP F7

Inside this fine stone house is a series of period rooms from the 1820s, meticulously restored by the Colonial Dames of America (an association of women who can trace their ancestry back to colonial times). The Dames were attracted by a connection with Abigail Adams Smith (daughter of President John Adams), though recent research has revealed this to be tenuous; the property was part of an estate bought by Abigail and husband in 1795, but the family soon went bankrupt, and it was only completed as a carriage house in 1799 by the new owner. The house served as a hotel between 1826 and 1833.

GRACIE MANSION

East End Ave at E 88th St. Subway #4, #5, #6 to 86th St ☎ 311 or 212/639-9675 (outside NYC). Tours (45min) on Wed 10am, 11am, 1pm, 2pm. $7; reservations required. MAP P.137, POCKET MAP F4

One of the city's best-preserved colonial buildings, the 1799 **Gracie Mansion** has served as the official residence of the mayor of New York City since 1942 (though the current mayor, billionaire Michael Bloomberg, decided to forgo residence here). The mansion was meticulously restored in 2002, but other than a few antiques and the bold murals in the dining room, the house itself isn't particularly compelling, and the tours are most interesting for the effusive guides and the stories of past mayors.

Cafés and snacks

CAFÉ SABARSKY

1048 Fifth Ave at E 86th St. Subway #4, #5, #6 to 86th St. Mon & Wed 9am–6pm, Thurs–Sun 9am–9pm. MAP P.137, POCKET MAP D5

Try to get a table by the window at this sumptuous Viennese café with great pastries and coffees. Conveniently located in the Neue Galerie.

E.A.T.

1064 Madison Ave between E 80th and E 81st sts. Subway #6 to 77th St ☎212/772-0022. Daily 7am–10pm. MAP P.137, POCKET MAP D5

Expensive and crowded but the food at this New York deli is excellent (celebrated restaurateur and gourmet grocer Eli Zabar is the owner). Try the soups and breads, or the heavenly mozzarella, basil and tomato sandwiches.

SERENDIPITY 3

225 E 60th St between Second and Third aves. Subway N, R, #4, #5, #6 to 59th St. Sun–Thurs 11.30am–midnight, Fri 11.30am–1am, Sat 11.30am–2am. MAP P.137, POCKET MAP D7

CAFÉ SABARSKY

Adorned with Tiffany lamps, this long-established eatery/ice-cream parlour is celebrated for its frozen hot chocolate, ($8.95), which is out of this world; the wealth of sundaes (from $9.50) is a real treat, too, everything from banana split and cinnamon fudge, to fresh fruit and "Forbidden Broadway" (chocolate blackout cake, ice cream, hot fudge topped with whipped cream).

Restaurants

CAFÉ BOULUD

20 E 76th St between Madison and Fifth Ave, at the Surrey Hotel. Subway #6 to 77th St ☎212/772-2600. Mon–Thurs 7am–10am, noon–2.30pm & 5.45–10.30pm, Fri & Sat 7am–10am, noon–2.30pm & 5.45–11pm, Sun 8am–11am, noon–3pm & 5.45–10.30pm. MAP P.137, POCKET MAP D5

Exceptional French–American cuisine directed by celebrated chef Daniel Boulud, a slightly more casual version of his swanky *Daniel* (entrees $16–44).

DONGURI

309 E 83rd St between First and Second aves. Subway #4, #5, #6 to 86th St ☎212/7373-5656. Tues–Sun 5.30–9.30pm. MAP P.137, POCKET MAP E4

Hidden Japanese gem, close to the Met, serving exquisite sushi dinners in a tiny five-table space; superb seafood.

FLEX MUSSELS

174 E 82nd St, between Third and Lexington aves. Subway #4, #5, #6 to 86th St ☎212/717-7772. Mon–Thurs 5.30–11pm, Fri 5.30–11.30pm, Sat 5–11.30pm, Sun 5–10pm. MAP P.137, POCKET MAP E5

Serves mussels fresh from Prince Edward Island (Canada) with various sauces, from Dijon to Thai, ranging from $18–24. Don't miss the special hand-cut fries ($6).

HEIDELBERG

1648 Second Ave between E 85th and E 86th sts. Subway #4, #5, #6 to 86th St 212/628-2332. Mon–Thurs 11.30am–11pm, Fri & Sat 11.30am–midnight, Sun noon–11pm. MAP P.137, POCKET MAP E4

The atmosphere here is Mittel-European kitsch, with gingerbread trim and staff sporting traditional dirndls and lederhosen. The food is the real deal too.

JOJO

160 E 64th St between Lexington and Third aves. Subway F to Lexington Ave/63rd St 212/223-5656. Mon–Thurs noon–2.30pm & 5.30–10.30pm, Fri & Sat noon–2.30pm & 5.30–11pm, Sun noon–2.30pm & 5.30–10pm. MAP P.137, POCKET MAP E6

Lavish townhouse restaurant created by feted chef Jean-Georges Vongerichten, serving excellent French fusion cuisine with the freshest ingredients.

Bars

AUCTION HOUSE

300 E 89th St between First and Second aves. Subway #4, #5, #6 to 86th St. Mon–Thurs & Sun 7.30pm–3am, Fri & Sat 7.30pm–4am. MAP P.137, POCKET MAP E4

This is a cosier, smarter alternative to the frat-boy pubs that dominate this part of town. The two quiet candlelit rooms decked out like Victorian parlours are perfect for couples.

METROPOLITAN MUSEUM OF ART BALCONY BAR & ROOF GARDEN CAFÉ

1000 Fifth Ave at E 82nd St. Subway #4, #5, #6 to 86th St. Sun & Tues–Thurs 10am–4.30pm, Fri & Sat 10am–8pm. MAP P.137, POCKET MAP D5

It's hard to imagine a more romantic spot to sip a glass of wine, whether on the *Roof Garden Café* (open May–Oct), which has some of the best views in the city, or in the *Balcony Bar* overlooking the Great Hall (Fri–Sat 4–8.30pm).

THE BALCONY BAR, METROPOLITAN MUSEUM OF ART

SUBWAY INN

143 E 60th St at Lexington Ave. Subway N, R, #4, #5, #6 to Lexington Ave/59th St. Mon–Sat 11am–4am, Sun noon–4am. MAP P.137, POCKET MAP E7

A neighbourhood anomaly since 1937, this downscale dive bar is great for a late-afternoon beer – and the perfect retreat after a visit to Bloomingdale's.

Live music

CAFÉ CARLYLE

The Carlyle Hotel, 35 E 76th St at Madison Ave. Subway #6 to 77th St 212/570-7175, www.thecarlyle.com. Mon–Sat 6.30pm–midnight. MAP P.137, POCKET MAP D5

This stalwart venue is home to Woody Allen, who plays the clarinet with his jazz band here on Monday nights (Jan–June; $135 cover). Other shows cost $40–100, but it's free if you book a table for dinner. Sets are at 8.45pm (plus 10.45pm Thurs–Sat).

The Upper West Side

The Upper West Side has traditionally exuded a more unbuttoned vibe than its counterpart across Central Park, though there is plenty of money in evidence, especially in the dazzling late nineteenth-century apartment buildings along the lower stretches of Central Park West and Riverside Drive, and at Lincoln Center, New York's palace of culture. This is generally less true further north, though gorgeous – and occasionally landmarked – blocks pop up in the 80s, 90s and 100s. Along the way a few museums, most significantly the Natural History Museum, are worth your time. At its northern edge, marked by the monolithic Cathedral of St John the Divine, Morningside Heights is a diverse area with a youthful buzz from Columbia University; most action revolves around Broadway.

LINCOLN CENTER FOR THE PERFORMING ARTS

W 62nd St to W 66th St between Broadway, Amsterdam and Columbus aves. Subway #1 to 66th St-Lincoln Center ⓣ212/875-5000, ⓦwww.lc.lincolncenter.org. MAP P.147, POCKET MAP C6

This marble assembly of early 1960s buildings, which received a substantial facelift for its 50th birthday, hosts New York's most prestigious performing arts groups.

At the centre of the complex, the world-class **Metropolitan Opera House** is an impressive marble and glass building, with murals by Marc Chagall. Flanking the Met are **Avery Fisher Hall**, home to the New York Philharmonic, and Philip Johnson's elegant **David H Koch Theater**, home to the New York City Ballet. The fountain in the middle serves as a meeting place; other spaces include an arts library, three theatres, and parks and plazas for summer events. Informative tours (60–90min, 2–6 tours daily, 10.30am–4.30pm; $15; ⓣ212/875-5350) leave from the attractive Atrium, on Broadway between 62nd and 63rd streets.

METROPOLITAN OPERA HOUSE, LINCOLN CENTER

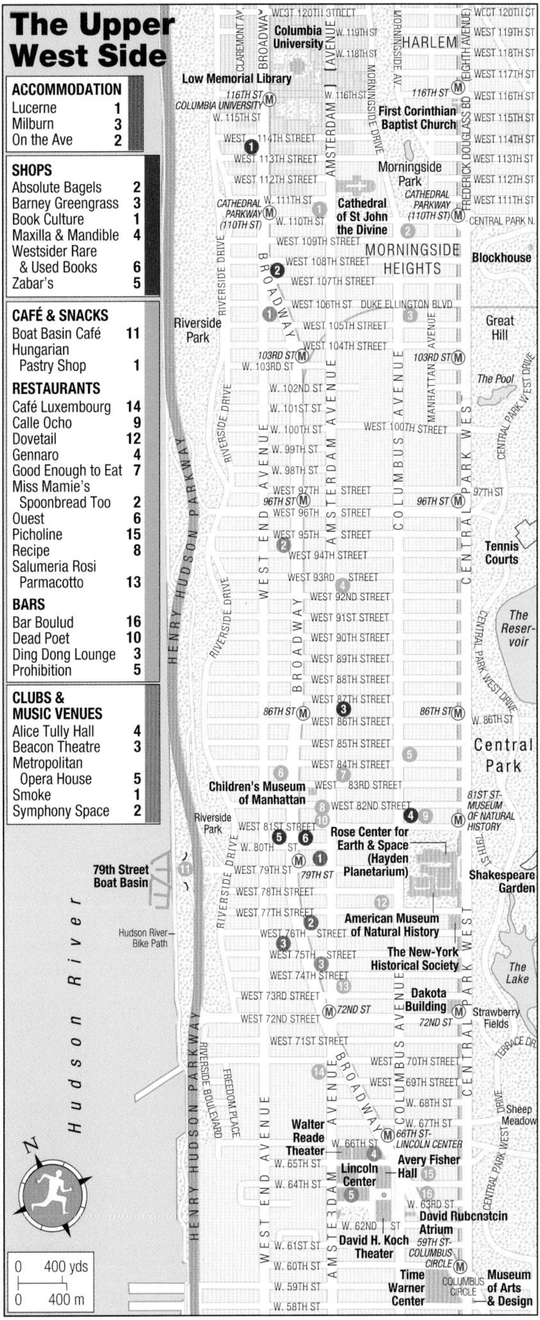
The Upper West Side
ACCOMMODATION
Lucerne 1
Milburn 3
On the Ave 2
SHOPS
Absolute Bagels 2
Barney Greengrass 3
Book Culture 1
Maxilla & Mandible 4
Westsider Rare & Used Books 6
Zabar's 5
CAFÉ & SNACKS
Boat Basin Café 11
Hungarian Pastry Shop 1
RESTAURANTS
Café Luxembourg 14
Calle Ocho 9
Dovetail 12
Gennaro 4
Good Enough to Eat 7
Miss Mamie's Spoonbread Too 2
Ouest 6
Picholine 15
Recipe 8
Salumeria Rosi Parmacotto 13
BARS
Bar Boulud 16
Dead Poet 10
Ding Dong Lounge 3
Prohibition 5
CLUBS & MUSIC VENUES
Alice Tully Hall 4
Beacon Theatre 3
Metropolitan Opera House 5
Smoke 1
Symphony Space 2
Columbia University
Low Memorial Library
HARLEM
First Corinthian Baptist Church
Morningside Park
Cathedral of St John the Divine
MORNINGSIDE HEIGHTS
Blockhouse
Riverside Park
Great Hill
The Pool
Tennis Courts
The Reservoir
Central Park
Children's Museum of Manhattan
Rose Center for Earth & Space (Hayden Planetarium)
79th Street Boat Basin
Shakespeare Garden
American Museum of Natural History
Hudson River Bike Path
The New-York Historical Society
The Lake
Dakota Building
Strawberry Fields
Hudson River
Sheep Meadow
Walter Reade Theater
Lincoln Center
Avery Fisher Hall
David Rubenstein Atrium
David H. Koch Theater
Time Warner Center
Museum of Arts & Design
HENRY HUDSON PARKWAY
BROADWAY
AMSTERDAM AVENUE
COLUMBUS AVENUE
CENTRAL PARK WEST
WEST END AVENUE
RIVERSIDE DRIVE
0 400 yds
0 400 m

THE DAKOTA BUILDING

1 W 72nd St at Central Park West. Subway B, C to 72nd St. MAP P.147, POCKET MAP C5

An early co-op finished in 1884, this grandiose German Renaissance-style mansion, with turrets, gables and ornate railings, was built to persuade wealthy New Yorkers that life in an apartment could be just as luxurious as in a private house. Plenty of celebrities have called it home, but the best-known residents were John Lennon and his wife Yoko Ono (who still lives here). It was outside the Dakota, on the night of December 8, 1980, that the ex-Beatle was shot.

THE NEW-YORK HISTORICAL SOCIETY

170 Central Park West at W 77th St. Subway B, C to 81st St ⓣ212/873-3400, Ⓦwww.nyhistory.org. Tues–Thurs & Sat 10am–6pm, Fri 10am–8pm, Sun 11am–5pm. $15, children 7–13 $5, Fri 6–8pm free. MAP P.147, POCKET MAP C5

The **New-York Historical Society** holds an extensive collection of books, prints, drawings, portraits and manuscripts. Among the highlights are all 435 existing original watercolours of James Audubon's landmark *Birds of America* . Elsewhere you'll find a broad cross-section of nineteenth-century American painting. The **Henry Luce Center** contains cultural and historical odds-and-ends that help make the museum seem more one of American than New York history: advertising ephemera, Tiffany lamps and the like. A recent overhaul saw the opening of the **DiMenna Children's History Museum**, which means to teach history to children through the history *of* children.

THE AMERICAN MUSEUM OF NATURAL HISTORY

Central Park West at W 79th St. Subway B, C to 81st St ⓣ212/769-5100, Ⓦwww.amnh.org. Daily 10am–5.45pm. Suggested admission $19, children 2–12 $10.50, IMAX films, space show & special exhibits extra ($14, children $10 to cover all). MAP P.147, POCKET MAP C5

This elegant giant fills four blocks with a strange architectural melange of heavy Neoclassical and rustic Romanesque styles that was built in several stages, the first by Calvert Vaux and Jacob Wrey Mould in 1872. The museum boasts 32 million items in its holdings, superb nature dioramas and anthropological collections, interactive and multimedia displays, and an awesome assemblage of bones, fossils and models. Top billing

DAKOTA BUILDING

AMERICAN MUSEUM OF NATURAL HISTORY

goes to the crowded **Dinosaur Halls. The Hall of Diversity,** focuses on both the ecological and evolutionary aspects of nature, while other delights include the massive totems in the **Hall of Northwest Coast Indians**, the taxidermal marvels in North American Mammals and the giant whale suspended in the **Hall of Ocean Life**.

The **Hall of Planet Earth**, a multimedia exploration, takes on the formation of planets, earthquake-tracking and carbon dating. The centrepiece is the **Dynamic Earth Globe**, where you can watch the earth via satellite.

Housed inside a metal and glass sphere, the **Hayden Planetarium** is one of the prime features of the **Rose Center for Earth and Space**; it screens a 3D film narrated by Whoopi Goldberg (every 30min; 25min) and offers a trip-to-the-moon simulator.

CHILDREN'S MUSEUM OF MANHATTAN

212 W 83rd St between Broadway and Amsterdam. Subway #1 to 79th or 86th St ⊙ 212/721-1234, ⊙ www.cmom.org. Tues–Fri & Sun 10am–5pm, Sat 10am–7pm. $11. MAP P.147, POCKET MAP B4

This delightful five-storey space offers interactive exhibits that stimulate learning in a fun, relaxed environment for kids (and babies) of all ages. If you've got a very little one in tow, check out the educational playspace **Playworks**.

RIVERSIDE PARK

Along the Hudson River and West Side Highway from W 72nd to W 158th sts. Subway #1, #2, #3, various stops along the Upper West Side. MAP P.147, POCKET MAP B1–B5

Not as imposing or spacious as Central Park, the waterfront **Riverside Park** was designed in the English pastoral style by the same team of architects, Olmsted and Vaux. The main stretch runs from 72th to 125th and slopes down from Riverside Drive, along wild paths and over great open patches of greenery. The **79th Street Boat Basin** is a lovely retreat as well as a nice summer eating option (see p.152).

Riverside Drive itself is flanked by palatial townhouses and apartment buildings constructed in the early twentieth century by those not quite rich enough to compete with the folks on Fifth Avenue. The architecturally distinctive landmark district of Riverside Drive–West End Historic District lies alongside, from 86th to 95th streets.

THE CATHEDRAL OF ST JOHN THE DIVINE

1047 Amsterdam Ave at W 112th St. Subway B, C, #1 to 110th St ☎ 212/316-7490, tour info ☎ 212/932-7347 Ⓦ www.stjohndivine.org. Mon–Sat 7am–6pm, Sun 7am–7pm. MAP P.147, POCKET MAP C2

The largest Gothic cathedral in the world holds that title despite being only two-thirds finished. A curious mix of Romanesque and Gothic styles, **St John the Divine** was begun in 1892, but its full 601ft length was completed only in 1941, after which construction stopped, to proceed sporadically between the late 1970s and 1997. The towers and transepts need finishing, but no further building plans are in the works. As it stands, St John is big enough to swallow Notre Dame and Chartres whole. Inside, note the intricately carved wood Altar for Peace, the Poets' Corner (with the names of American poets carved into its stone block floor), the octagonal baptistry and the triptych by Keith Haring – his final finished work. The amazing stained-glass windows include scenes from American history among biblical ones. Highlight tours (Tues–Sat usually 11am & 2pm; $6), 'vertical' tours to the roof (Sat noon & 2pm; $15) and a variety of other programmes are regularly available.

COLUMBIA UNIVERSITY

Between Broadway and Morningside Drive from 114th to 120th sts. Subway #1 to 116th St. MAP P.147, POCKET MAP B1

The epicentre of Morningside Heights, **Columbia University**'s campus fills 36 acres. Established in 1754, it is the oldest and most revered university in the city and one of the most prestigious academic institutions in the country. Well-known alumni include Barack Obama, Isaac Asimov, Ruth Bader Ginsburg, Lou Gehrig and Kathryn Bigelow.

McKim, Mead and White led the way in designing its new Italian Renaissance-style campus after it moved from midtown in 1897, with the domed and colonnaded **Low Memorial Library** as the focal point. Hour-long tours (☎ 212/854-4900; free) of the campus leave regularly Monday to Friday during the school year from the information office on the corner of 116th Street and Broadway.

COLUMBIA UNIVERSITY

Shops

ABSOLUTE BAGELS

2788 Broadway between 107th and 108th sts. Subway #1 to 110th St–Cathedral Parkway. Daily 6am–9pm. MAP P.147, POCKET MAP B2

This tiny shop, rather unusually (for the product) Thai-owned, bakes hot, fresh, chewy bagels that some claim as the best in the city. After tasting one – whether loaded with egg salad, smeared with lox spread or just au naturel – you'll find it hard to disagree.

BARNEY GREENGRASS

541 Amsterdam Ave between W 86th and W 87th sts. Subway #1 to 86th St ☎ 212/724-4707. Tues–Sun 8am–6pm, restaurant Mon–Fri 8.30am–4pm, Sat & Sun 8.30am–5pm. MAP P.147, POCKET MAP C4

Around the dawn of time, or at least a hundred years ago, the self-styled Sturgeon King began providing Upper West Siders with a beautiful array of smoked fish, cheese blintzes and the like. Be thankful that this deli-restaurant shows no sign of letting up.

BOOK CULTURE

2915 Broadway at 114th St. Subway #1 to 110th St. Daily 10am–8pm. MAP P.147, POCKET MAP B2

One of the top independent bookstores left in the city, Book Culture offers an airy space conducive to browsing and a downstairs kids' room; the original branch at 536 112th Street carries mainly academic titles (on its second floor).

MAXILLA & MANDIBLE

451 Columbus Ave between W 81st and W 82nd sts. Subway B, C to 81st St. Mon–Sat 11am–7pm, Sun 1–5pm. MAP P.147, POCKET MAP C5

After a visit to the nearby

MAXILLA & MANDIBLE

Natural History museum, get your souvenirs here: coyote skulls, ostrich eggs and polished shells. For scientists or just the plain curious.

WESTSIDER RARE & USED BOOKS

2246 Broadway between 80th and 81st sts. Subway #1 to 79th St. Daily 10am–10pm. MAP P.147, POCKET MAP B5

All manner of titles (especially strong on art books) are crammed floor to ceiling and into every nook and cranny of this eclectic bookshop, which is ripe for browsing; pretty much all of them are in good shape and sold at reasonable prices. There's a related record store down on 72nd St.

ZABAR'S

2245 Broadway at W 80th St. Subway #1 to 79th St. Mon–Fri 8am–7.30pm, Sat 8am–8pm, Sun 9am–6pm, café opens slightly earlier. MAP P.147, POCKET MAP B5

A veritable Upper West Side institution, this beloved family store offers a quintessential taste of New York: bagels, lox and all manner of *schmears*, not to mention a dizzying selection of gourmet food. An attached café means you can sample the goods right away if you wish.

Café and snacks

BOAT BASIN CAFÉ

W 79th St at the Hudson River with access through Riverside Park. Subway #1 to 79th St ☎ 212/496-5542. June–Aug Mon–Wed noon–11pm, Thurs & Fri noon–11.30pm, Sat 11am–11.30pm, Sun 11am–10pm, Late March to May, Sept & Oct daily noon until dusk; all weather permitting. MAP P.147, POCKET MAP B5

This inexpensive outdoor restaurant with long views of the Hudson River serves standard burgers with fries, hot dogs, sandwiches and a few more serious entrees. Live music on weekend afternoons.

HUNGARIAN PASTRY SHOP

1030 Amsterdam Ave between W 110th and 111th sts. Subway B, C, #1 to 110th St. Mon–Fri 7.30am–11.15pm, Sat 8.30am–11.15pm, Sun 8.30am–10.30pm. MAP P.147, POCKET MAP B2

If you're looking for a place to stop and relax near St John the Divine or Columbia, you won't do better than this simple coffeehouse. Sip your espresso and read all day if you like – the only problem is choosing among the home-made pastries, cookies and cakes.

Restaurants

CAFÉ LUXEMBOURG

200 W 70th St between Amsterdam and West End aves. Subway #1, #2, #3 to 72nd St ☎ 212/873-7411. Mon & Tues 8am–11pm, Wed–Fri 8am–midnight, Sat 9am–midnight, Sun 9am–11pm. MAP P.147, POCKET MAP B6

Popular Lincoln Center area bistro that packs in a slightly sniffy crowd to enjoy first-rate, contemporary French food. Entrees in the high $20s, the brasserie menu is a bit cheaper.

CALLE OCHO

45 W 81st St, between Columbus Ave and Central Park West in the Excelsior Hotel. Subway B, C to 81st St ☎ 212/873-5025. Mon–Thurs 6–10.30pm, Fri 6–11.30pm, Sat noon–3pm & 5–11.30pm, Sun noon–3pm & 5–10pm. MAP P.147, POCKET MAP C5

Very tasty Latino fare, such as *ceviches* ($13–18) and *chimichurri* steak ($25), is served in a colourfully decked-out restaurant with a hopping bar. The mojitos are as potent as any in the city.

DOVETAIL

103 W 77th St. Subway B, C to 81st St-Museum of Natural History ☎ 212/362-3800. Mon 5.30–10pm, Tues–Sat 5.30–11pm, Sun 11.30am–2.30pm & 5.30–10pm. MAP P.147, POCKET MAP C5

BOAT BASIN CAFÉ

A rare Michelin-starred (and worth it) restaurant in this area, with bold, fresh market-driven dishes like Brussels sprouts salad ($20), scallops and lobster with celery root ($46) and steak with beef cheek lasagne ($40); Sunday "suppas" offer a great prix-fixe (three courses $46).

GENNARO

665 Amsterdam Ave between W 92nd and W 93rd sts. Subway #1, #2, #3 to 96th St ☎212/665-5348. Mon–Thurs & Sun 5–10.30pm, Fri & Sat 5–11pm. MAP P.147, POCKET MAP C4

A rare outpost of good Italian food around these parts, though you'll have a wait for a table. Reasonably priced standouts include a warm potato, mushroom and goat cheese tart.

GOOD ENOUGH TO EAT

483 Amsterdam Ave between W 83rd and W 84th sts. Subway #1 to 86th St ☎212/496-0163. Mon–Thurs 8am–10.30pm, Fri 8am–11pm, Sat 9am–11pm, Sun 9am–10pm. MAP P.147, POCKET MAP C4

Cutesy Upper West Side restaurant known for its cinnamon-swirl French toast ($10.25), meatloaf ($17.95) and weekend brunch specials.

MISS MAMIE'S SPOONBREAD TOO

336 W 110th St between Columbus and Manhattan aves. Subway B, C to Cathedral Parkway (110th St) ☎212/865-6744. Mon–Thurs 11.30am–10pm, Fri & Sat 11.30am–11pm, Sun 11.30am–9.30pm. MAP P.147, POCKET MAP C2

Excellent soul-food restaurant with a 1950s-themed interior, addictive North Carolina ribs ($15.95) and some of the best fried chicken ($13.95) in the city.

OUEST

2315 Broadway between W 83rd and W 84th sts. Subway #1 to 86th St ☎212/580-8700. Mon 5–9.30pm, Tues & Wed 5–10pm, Thurs 5–10.30pm, Fri & Sat 5–11pm, Sun 11am–2pm & 5–9pm. MAP P.147, POCKET MAP B4

GENNARO

This New American restaurant has earned a loyal following for its celeb spottings and exceptional gourmet comfort food such as pan-roasted squab with risotto and stewed tripe. There's also a $38 three-course prix-fixe (Mon–Fri 5–6.30pm).

PICHOLINE

35 W 64th St between Broadway and Central Park West. Subway #1 to 66th St ☎212/724-8585. Mon–Thurs 5–10pm, Fri & Sat 5–11pm, Sun 5–9pm. MAP P.147, POCKET MAP C6

Popular with Lincoln Center audiences, this pricey French favourite ($115 for six-course tasting menu, $95 for four courses, $78 pre-theatre prix-fixe) executes Gallic fare with flair; the cheese plate is to die for. Jackets required.

RECIPE

425 Amsterdam Ave between 81st and 82nd sts. Subway #1 to 79th St ☎212/501-7755. Mon–Thurs 5–10.30pm, Fri 5–11.30pm, Sat 11am–3.30pm & 5–11.30pm, Sun 11am–3.30pm & 5–10.30pm. MAP P.147, POCKET MAP B5

Reasonable prices and farm-fresh ingredients help this locavore favourite pack them in; it's a mere slip of a restaurant, styled in industrial-meets-farmhouse decor. Go for the duck or roast game hen.

SALUMERIA ROSI PARMACOTTO

283 Amsterdam Ave, between 73rd and 74th sts. Subway #1, #2, #3 to 72nd St ☎ 212/877-4800. Mon–Thurs noon–10pm, Fri noon–11pm, Sat 11am–11pm, Sun 11am–10pm. MAP P.147, POCKET MAP C5

On your left as you enter is a deli counter with a dizzying array of gorgeous cured meats. Order lots of small plates: a selection of salumi and some cheeses (each choice $5–8, platters $15–26); escarole and anchovy salad ($11); pasta ($9–12); meatballs (if available).

Bars

BAR BOULUD

1900 Broadway, between 63rd and 64th sts. Subway A, B, C, D, #1 to 59th St-Columbus Circle; #1 to 66th St-Lincoln Center ☎ 212/595-0303. Mon–Thurs noon–4pm & 5–11pm, Fri noon–4pm & 5pm–midnight, Sat 11am–3.30pm & 5pm–midnight, Sun 11am–4pm & 5–10pm. MAP P.147, POCKET MAP C6

Treat this Daniel Boulud restaurant like a pre- or post-theatre wine bar, and zoom in on the home-made patés, terrines and charcuterie, accompanied by a glass – or bottle – from the Rhône.

DING DONG LOUNGE

DEAD POET

450 Amsterdam Ave between W 81st and W 82nd sts. Subway #1 to 79th St. Mon–Sat 10am–4am, Sun noon–4am. MAP P.147, POCKET MAP B5

You'll be waxing poetic and then dropping down dead if you stay for the duration of this sweet little bar's daily specials – usually involving $4 or $5 pints. The backroom has armchairs, books and a pool table.

DING DONG LOUNGE

929 Columbus Ave between W 105th and W 106th sts. Subway B, C, #1 to 103rd St. Daily 4pm–4am. MAP P.147, POCKET MAP C2

A punk bar with DJs and occasional concerts – attracts a vibrant mix of graduate students, neighbourhood Latinos and stragglers attracted by the anything-goes ethos. Cheap draughts 4–8pm.

PROHIBITION

503 Columbus Ave at W 84 St. Subway B, C to 86th St. Mon–Tues & Sun 5pm–2/3pm, Wed–Sat 5pm–4am. MAP P.147, POCKET MAP C4

Stylish bar and lounge with a funky, retro decor (check out the lamps in suspended wine bottles), nice array of draught beers and diabolical Martinis. Free live music nightly (usually beginning at 9.30pm or 10.30pm.

Clubs and music venues

ALICE TULLY HALL

1941 Broadway at 65th St, Lincoln Center. Subway A, B, C, D, #1 to 59th St-Columbus Circle; #1 to 66th St-Lincoln Center ☎ 212/671-4050, 🌐 new.lincolncenter.org. Tickets $20–90. MAP P.147, POCKET MAP C6

A small performance hall for top chamber orchestras, string quarters and instrumentalists.

BEACON THEATRE

BEACON THEATRE

2124 Broadway at W 74th St. Subway #1, #2, #3 to 72nd St ☎ 212/465-6500, tickets ☎ 1-866/858-0008, 🌐 www.beacontheatre.com. Tickets $25–100. MAP P.147, POCKET MAP B5

This beautifully restored theatre caters to a mature rock crowd One of the more established music venues in town, plenty of big names play here.

METROPOLITAN OPERA HOUSE

Lincoln Center, Columbus Ave at 64th St. Subway A, B, C, D, #1 to 59th St–Columbus Circle; #1 to 66th St–Lincoln Center ☎ 212/362-6000, 🌐 www.metopera.org. Tickets $20–495. MAP P.147, POCKET MAP C6

New York's premiere opera venue is home to the world-renowned Metropolitan Opera Company from September to May. Seats are expensive and nearly impossible to get, though $22 standing-room tickets are made available at 10am the day of a performance (call for info).

SMOKE

2751 Broadway at W 106th St. Subway #1 to 103rd St ☎ 212/864-6662, 🌐 www.smokejazz.com. Mon–Fri 5pm–2am, Sat & Sun 11am–2am (jazz brunch sets 11.30am, 1pm & 2.30pm); evening sets start 7pm Mon–Thurs & Sun, 8pm Fri & Sat. Cover free to $30, occasional $20 minimums. MAP P.147, POCKET MAP B2

This Upper West Side jazz joint is a real neighbourhood treat – nice bar, intimate seating, smooth sounds – and does credible bistro-style dinners.

SYMPHONY SPACE

2537 Broadway at W 95th St. Subway #1, #2, #3 to 96th St ☎ 212/864-5400, 🌐 www.symphonyspace.org. Tickets free to $50. MAP P.147, POCKET MAP B3

One of New York's primary performing arts centres, with regular short-story readings, as well as classical and world-music performances. It is perhaps best known for its free, uninterrupted reading of James Joyce's *Ulysses* every Bloomsday (June 16).

Harlem and north Manhattan

The most famous black community in America, Harlem has been the bedrock of African-American culture since the 1920s, when poets, activists and jazz blended in the Harlem Renaissance. Though it acquired a notoriety for street crime in the 1970s, it is now a neighbourhood on the rise. Indeed, Harlem's streets are as safe as any other in New York. Though most tourists still visit Harlem solely to see its wonderful Gospel choirs on Sundays, you'll also find some fabulous West African and soul-food restaurants, a vibrant local jazz scene, plenty of historic sights and some of the prettiest streets in the city. Explore African-American history at the Schomburg Center, or visit contemporary temples of black culture: the Apollo Theater and Abyssinian Baptist Church. North of Harlem lies Washington Heights and Inwood, home to the largest Dominican population in the United States.

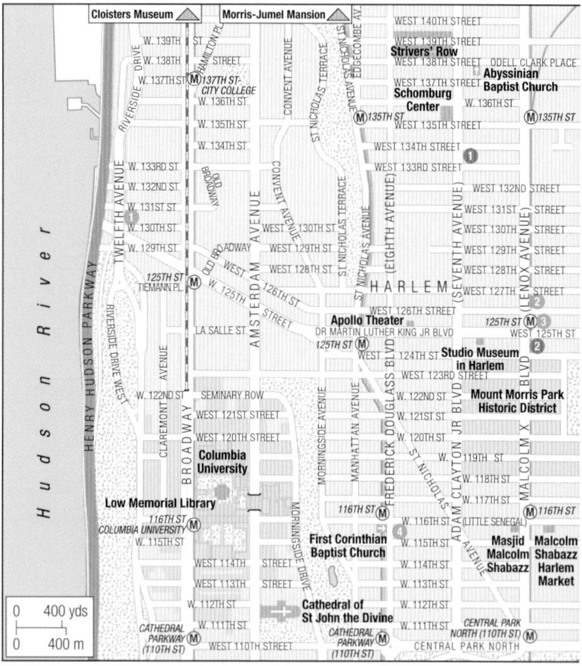

116TH STREET

Subway B, C, #2, #3, #6 to 116th St.

MAP P.156–157, POCKET MAP C1–D1

Harlem lies north of 110th St, but the first area of interest lies along **116th Street**; it's here that the spirit of the late Malcolm X is perhaps the most palpable. Look for the green onion-dome of the **Masjid Malcolm Shabazz**, 102 West 116th St at Lenox Ave; the mosque was renovated in the 1960s and named after him. Between Lenox and Fifth avenues, at no. 52, you'll pass the bazaar-like **Malcolm Shabazz Harlem Market** (daily 10am–8pm), its entrance marked by colourful fake minarets. The market's offerings include textiles, jewellery and clothing, all with a distinctly Afro-centric flavour. The stretch of 116th St between Lenox and Manhattan avenues has become a hub for West African immigrants and is unofficially known as **Little Senegal**; it's lined with shops, beauty parlours and African restaurants. There are also some African-influenced buildings nearby, including the fanciful blue-and-white Moorish-style First Corinthian Baptist Church, 1912 Powell Blvd at 116th Street.

MURAL, HARLEM

MOUNT MORRIS PARK HISTORIC DISTRICT

Subway #2, #3 to 116th St or 125th St.
MAP P.156–157, POCKET MAP D1

Centred on Malcolm X Blvd (aka Lenox Ave) between W 118th and 124th streets, this 16-block area, which is full of magnificent, four- to five-storey late nineteenth-century brownstones and quiet streets, was one of the first to attract residential development after the elevated railroads were constructed – it remains a relatively exclusive neighbourhood, with the likes of writer Maya Angelou and basketball legend Kareem Abdul-Jabbar living here.

125TH STREET

Subway A, B, C, D, #2, #3 to 125th St.
MAP P.156–157

125th Street between Broadway and Fifth Avenue is the working centre of Harlem and its main commercial drag. It's here that recent investment in the area is most obvious – note the presence of numerous chain stores and fashion retailers – spurred by the establishment of former president Bill Clinton's offices at 55 W 125th St in 2001. The celebrated Apollo Theater is still going strong, but make time also for the **Hip Hop Cultural Center**, 2309 Fredrick Douglass Blvd at 124th St (call to check opening times; T 212-234-7171), which has an exhibition of rare hip-hop footage, graffiti, photos and music demonstrations; and the **National Jazz Museum** (Mon–Fri 10am–4pm; W www.jazzmuseuminharlem.org) at 104 E 126th St near Park Ave, which organizes courses and live jazz, and has a small exhibit of old jazz memorabilia.

THE STUDIO MUSEUM IN HARLEM

144 W 125th St between Lenox and Seventh aves. Subway #2, #3 to 125th St T 212/864-4500, W www.studiomuseum.org. Thurs–Fri noon–9pm, Sat 10am–6pm, Sun noon–6pm. $7, free Sun. MAP P.156–157

The **Studio Museum in Harlem** has over 60,000 square feet of exhibition space dedicated to showcasing contemporary African-American painting, photography and sculpture. The superb permanent collection is displayed on a rotating basis and includes works by Harlem Renaissance-era photographer James Van Der Zee.

APOLLO THEATER

THE APOLLO THEATER

253 W 125th St. Subway A, B, C, D, #2, #3 to 125th St ⓣ 212/531-5300, ⓦ www.apollotheater.com. Tours Mon, Tues, Thurs & Fri 11am, 1pm, 3pm, Wed 11am, Sat & Sun 11am & 1pm. $16 Mon–Fri, $18 Sat & Sun. MAP P.156–157

From the 1930s to the 1970s, the **Apollo Theater** was the centre of black entertainment in northeastern America. Almost all the great figures of jazz and blues played here along with singers, comedians and dancers. Past winners of its famous Amateur Night (still running on Wed at 7.30pm; from $19) have included Ella Fitzgerald, Billie Holiday, the Jackson Five, Sarah Vaughan, Marvin Gaye and James Brown. Hip-hop diva Lauren Hill was actually booed at her debut as a young teen. Yet the Apollo has also become the spiritual heart of black America; James Brown's casket lay in state in the theatre, and when Michael Jackson died in 2009, an official exhibit was arranged inside a few days later.

SCHOMBURG CENTER FOR RESEARCH IN BLACK CULTURE

515 Malcolm X Blvd at W 135th St. Subway B, C, #2, #3 to 135th St ⓣ 212/491-2200, ⓦ www.nypl.org/research/sc. Exhibitions Mon–Sat 10am–6pm. Free. MAP P.156–157

Primarily a research library, the **Schomburg Center** also holds enlightening temporary exhibitions held in three galleries on site – recent topics have included the struggle to end segregation in US schools. The library itself was created in 1925 by Arthur Schomburg, a black Puerto Rican obsessed with documenting black culture. Further enriching the site are the ashes of poet Langston Hughes, perhaps most famous for publishing *The Negro Speaks of Rivers* in 1921.

ABYSSINIAN BAPTIST CHURCH

The poem inspired the terrazzo and brass "cosmogram" in the atrium beyond the main entrance. Seven lines radiate out from a circle, and the last, "My soul has grown deep like the rivers", located in the centre, marks where he is interred.

ABYSSINIAN BAPTIST CHURCH

132 Odell Clark Place (W 138th St) off Adam Clayton Powell Jr Blvd. Subway #2, #3 to 135th St ⓣ 212/862-7474, ⓦ www.abyssinian.org. Tourists are welcome to the Sun 11am service only (1hr 30min). Free. MAP P.15

With its roots going back to 1808, the **Abyssinian Baptist Church** houses one of the oldest (and biggest) Protestant congregations in the country. In the 1930s, its pastor, Reverend Adam Clayton Powell Jr, was instrumental in forcing the mostly white-owned, white-workforce stores of Harlem to employ the blacks whose patronage ensured the stores' economic survival. It's worth a trip here for its revival-style Sunday-morning services and gut-busting choir. Dress formally and remember that this is a religious service and not a show.

STRIVERS' ROW

Subway B, C, #2, #3 to 135th St. MAP P.156-157

On W 138th and 139th sts (between Adam Clayton Powell Jr and Frederick Douglass blvds), **Strivers' Row** comprises three of the finest blocks of Renaissance-influenced rowhouses in Manhattan. Commissioned in 1891 during a housing boom, this dignified development within the burgeoning black community came to be the most desirable place for ambitious professionals to reside at the turn of the twentieth century – hence its name. Today it remains an extremely posh residence for professionals of all backgrounds.

MORRIS–JUMEL MANSION

65 Jumel Terrace at W 160th St between St Nicholas and Edgecombe aves. Subway C to 163rd St ⊕ 212/923-8008, ⓦ www.morrisjumel.org. Wed–Sun 10am–4pm. $5. MAP P.163

This 1765 mansion, the oldest house in Manhattan, features proud Georgian outlines and a Federal portico, and served briefly as George Washington's headquarters before it fell to the British in 1776. Later, wine merchant Stephen Jumel bought the mansion and refurbished it for his wife Eliza, formerly a prostitute and his mistress. On the top floor, you'll find a magnificently fictionalized account of her "scandalous" life.

CLOISTERS MUSEUM

99 Margaret Corbin Drive, Fort Tryon Park. Subway A to 190th St ⊕ 212/923-3700, ⓦ www.metmuseum.org/cloisters. Tues–Sun 9.30am–5.15pm, closes 4.45pm Nov–Feb. Suggested donation $25, free with same-day Met Museum entry. MAP P.163

This reconstructed monastic complex houses the pick of the Metropolitan Museum's medieval collection. Most prized are the mystery-shrouded **Unicorn Tapestries**, seven elaborate panels thought to have been created in the late thirteenth century in France or Belgium. Among the Cloisters Museum's larger artefacts are a monumental Romanesque hall made up of French remnants and a frescoed Spanish Fuentiduena chapel, both thirteenth century. At the centre of the museum is the **Cuxa Cloister** from a twelfth-century Benedictine monastery in the French Pyrenees; its capitals are brilliant works of art, carved with weird, self-devouring grotesque creatures.

CLOISTERS MUSEUM

Restaurants

AFRICA KINE

256 W 116th St between Douglass and Powell blvds. Subway B, C to 116th St ☎212/666-9400. Daily 12.30pm–2am. MAP P.156–157, POCKET MAP C1

The best place on the emerging Little Senegal strip to try authentic West African dishes, lamb curry, and spicy fish and okra stews, served with heaps of rice, all for around $10.

DINOSAUR BAR B QUE

646 W 131st St at 12th Ave. Subway #1 to 125th St ☎212/694-1777. Mon–Thurs 11.30am–11pm, Fri & Sat 11.30am–midnight, Sun noon–10pm. MAP P.156–157

Get some of the best slow pit-smoked ribs here, smothered in a home-made sauce you'll delightfully taste for days after your meal. Or sample the "Big Ass Pork Plate" for $15.50.

RED ROOSTER

310 Malcolm X Blvd, between W 125th and W 126th sts. Subway #2, #3 to 125th St ☎212/792-9001. Mon–Thurs 11.30am–3pm & 5.30–10.30pm, Fri 11.30am–3pm & 5.30–11.30pm, Sat 10am–3pm & 5.30–11.30pm, Sun 10am–3pm & 5–10pm. MAP P.156–157

Marcus Samuelsson's restaurant opened in 2011, bringing a touch of class to Harlem with a sophisticated take on Southern comfort food. Sandwiches cost from $14–17, while mains such as lamb and sweet potato hash are $16–35. Leave room for the coconut rice pudding ($9).

SYLVIA'S RESTAURANT

328 Lenox Ave between W 126th and W 127th sts. Subway #2, #3 to 125th St. ☎212/996-0660. Mon–Sat 8am–10.30pm, Sun 11am–8pm. MAP P.156–157

So famous that Sylvia has her own package food line, this is Harlem's premier soul-food landmark. While the BBQ ribs ($16.95) are exceptional and the candied yams are justly celebrated, *Sylvia's* has become a bit of a tourist trap – try to avoid Sundays when tour groups arrive for the Gospel brunch.

Live music

LENOX LOUNGE

288 Lenox Ave at W 125th St. Subway #2, #3 to 125th St ☎212/427-0253, Ⓦwww.lenoxlounge.com. Daily noon–4am. MAP P.156–157

Entertaining Harlem since the 1930s, this historic jazz lounge has an over-the-top Art Deco interior (check out the Zebra Room). Most shows starts at 8pm, with three sets Fri and Sat (9pm, 10.30pm and midnight). Cover $20, with a $16 drink minimum.

SHRINE BAR

2271 Powell Blvd between 133rd and 134th sts. Subway B, #2, #3 to 135th St ☎212/690-7807, Ⓦwww.shrinenyc.com. Daily 4pm–4am. MAP P.156–157

Funky bar, restaurant and live music venue (mostly jazz and world music), which also hosts comedy and poetry nights; shows start at 6pm most nights, and at 1pm on Sundays.

DINOSAUR BAR B QUE

The outer boroughs

New York City doesn't end with Manhattan. There are four other boroughs to explore: Brooklyn, Queens, The Bronx and Staten Island. They cover an enormous area and you'll naturally want to pick your attractions carefully, although some of the more alluring parts of Brooklyn and Queens, like Brooklyn Heights and Long Island City, are just a subway stop away from downtown or midtown. Staten Island is the only borough that lacks an essential must-see sight or dynamic neighbourhoods for great ethnic food – the free ferry ride back and forth, with its views of downtown and the Statue of Liberty, is excitement enough. Otherwise, between the Bronx Zoo, Coney Island, Prospect Park, Greek Astoria and much more, you'll be torn in which direction to head.

BROOKLYN HEIGHTS

MAP P.165, POCKET MAP G15

From Manhattan, simply walk over the Brooklyn Bridge, take the left fork near the pedestrian path's end and emerge in one of New York City's most beautiful, historic and coveted neighbourhoods. The original New York City suburb, this peaceful, tree-lined area was settled by financiers from Wall Street, has been home to literary figures such as Truman Capote, Tennessee Williams and Norman Mailer and retains an exclusive air. Make sure you take in the **Promenade**, a terrace with terrific views of lower Manhattan, the East River and the Brooklyn Bridge.

DUMBO

MAP P.165, POCKET MAP G15

An acronym for Down Under Manhattan Bridge Overpass, **DUMBO** is a walk downhill from Brooklyn Heights Promenade and fronts the East River. It was a busy hub for ferries and trade in the nineteenth century, but the

WILLOW STREET, BROOKLYN

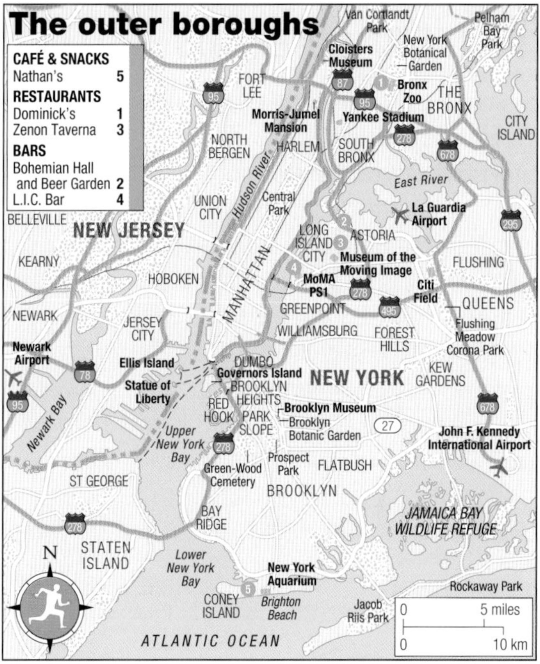

opening of the Brooklyn Bridge in 1883 led to the area's demise. In the past two decades luxury condo conversions and multipurpose art galleries have made it lively again. Check out the shops on Water, Main, Washington and Front streets before drinking in the views from the water's edge.

BROOKLYN BRIDGE PARK

Subway #2, #3 to Clark St, A, C to High St www.brooklynbridgepark.org. MAP P.165, POCKET MAP F15

The latest attempt to reimagine New York's waterfront, **Brooklyn Bridge Park** begins around Fulton Ferry Landing and runs alongside Brooklyn Heights down to Atlantic Avenue. **Empire-Fulton Ferry State Park** boasts a carousel (Mon & Wed–Sun 11am–7pm; $2) and brilliant views of the bridges, while Pier 6 has a cool water-play area, huge sandpit, steep slides and ferries to Governors Island (see p.40). There's also boating, volleyball and outdoor movies.

NEW YORK TRANSIT MUSEUM

Intersection of Boerum Place and Schermerhorn St, downtown Brooklyn. Subway #2, #3, #4, #5 to Borough Hall; A, C, F, R to Jay Street-MetroTech 718/694-1600, www.mta.info/mta/museum. Tues–Fri 10am–4pm, Sat & Sun 11am–5pm. $7, children 2–17 $5. MAP P.165, POCKET MAP G16

Housed in an abandoned 1930s subway station, the **Transit Museum** offers more than one hundred years' worth of transportation history and memorabilia, including antique turnstiles, and more than twenty restored subway cars and buses that you can hop on and off of. It's an excellent place for kids.

RED HOOK

MAP P.165

This waterfront district, a former shipping centre, was once one of the more rough-and-tumble in the city, but now holds artists' galleries, unique restaurants, converted warehouses and, to some folks' chagrin, twin giants in IKEA and Fairway. Cut off from the subway system, **Red Hook** can be reached by water taxi or bus, a worthwhile venture to hit the Red Hook Ball Fields on summer weekends, where you can sample Latin American street food and watch soccer, or to take in fabulous views of the Statue of Liberty and lower Manhattan from the piers, while snacking on a Key Lime Pie from *Steve's Authentic Key Lime Pies* (204 Van Dyke St).

THE BROOKLYN MUSEUM

200 Eastern Parkway, Prospect Heights, Brooklyn. Subway #2, #3 to Eastern Parkway ⓣ718/638-5000, ⓦwww.brooklynmuseum.org. Wed & Fri–Sun 11am–6pm, Thurs 11am–10pm, first Sat of every month 11am–11pm. Free from 5pm, suggested donation $12. MAP P.163

One of the largest museums in the country, the **Brooklyn Museum** boasts 1.5 million objects and five floors of exhibits in its McKim, Mead and White-designed Neoclassical home. A changing selection of Rodin sculptures greets you inside the door, though the highlight on this floor is the African Art collection. The third floor holds arguably the museum's crown jewel in its delicately carved "Brooklyn Brown Head", one of 1200 pieces in the Ancient Egyptian Art section. A flight up, Judy Chicago's *Dinner Party* installation marks an important moment in feminist art, while the fifth floor tops things off

BROOKLYN BOTANIC GARDEN

with the big-name-driven but uneven "American Identity" exhibit. Head instead for the Visible Storage section on the same level, packed with Tiffany lamps, antique furniture and paintings that the museum doesn't have room to display in its main galleries.

BROOKLYN BOTANIC GARDEN

Entrance on Eastern Parkway, next to Brookyn Museum. Subway #2, #3 to Eastern Parkway; B, Q, S to Prospect Park ⓣ718/623-7200, ⓦwww.bbg.org. Mid-March to Oct Tues–Fri 8am–6pm, Sat & Sun 10am–6pm, Nov to mid-March Tues–Fri 8am–4.30pm, Sat & Sun 10am–4.30pm. $10, children under 12 free. MAP P.163

The **Brooklyn Botanic Garden** is one of the most enticing park spaces in the city and a relaxing place to unwind after a couple of hours in the museum next door. Though smaller, it is more immediately likeable than its more celebrated cousin in the Bronx (see p.169). Some 12,000 plants from around the world occupy 52 acres of manicured terrain. Highlights are mostly seasonal, but include the Rose Garden, Japanese Garden, Cherry Esplanade and Celebrity Path, honouring Brooklyn's famous sons and daughters.

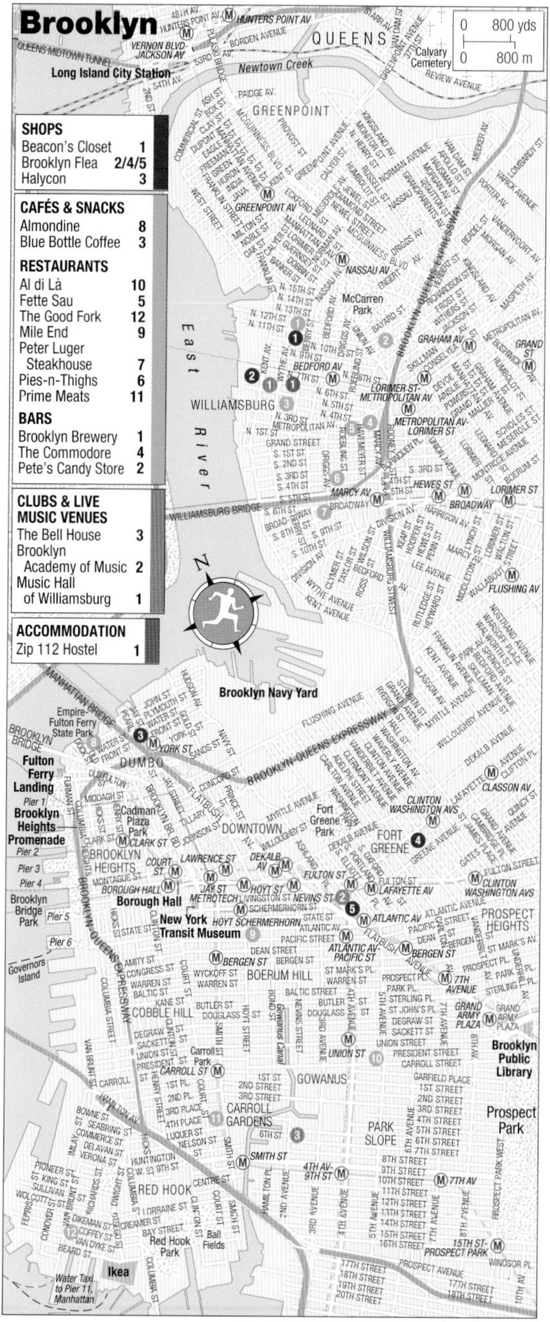
Brooklyn
SHOPS
Beacon's Closet 1
Brooklyn Flea 2/4/5
Halycon 3
CAFÉS & SNACKS
Almondine 8
Blue Bottle Coffee 3
RESTAURANTS
Al di Là 10
Fette Sau 5
The Good Fork 12
Mile End 9
Peter Luger Steakhouse 7
Pies-n-Thighs 6
Prime Meats 11
BARS
Brooklyn Brewery 1
The Commodore 4
Pete's Candy Store 2
CLUBS & LIVE MUSIC VENUES
The Bell House 3
Brooklyn Academy of Music 2
Music Hall of Williamsburg 1
ACCOMMODATION
Zip 112 Hostel 1
0 800 yds
0 800 m
QUEENS
Long Island City Station
Newtown Creek
Calvary Cemetery
GREENPOINT
McCarren Park
WILLIAMSBURG
East River
WILLIAMSBURG BRIDGE
BROOKLYN-QUEENS EXPRESSWAY
Brooklyn Navy Yard
MANHATTAN BRIDGE
BROOKLYN BRIDGE
Empire-Fulton Ferry State Park
DUMBO
Fulton Ferry Landing
Brooklyn Heights Promenade
Cadman Plaza Park
DOWNTOWN
Fort Greene Park
FORT GREENE
BROOKLYN HEIGHTS
Borough Hall
New York Transit Museum
Brooklyn Bridge Park
Governors Island
BOERUM HILL
PROSPECT HEIGHTS
COBBLE HILL
Gowanus Canal
GOWANUS
CARROLL GARDENS
PARK SLOPE
Brooklyn Public Library
Prospect Park
RED HOOK
Red Hook Park
Ball Fields
Ikea
Water Taxi to Pier 11, Manhattan

PROSPECT PARK

Flatbush Ave and Prospect Park West, Brooklyn. Subway #2, #3 to Grand Army Plaza; F to 7th Ave or 15th St; B, Q to Prospect Park ☎718/965-8951, www.prospectpark.org. MAP P.163

Energized by their success with Central Park, architects Olmsted and Vaux landscaped 526-acre **Prospect Park** in the early 1860s, completing it just as the finishing touches were being put to Grand Army Plaza outside (home to an excellent farmers' market Sat 8am–4pm). Focal points include the Lefferts Homestead, an eighteenth-century colonial farmhouse that is open free of charge on weekends; the Prospect Park Zoo (April–Oct Mon–Fri 10am–5pm, Sat and Sun 10am–5.30pm; Nov–March daily 10am–4.30pm; $7); the Audubon House, holding nature exhibits and situated by a duck-filled pond, the carousel (April–Oct Thurs–Sun noon–5pm; $2); and the ninety-acre Long Meadow, which cuts through the centre.

PROSPECT PARK

PARK SLOPE

MAP P.163

The western exits of Prospect Park abut the largest landmark district in Brooklyn: **Park Slope**, an area settled in the seventeenth century by Dutch farmers but that blossomed after streetcars were extended to the neighbourhood in the 1870s. Once the home of Irish immigrants and Ansonia Clock factory workers, Park Slope is almost totally gentrified, sporting historic brownstones inhabited mostly by young professional couples with small children, along with some well-known literary types such as Paul Auster and Jonathan Safran Foer; the quiet, tree-lined cross streets rival those of Brooklyn Heights for attractiveness and property value. Fifth Avenue holds the most interesting cafés, boutiques, wine stores and restaurants.

CONEY ISLAND

Subway D, F, N, Q to Coney Island-Stillwell Ave or F, Q to W 8th St-NY Aquarium. www.coneyisland.com. Boardwalk open year-round, rides are seasonal (roughly April–Sept). MAP P.163

Generations of working-class New Yorkers came to relax at one of Brooklyn's farthest points: **Coney Island**, which at its height accommodated 100,000 people daily. It's now down-and-out and the Astroland amusement park has shut, replaced by **Luna Park**, which complements the 90-year-old Wonder Wheel and the almost-that-old wooden roller coaster, the Cyclone. Other summertime highlights include the Fourth of July Hot Dog Eating Contest at *Nathan's* (see p.171) and the annual Mermaid Parade (3rd or 4th Sat in June).

WILLIAMSBURG

NEW YORK AQUARIUM

Surf Ave and W 8th St, Coney Island, Brooklyn. Subway F, Q to West 8th St; D, F, N, Q to Surf Ave 718/265-3474, www.nyaquarium.com. April, May, Sept & Oct Mon–Fri 10am–5pm, Sat & Sun 10am–5.30pm; June–Aug Mon–Fri 10am–6pm, Sat & Sun 10am–7pm; Nov–March daily 10am–4.30pm. $14.95, children 3–12 $10.95. MAP P.163

On Coney Island's boardwalk stands the seashell-shaped **New York Aquarium**. More than ten thousand creatures – none more eye-grabbing than the otherworldly jellyfish and anemones in the Alien Stingers exhibit – reside here in an array of tanks and pools. Check out the latest additions, Conservation Hall and Glovers Reef, where you'll see rays and piranhas, and learn about coral.

BRIGHTON BEACH

MAP P.163

At Brooklyn's southernmost end, **Brighton Beach** was developed in 1878 and named after the English resort. It's home to the country's largest community of Russian Jewish émigrés, many of whom arrived in the 1970s following a relaxation of restrictions on Soviet citizens entering the United States. The main drag, Brighton Beach Avenue, parallels the boardwalk underneath the elevated subway; the street is a bustling mixture of food outlets, appetizing restaurants and Russian souvenir shops. In the evening its cabaret-restaurants (like *Primorski)* become a near-parody of a rowdy Russian night out.

WILLIAMSBURG

MAP P.165, POCKET MAP J11

With easy access to Manhattan and excellent waterfront views, it's not hard to see why **Williamsburg** has become one of the city's most happening spots. The L train to Bedford Avenue will land you on the main stretch of coffee, record, book and vintage shops.

After the opening of the Williamsburg Bridge in 1903, working-class Jews seeking more spacious homes flooded the neighbourhood from the Lower East Side. Many Hasidic Jews live in the southwest part of the district, centred on Lee Avenue.

McCarren Park separates northern Williamsburg from the fashionable Polish enclave of Greenpoint, and the park serves as a big hangout, with summer concerts. Its historic pool, restored in 2012, is a focus for summer fun and music events.

ASTORIA

MAP P.163, POCKET MAP J3

Developed in 1839 and named after John Jacob Astor, **Astoria**, Queens is known for two things: filmmaking and the fact that it has the largest concentration of Greeks outside Greece – or so it claims. Between 1920 and 1928, Astoria, where Paramount had its studios, was the capital of the silent film era and continued to blossom until the 1930s, when the lure of Hollywood's reliable weather left Astoria largely empty.

Greek Astoria stretches from Ditmars Boulevard to Broadway, and from 31st Street across to Steinway Street, though plenty of Moroccans, Egyptians, Brazilians and others have moved in; it makes for a foodie haven, evidenced in the patisseries, fresh seafood restaurants and kebab stands.

THE MUSEUM OF THE MOVING IMAGE

35th Ave at 37th St, Astoria, Queens. Subway N, Q to 36th St; M, R to Steinway St ☎718/784-0077, www.movingimage.us. Tues–Thurs 10am–5.30pm, Fri 10.30am–8.30pm, Sat & Sun 10.30am–7pm. $12, children 3–18 $6. MAP P.163, POCKET MAP J5

Part of the old Paramount complex, the recently expanded **Museum of the Moving Image** tells the fascinating story of cinema through state-of-the-art theatres, interactive exhibits and vintage props. The museum's core collection, "Behind the Screen", holds old movie cameras and special-effects equipment; sketches and set models from *The Silence of the Lambs*; and enough *Star Wars* action figures to make an obsessed fan drool with envy. To get hands-on, you can create a short animated film and add your own sound effects to well-known movie scenes.

ISAMU NOGUCHI GARDEN MUSEUM

9-01 33rd Rd at Vernon Blvd, Long Island City, Queens. Subway N, Q, W to Broadway; F to Queensbridge–21st St ☎718/204-7088, www.noguchi.org. Wed–Fri 10am–5pm, Sat & Sun 11am–6pm. $10. MAP P.163, POCKET MAP G5

While hard to reach, the **Isamu Noguchi Garden Museum** easily repays curiosity. The museum is devoted to the "organic" sculptures, drawings, modern dance costumes and Akari light sculptures of the prolific Japanese-American abstract sculptor Isamu Noguchi (1904–88), whose studio was here. His pieces, in stone, bronze and wood, exhibit a sublime simplicity.

BRONX ZOO

YANKEE STADIUM

and tours (daily except home game days noon–1.40pm, every 20min; $20, children 14 and under $15 if purchased at box office; ⓣ646/977-8687) take in these, the dugout, the clubhouse and batting cages.

MoMA PS1

22-25 Jackson Ave at 46th Ave, Long Island City. Subway #7 to 45 Rd–Courthouse Square; E, G to 23rd St–Ely Ave. ⓣ718/784-2084, ⓦwww.momaps1.org. Thurs–Mon noon–6pm. Suggested admission $10 (free with same-day MoMA ticket). MAP P.163, POCKET MAP I8

MoMA PS1 is one of the oldest and biggest organizations in the United States devoted exclusively to contemporary art and to showing leading emerging artists. Since its founding in 1971, this public school-turned-exhibition space has hosted some of the city's most exciting art displays.

YANKEE STADIUM

161st St and River Ave. Subway B, D, #4 to Yankee Stadium ⓣ212/926-5337, ⓦnewyork.yankees.mlb.com. Tickets $15–300. MAP P.163

Yankee Stadium is home to the New York Yankees, 27-time World Series champs and the most famous franchise in sports. Babe Ruth, Lou Gehrig, Joe DiMaggio and dozens more have formed a continuous line of superstars up to present-day heroes Derek Jeter and Robinson Cano. A brand-new stadium, inaugurated for the 2009 season, replaced the "House That Ruth Built"; the team's heroes are enshrined with plaques and monuments,

BRONX ZOO

Main gate on Fordham Rd. Subway #2, #5 to East Tremont Ave/West Farms Square. ⓣ718/220-5100, ⓦwww.bronxzoo.com. April–Nov Mon–Fri 10am–5pm, Sat & Sun 10am–5.30pm, Dec–March daily 10am–4.30pm. $16, children 3–12 $12; special rides and attractions extra, though discount for Total Experience tickets; Wed "pay what you wish". MAP P.163

The largest urban zoo in the United States, which first opened its gates in 1899, houses over four thousand animals and was one of the first institutions of its kind to realize its inhabitants both looked and felt better out in the open. The "Wild Asia" exhibit is an almost forty-acre wilderness through which tigers, elephants and deer roam relatively free, visible from a monorail (May–Oct; $4). Check out exotic species and daily penguin feeding in the "Sea Bird Colony".

NEW YORK BOTANICAL GARDEN

Entrance across the road from the zoo's main gate. Subway B, D, #4 to Bedford Park Blvd, though Metro-North from Grand Central to Botanical Garden Station is easier ⓣ718/817-8700, ⓦwww.nybg.org. Tues–Sun 10am–6pm. All garden $20, children 2–12 $8; grounds only $10, children 2–12 $2. MAP P.163

The late nineteenth-century **New York Botanical Garden** is a brilliant companion piece to the zoo opposite. Near the main entrance, the Enid A. Haupt Conservatory, a landmark crystal palace, showcases jungle and desert ecosystems, a palm court and a fern forest, among other seasonal displays. Close by are herb and perennial gardens.

Shops and galleries

BEACON'S CLOSET

88 N 11th St between Wythe and Berry, Williamsburg, Brooklyn; other locations in Park Slope and the Village. Subway L to Bedford Ave. Mon–Fri noon–9pm, Sat & Sun 11am–8pm. MAP P.163, POCKET MAP I11

One of the signature Williamsburg stores, this huge clothing exchange is great for finding excellent deals on vintage designer duds or making a bit of cash if you've got used stuff in good condition to spare.

BEACON'S CLOSET

BROOKLYN FLEA

176 Lafayette Ave, between Clermont and Vanderbilt aves, Fort Greene (April–Nov Sat 10am–5pm); 27 N 6th St, between Kent Ave and the East River, Williamsburg (April–Nov Sun 10am–5pm). Subway C to Lafayette Ave; G to Clinton–Washington aves; L to Bedford Ave Ⓦ brooklynflea.com. MAP P.165, POCKET MAP J15, J16 & H11

The "flea" epithet is a bit of a misnomer, as this is as much a high-quality arts and crafts fair as second-hand fair, with two hundred stalls and superb artisan food. During the winter (Dec–March), the market moves indoors to 1 Hanson Place. From April to November, the Williamsburg location spends Saturdays as Smorgasburg, an outdoor food extravaganza.

HALCYON

57 Pearl St at Water St, Dumbo, Brooklyn. Subway A, C to High St; F to York St. Mon, Wed & Sat noon–8pm, Tues, Thurs & Fri noon–9pm, Sun noon–6pm. MAP P.165, POCKET MAP H13

A reliable source for dance music and much more, Halcyon serves as an underground community centre of sorts. Come listen to whatever you like, check out some art then find your way to a Halcyon-sponsored event.

Cafés and snacks

ALMONDINE

85 Water St, Dumbo, Brooklyn. Subway A, C to High St; F to York St. Mon–Sat 7am–7pm, Sun 10am–6pm. MAP P.165, POCKET MAP G13

It just might be the best bakery in the city, with its exquisite chocolate cakes and fruit tarts, buttery croissants and tasty salami sandwiches. Eat in or, better yet, take it to the nearby park between the bridges.

BLUE BOTTLE COFFEE

160 Berry St, between Fourth and Fifth sts, another location in Chelsea. Subway L to Bedford Ave. Mon–Fri 7am–7pm, Sat & Sun 8am–7pm. MAP P.165, POCKET MAP H12

The first New York outpost of a well-regarded San Francisco coffee roaster. A cross between a café and a lab, the java used for iced coffee drips in giant bulbous tubes. Filters are lined up to make coffee to order and a working roastery fills the back.

NATHAN'S

1310 Surf Ave at Schweiker's Walk, Coney Island, Brooklyn. Subway D, F, N, Q to Coney Island–Stillwell Ave ☎718/946-2202. Mon–Thurs & Sun 8am–1am, Fri & Sat 8am–2am. MAP P.163

Home of the "famous Coney Island hot dog", served since 1916, *Nathan's* is a bona fide New York experience. It holds an annual Hot Dog Eating Contest on July 4.

Restaurants

AL DI LÀ

248 Fifth Ave at Carroll St, Park Slope, Brooklyn. Subway R to Union St ☎718/783-4565. Mon–Thurs noon–3pm & 6–10.30pm, Fri noon–3pm & 6–11pm, Sat 11am–3.30pm & 5.30–11pm, Sun 11am–3.30pm & 5–10pm. MAP P.163

Venetian country cooking at its finest at this husband-and-wife-run restaurant. Standouts include beet ravioli, Swiss chard gnocchi, grilled sardines and braised rabbit. Expect an hour-long wait (no reservations).

DOMINICK'S

2335 Arthur Ave at 187th St, the Bronx. Subway B, D to Fordham Rd ☎718/733-2807. Mon & Wed–Sun noon–midnight. MAP P.163

All you could hope for in a Belmont neighbourhood Italian: great, rowdy atmosphere, communal seating, wonderful food and low(ish) prices. Stuffed baby squid, veal *parmigiana* and chicken *scarpariello* are standouts. Cash only.

FETTE SAU

345 Metropolitan Ave, at Havemeyer St, Williamsburg, Brooklyn. Subway L to Bedford Ave; G to Metropolitan Ave ☎718/963-3404. Mon–Fri 5pm–2am, Sat & Sun noon–midnight. MAP P.163, POCKET MAP J12

The industrial-chic vibe (it's in an old auto repair shop) of this barbecue specialist fits the neighbourhood. Order your meat by the pound (beef brisket, pork shoulder or pork belly $16), tack on a couple of sides (burnt end baked beans $5.25) and wash it down with a microbrew ($6 pints).

THE GOOD FORK

391 Van Brunt St, Red Hook, Brooklyn. Subway F, G to Smith–9th sts ☎718/643-6636. Tues–Fri 5.30–10.30pm, Sat 10am–3pm & 5.30–10.30pm, Sun 10am–3pm & 5.30–10pm. MAP P.163

Though it's a neighbourhood restaurant at heart (in an out-of-the-way spot), it's worth making the effort for the inventive cocktails, delectable dumplings and Korean-inspired take on steak and eggs.

MILE END

97A Hoyt St between Pacific and Atlantic, Boerum Hill, Brooklyn. Subway F to Bergen; A, C, G to Hoyt-Schermerhorn. Mon–Thurs 8am–4pm & 5.30–10pm, Fri 8am–4pm & 5.30–11pm, Sat 10am–4pm & 5.30–11pm, Sun 10am–4pm & 5.30–10pm. MAP P.165, POCKET MAP H16

This cosy Montreal-style Jewish deli serves smoked meat sandwiches that rival any in town, along with takes on Old World home cooking – for example, *kasha varnishkes* (buckwheat and pasta) with duck confit. A real treat.

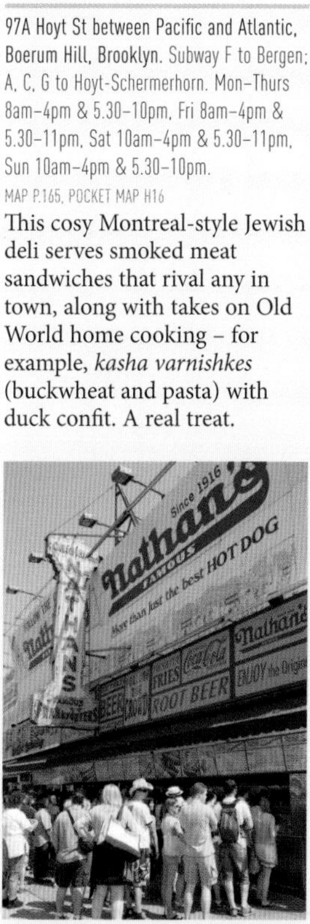

NATHAN'S

PETER LUGER STEAK HOUSE

178 Broadway at Driggs Ave, Williamsburg, Brooklyn. Subway J, M, Z to Marcy Ave ☎718/387-7400. Mon–Thurs 11.45am–9.45pm, Fri & Sat 11.45am–10.45pm, Sun 12.45–9.45pm. MAP P.165, POCKET MAP J13

Catering to carnivores since 1873, *Peter Luger's* may just be the city's finest steakhouse. The service is surly and the decor plain, but the porterhouse steak – essentially the only cut served – is divine. Make sure to order the bacon starter too. Cash only, and expensive; tabs can easily run to $100 or so per person.

PIES-N-THIGHS

166 S 4th St, at Driggs Ave. Subway J, M, Z to Marcy Ave, Williamsburg, Brooklyn ☎347/529-6090. Mon–Fri 9am–4am & 5pm–midnight, Sat & Sun 10am–4pm & 5pm–midnight. MAP P.165, POCKET MAP J12

Tucked in a bright corner location, *P-n-T* do exemplary southern-style food: great chicken biscuits (a scone with a fried chicken filling; $6), expertly fried chicken ($13 with a side dish and a changing rotation of pies (Key Lime is a favourite; slices $5). Cash only.

PRIME MEATS

465 Court St, at Luquer St, Carroll Gardens, Brooklyn. Subway F, G to Carroll St ☎718/254-0327. Mon–Wed & Sun 11am–1am, Thurs–Sat 8am–2am. MAP P.165

Popular spot serving up excellent steaks ($32 for a NY strip), burgers ($18) and roasted bone marrow ($18) in a room that feels decades old. Earlier in the day, you can enjoy mushrooms, eggs and bratwurst ($13).

ZENON TAVERNA

34-10 31st Ave, Astoria, Queens. Subway N, Q to 30th Ave; R to Steinway St ☎718/956-0133. Daily noon–11pm. MAP P.163, POCKET MAP J4

Charred octopus, grilled meatballs and taramasalata dip will get your meal off on the right foot at the super-friendly Greek-Cypriot tavern; whole fish or one of the lamb specials keep it headed in the right direction.

Bars

BOHEMIAN HALL AND BEER GARDEN

29-19 24th Ave between 29th and 30th sts, Astoria, Queens. Subway N, Q, W to Astoria Blvd. Mon–Wed & Sun noon–2am, Thurs–Sat noon–3am. MAP P.163, POCKET MAP J3

This Czech bar is the real deal, catering to old-timers and serving a good selection of pilsners as well as hard-to-find brews. Out the back, there's a very large beer garden, complete with picnic tables, trees, burgers and sausages, and a bandshell for polka groups.

BROOKLYN BREWERY

79 N 11th St, Williamsburg, Brooklyn. Subway L to Bedford Ave. Fri 6–11pm, Sat noon–8pm, Sun noon–6pm. MAP P.163, POCKET MAP I11

After wandering Williamsburg, check out this stellar microbrewery, which hosts events year-round; hang out in their tasting room on Fridays or take a free tour on Saturdays or Sundays (and less occasionally on weekdays).

PETE'S CANDY STORE

THE COMMODORE

366 Metropolitan Ave, at Havemeyer St, Williamsburg, Brooklyn. Subway L to Lorimer St; G to Metropolitan Ave. Daily 4pm–4am. MAP P.165, POCKET MAP J12

Straight out of Williamsburg central casting: a retro-style rec room vibe; better-than-expected bar food (fried chicken, grilled cheese and poblano sandwich, sautéed kale); inexpensive cocktails and pitchers; a hip, young crowd playing old video games… somehow it all works perfectly.

L.I.C. BAR

45–58 Vernon Blvd, at 46th Ave, Long Island City, Queens. Subway #7 to Vernon Blvd–Jackson Ave or 45th Rd–Courthouse Square; G to 21st St ⓣ718/786-5400. Mon–Fri 4pm–2am, Sat & Sun 1pm–2am. MAP P.163, POCKET MAP G8

A friendly, atmospheric place for a beer, burger and some free live music (Mon & Wed); hunker down at the old wooden bar or in the pleasant outdoor garden.

PETE'S CANDY STORE

709 Lorimer St between Frost and Richardson sts, Williamsburg, Brooklyn. Subway L to Lorimer St; G to Metropolitan Ave. Mon–Thurs 5pm–2am, Fri & Sat 4pm–4am, Sun 3.30pm–2am. MAP P.163, POCKET MAP J11

This terrific little spot to tipple was once a real candy store. There's free live music every night, a reading series, Scrabble and Bingo nights, pub quizzes and some well-poured cocktails.

Clubs and live music venues

THE BELL HOUSE

149 7th St between Second and Third aves, Gowanus, Brooklyn. Subway F, G, R to Fourth Ave–9th St ⓣ718/643-6510, ⓦwww.thebellhouseny.com. MAP P.163

A converted printing house on a bleak stretch in no-man's Gowanus land provides the setting for indie band performances and wacky events – cookoffs, Burt Reynolds' film celebrations and so on. The front-room bar (daily 5pm–4am) is a pleasantly spacious place to drink.

BROOKLYN ACADEMY CF MUSIC

BROOKLYN ACADEMY OF MUSIC

30 Lafayette St between Ashland Place and St Felix St, Brooklyn. Subway 2, 3, 4, 5, B, Q to Atlantic Ave; D, M, N, R to Pacific St ⓣ718/636-4100, ⓦwww.bam.org. MAP P.165, POCKET MAP J16

America's oldest performing arts academy (1859) and one of the most daring producers in New York – definitely worth crossing the river for, especially to catch Alvin Ailey dance creations, European theatre troupes and rare movie screenings.

MUSIC HALL OF WILLIAMSBURG

66 N 6th St at Kent, Williamsburg, Brooklyn. Subway L to Bedford Ave ⓣ718/486-5400, ⓦwww.musichallofwilliamsburg.com. Tickets $10–30. MAP P.163, POCKET MAP I11

A large performance space with excellent acoustics. Set in an old factory this is one of the city's best spots for live music and indie-rock.

ACCOMMODATION

Hotels

Accommodation prices in New York City are extremely high: many hotels charge more than $200 a night for a double room; $400–500 in high season can be common. The traditional centre of hotel life is midtown Manhattan, but more and more new places are being built below 34th Street. Booking ahead is near essential, and at certain times of the year – early to mid-autumn or the weeks leading up to Christmas – the city can seem sold out. There's hardly such a thing as a fixed room price. Rates in this chapter refer to the cost of the cheapest double room at peak times; be aware that prices can change on a daily basis, depending on a hotel's occupancy and other factors subject to the whims of the booking computer. For some places, rates might be up to half as much as what's listed here, depending on when you check; booking online – whether directly with the hotel or through a third-party travel site – can save lots of money, too. Taxes add 14.75 percent to your bill, plus $3.50 per night in "occupancy tax" and room fees.

Financial District

RITZ-CARLTON > 2 West St, Battery Park. Subway #1 to Rector St; #4, #5, to Bowling Green T 212/344-0800, W www.ritzcarlton.com. MAP P.34–35, POCKET MAP C24 The views of New York Harbor and the Statue of Liberty don't get much better than from this elegant high-rise hotel. It features a lively bar, 425-square-foot rooms with soothing muted tones – all with dazzling vistas and "bath butlers" to draw baths and provide warm towels. Weekend discounts. **$595.**

Soho and Tribeca

COSMOPOLITAN > 95 W Broadway at Chambers St. Subway A, C, #1, #2, #3 to Chambers St T 1-888/895-9400 or 212/566-1900, W www.cosmohotel.com. MAP P.45, POCKET MAP C21 Great Tribeca location, with smart, well-maintained rooms at reasonable prices, this is one of the best of the conventional hotels downtown. **$359.**

CROSBY STREET HOTEL > 79 Crosby St between Spring and Prince sts. Subway N, R to Prince St; #6 to Spring St T 212/226-6400, W www.firmdale.com. MAP P.45, POCKET MAP D19 It's expensive, but you get bright and spacious rooms set around a courtyard on the edge of trendy Soho, with luxurious bathrooms, floor-to-ceiling windows and contemporary art throughout. Rooms on the higher floors have spectacular views. Afternoon tea ($34) is served all day in the drawing room. **$595.**

SMYTH TRIBECA > 85 W Broadway between Warren and Chambers sts. Subway A, C, #1, #2, #3 to Chambers St T 212/587-7000, W www.thompsonhotels.com. MAP P.45, POCKET MAP C21 One of the trendier boutiques in this part of town, with plush, contemporary design and furnishings with classical and Art Deco touches; iPod docking station, plasma TV and large bathroom (with Kiehl products) included. **$459.**

TRIBECA GRAND HOTEL > **2 Sixth Ave, between White and Walker sts. Subway #1 to Franklin St ⓣ1-877/519-6600 or 212/519-6600, ⓦwww.tribecagrand.com.** MAP P.45, POCKET MAP C20 Beckoning with a warm orange glow, the *Church Lounge* is one of the more striking hotel public spaces and a great place to have a drink. Rooms are stylish, yet understated, though each bathroom boasts a phone and built-in TV. **$429.**

The Lower East Side

BLUE MOON > **100 Orchard St between Delancey and Broome sts. Subway F to Delancey St; J, M, Z to Essex St ⓣ 212/533-9080, ⓦ www.bluemoon-nyc.com.** MAP P.63, POCKET MAP E19 Five-storey Lower East Side tenement transformed into a luxurious boutique, with rooms named after 1930s and 1940s celebrities and decked out with period iron-frame beds and the odd antique – rooms on the 6th, 7th and 8th floors also come with fabulous views across the city. Continental breakfast and wi-fi included. **$350.**

HOTEL 91 > **91 E Broadway. Subway F to E Broadway ⓣ 212/266-6800, ⓦ www.thehotel91.com.** MAP P.63, POCKET MAP E21 Funky Lower East Side boutique, with a slight Asian theme – orchids grace every room, and a statue of Buddha sits in the lobby. Rooms are compact but well equipped, with LCD TVs and marble bathrooms. Free wi-fi. **$179.**

The East Village

BOWERY HOTEL > **335 Bowery at E 3rd St. Subway #6 to Bleecker St ⓣ212/505-9100, ⓦwww.theboweryhotel.com.** MAP P.70–71, POCKET MAP D18 This fabulous, but pricey, boutique property oozes sophistication and tempts guests with iPod docks, floor-to-ceiling windows, marble tubs with a view and a hip lounge bar. **$495.**

The West Village

LARCHMONT > **27 W 11th St between Fifth and Sixth aves. Subway F, M, L to 14th St ⓣ212/989-9333, ⓦwww.larchmonthotel.com.** MAP P.82–83, POCKET MAP C17 This budget hotel, with a terrific location on a tree-lined street in Greenwich Village, has small but nice clean rooms – it's a bargain, but the bathrooms are shared. Slightly more expensive on weekends. **$135.**

Chelsea and the Meatpacking District

CHELSEA LODGE > **318 W 20th St between Eighth and Ninth aves. Subway C, E to 23rd St ⓣ212/243-4499 or 1-800/373-1116, ⓦwww.chelsealodge.com.** MAP P.93, POCKET MAP C10 Step through the (unmarked) door of this gem, a converted boarding house, and you'll be greeted with cheery Early American/Sportsman decor. The "lodge" rooms, with in-room showers and sinks (shared toilets), are a little small for two, but the few deluxe rooms are great value and have full bathrooms. Two of the suites share a leafy private garden. **$145.**

CHELSEA PINES INN > **317 W 14th St, between Eighth and Ninth aves. Subway A, C, E to 14th St ⓣ1-888/546-2700 or 212/929-1023, ⓦwww.chelseapinesinn.com.** MAP P.93, POCKET MAP A17 Housed in an old brownstone, this super-friendly hotel offers clean, comfortable, shabby-chic rooms, all done with a movie motif and recently renovated. Long popular with a gay and lesbian clientele. Best to book in advance. **$269.**

HÔTEL AMERICANO > **518 W 27th St, between Tenth and Eleventh aves. Subway #1 to 28th St ⓣ 212/216-0000, ⓦ www.hotel-americano.com.** MAP P.93, POCKET MAP B10 The first venture outside of Mexico by boutique developers Grupo Habita, the eye-catching *Americano* sits right on the High Line, with a sleek, modern style all its own. Some evidence: Japanese-style platform beds, showers looking out onto the skyline and separate elevators for guest and public use. **$399.**

Union Square, Gramercy Park and the Flatiron District

ACE > 20 W 29th St at Broadway. Subway N, R to 28th St 212/679-2222, www.acehotel.com/newyork. MAP P.101, POCKET MAP D10 Capturing the spirit of old New York, yet fully modern, the *Ace Hotel* sets a new standard for bohemian chic. A whole host of different room styles are on offer (including bunks), with retro-style fridges, guitars, muted tones and cool artwork. **$479.**

GIRAFFE > 365 Park Ave at 26th St. Subway #6 to 28th St 212/685-7700, www.hotelgiraffe.com. MAP P.101, POCKET MAP E10 A small, boutique hotel with a personal touch, the *Giraffe* offers deluxe rooms with tiny terraces and all the amenities; there's a wine and cheese hour (Mon–Sat 5–8pm) in the lobby with live music accompaniment. **$489.**

GRAMERCY PARK > 2 Lexington Ave at E 21st St. Subway #6 to 23rd St 212/475-4320, www.gramercyparkhotel.com. MAP P.101, POCKET MAP E10 An Ian Schrager overhaul gave new life to this once bohemian hotel, located in a prime Gramercy spot with access to the private park. The rooms are bold and luxurious. **$495.**

ROGER WILLIAMS > 131 Madison Ave at 31st St. Subway #6 to 33rd St 1-888/448-7788 or 212/448-7000, www.therogernewyork.com. MAP P.101, POCKET MAP D9 The first thing you'll notice is the use of colour: the lobby is awash with it, and the Scandinavian/Japanese fusion rooms feature both mellow and vibrant tones. Some come with small terraces with views of the Empire State Building. **$450.**

SEVENTEEN > 225 E 17th St between Second and Third aves. Subway L, N, Q, R, #4, #5, #6 to 14th St–Union Square 212/475-2845, www.hotel17ny.com. MAP P.101, POCKET MAP E11 *Seventeen*'s rooms feature a/c, cable TV and phones, though many share baths. It's clean, friendly and nicely situated on a pleasant tree-lined street minutes from Union Square and the East Village. **$150.**

Midtown

70 PARK AVENUE HOTEL > 70 Park Ave, at 38th St. Subway S, #4, #5, #6, #7 to 42nd St-Grand Central 1-877/707-2752 or 212/973-2400 www.70parkave.com. MAP P.109, POCKET MAP D9 This classy boutique hotel is adorned with re-creations of classical friezes and frescoes, and original lighting and furnishing design featuring rich woods and muted earth tones. Extras include CD/DVD players, flat-screen TVs, wi-fi and a nightly wine reception. Pet-friendly. **$429.**

AFFINIA SHELBURNE > 303 Lexington Ave between E 37th and E 38th sts. Subway #4, #5, #6, #7 to 42nd St-Grand Central 212/689-5200, www.affinia.com. MAP P.109, POCKET MAP E9 Luxurious hotel in the most elegant part of Murray Hill. All the rooms have kitchenettes, and its restaurant *Rare* specializes in gourmet burgers. **$359.**

THE ALEX > 205 E 45th St, between Second and Third aves. Subway #4, #5, #6, #7 to 42nd St 212/867-5100, www.thealexhotel.com. MAP P.109, POCKET MAP E8 This sleek, beige-toned place is a serene Midtown oasis. Rooms are bright and airy, with modern Scandinavian touches. **$420.**

ALGONQUIN > 59 W 44th St between Fifth and Sixth aves. Subway B, D, F, M to 42nd St 212/840-6800, www.algonquinhotel.com. MAP P.109, POCKET MAP D8 At New York's classic literary hangout (see p.113), you'll find a resident cat named Matilda, cabaret performances and suites with silly names. The bedrooms have been refurbished to good effect. **$479.**

CHAMBERS > 15 W 56th St between Fifth and Sixth aves. Subway F to 57th St 1-866/204-5656 or 212/974-5656, www.chambershotel.com. MAP P.109, POCKET MAP D7 Designed by architect

David Rockwell, *Chambers* is well placed for Central Park and MoMA, though you can just sit and admire the 500 original works in the hallways. Modern, tasteful rooms approximate a New York apartment, as do the mezzanine lounge spaces. The latest *Momofuku* offspring, *Má Pêche*, is on-site. **$425.**

IROQUOIS > **49 W 44th St between Fifth and Sixth aves. Subway B, D, F, M to 42nd St ⓣ1-800/332-7220 or 212/840-3080, ⓦwww.iroquoisny.com.** MAP P.109, POCKET MAP D8 A former haven for rock bands, this reinvented "boutique" hotel has comfortable, tasteful rooms with Italian marble baths and a health centre, library and a five-star restaurant. One of the hotel's noted visitors is immortalized in the lounge named after him: James Dean lived here from 1951 to 1953 (room #803). $529.

LIBRARY > **299 Madison Ave at E 41st St. Subway #4, #5, #6, #7 to 42nd St-Grand Central ⓣ212/983-4500, ⓦwww.libraryhotel.com.** MAP P.109, POCKET MAP D8 The *Library's* unusual concept, has each floor devoted to one of the ten major categories of the Dewey Decimal System. Coloured in shades of brown and cream, the rooms are average-sized but nicely appointed, with big bathrooms. The hotel throws a wine and cheese get-together every weekday evening. **$469.**

THE MANSFIELD > **12 W 44th St between Fifth and Sixth aves. Subway B, D, F, M to 42nd St ⓣ1-800/255-5167 or 212/277-8700, ⓦwww.mansfieldhotel.com.** MAP P.109, POCKET MAP D8 One of the loveliest, friendliest hotels in the city, the *Mansfield* is both grand and intimate. With its recessed floor spotlighting, copper-domed salon, clubby library and nightly jazz, there's a charming, quirky feel about the place. **$499.**

THE METRO > **45 W 35th St between Fifth and Sixth aves. Subway B, D, F, M, N, Q, R to 34th St ⓣ1-800/356-3870 or 212/947-2500, ⓦwww.hotelmetronyc.com.** MAP P.109, POCKET MAP D9 A very stylish hotel, with minimal Hollywood theming, a delightful seasonal rooftop terrace, clean rooms and free continental breakfast. **$340.**

MORGANS > **237 Madison Ave between E 37th and E 38th sts. Subway #6 to 33rd St ⓣ1-800/334-3408 or 212/686-0300, ⓦwww.morganshotel.com.** MAP P.109, POCKET MAP D9 Still one of the chicest flophouses in town; rooms come in soothing neutral tones and maple panelling, with specially commissioned photographs by the late Robert Mapplethorpe. **$419.**

POD > **230 E 51st St between Second and Third aves. Subway #6 to 51st St ⓣ1-800/742-5945 or 212/355-0300, ⓦwww.thepodhotel.com.** MAP P.109, POCKET MAP E8 This pleasant budget hotel is one of the best deals in Midtown. All 370 "pods" (solo, double, bunk, queen or "odd"; reminiscent of a ship's quarters) come with a/c, iPod docks, free wi-fi and LCD TVs, though some share baths. The open-air roof deck is a bonus, with stunning views. **$299.**

ROGER SMITH > **501 Lexington Ave at E 47th St. Subway #6 to 51st St ⓣ1-800/445-0277 or 212/755-1400, ⓦwww.rogersmith.com.** MAP P.109, POCKET MAP E8 Lots of style and personality: individually decorated rooms and bold artwork on display in the common areas. Breakfast is included. **$519.**

THE STRAND > **33 W 37th St, between Fifth and Sixth aves. Subway B, D, F, M, N, Q, R to 34th St–Herald Square ⓣ212/448-1024, ⓦwww.thestrandnyc.com.** MAP P.109, POCKET MAP D9 The rooms, some of which have views of the Empire State Building, are fresh and comfortable, but it's the soothing lobby and lovely roof-deck bar that help this hotel stand out. **$359.**

WALDORF ASTORIA > **301 Park Ave at E 50th St. Subway #6 to 51st St ⓣ1-800/925-3673 or 212/355-3000, ⓦwww.waldorfnewyork.com.** MAP P.109, POCKET MAP E8 One of the great names among New York hotels and restored to its 1930s glory, the *Waldorf* is a wonderful place to stay if you can afford it or someone else is paying. Even if you can't, it's worth dropping by for a look at the lobby (see p.110) and a drink at the mahogany bar downstairs. $549.

Times Square and the Theater District

414 > 414 W 46th St between Ninth and Tenth aves. Subway C, E to 50th St T 212/399-0006 or 1-866/414-HOTEL, W www.414hotel.com. MAP P.123, POCKET MAP C8 Popular with Europeans but welcoming to all, this guesthouse, which has larger-than-ordinary rooms in two townhouses, makes a nice camp a bit removed from Times Square's bustle. The backyard garden is a wonderful place to enjoy your morning coffee. **$255.**

AMERITANIA AT TIMES SQUARE > 54 230 W 54th St at Broadway. Subway B, D, E to Seventh Ave T 1-800/555-7555 or 212/247-5000, W www ameritaniahotelnewyork. com. MAP P.123, POCKET MAP C7. One of the coolest-looking hotels in the city, with well-furnished rooms with marble bathrooms; there's a bar/restaurant off the high-tech, Neoclassical lobby. **$299.**

CASABLANCA > 147 W 43rd St between Sixth Ave and Broadway. Subway B, D, F, M, #1, #2, #3 to 42nd St T 1-888/922-7225 or 212/869-1212, W www.casablancahotel.com. MAP P.123, POCKET MAP D8 Moorish tiles, ceiling fans and *Rick's Café* are all here in this unusual and understated theme hotel. While the feeling is 1940s Morocco, the rooms are all up to date. **$410.**

DISTRIKT > 342 W 40th St, between Eighth and Ninth aves. Subway A, C, E to 42nd St–Port Authority T 1-888/444-5610 or 212/706-6100, W www.distrikthotel.com. MAP P.123, POCKET MAP C9 With a city neighbourhood theme, the welcoming *Distrikt* has nice-sized rooms done in classy muted browns and beiges; choose one of the upper floors (eg "Harlem") for the best views. The street outside is on the unsalubrious side. **$409.**

FLATOTEL > 135 W 52nd St between Sixth and Seventh aves. Subway B, D, E to Seventh Ave T 1-800/352-8683 or 212/887-9400, W www.flatotel .com. MAP P.123, POCKET MAP D7 A comfortable, stylish hotel that highlights clean lines and motifs inspired by Frank Lloyd Wright. Though some might find it a dizzying place for a workout, check out the Sky Gym fitness centre on the 46th floor. **$340.**

GRACE > 125 W 45th St between Sixth and Seventh aves. Subway B, D, F, M, #1, #2, #3 to 42nd St T 212/354-2323, W www .room-matehotels.com. MAP P.123, POCKET MAP D8 You won't find many hotels like this one, with a lobby that more closely resembles a concession stand; a tiny glassed-in pool overlooked by a louche loungey bar; different, funky retro wallpaper on each floor; and ultra-modern rooms with platform beds. **$379.**

INK48 > 653 Eleventh Ave, between 47th and 48th sts. Subway C, E to 50th St T 800/843-8869 or 212/1757-0088 W www.ink48.com. MAP P.123, POCKET MAP B8 Located on an industrial strip, this old printing press has been re-made into a dashing hotel; all rooms face outwards – many to the Hudson – for splendid views (best from upper floor corner rooms), and have modern decor and lofty ceilings. The rooftop bar, *Press Lounge*, is a plus, as is the spa. Dog-friendly. **$449.**

LE PARKER MERIDIEN > 119 W 56th St between Sixth and Seventh aves. Subway F to 57th St T 212/245-5000, W www.parkermeridien.com. MAP P.123, POCKET MAP D7 This hotel maintains a shiny, clean veneer, with comfortably modern rooms, a huge fitness centre, rooftop swimming pool and 24hr room service. The tucked away, ground-floor *Burger Joint* (see p.128) is a fun place for a bite to eat. **$459.**

SALISBURY > 123 W 57th St between Sixth and Seventh aves. Subway F, N, Q, R to 57th St T 212/246-1300, W www .nycsalisbury.com. MAP P.123, POCKET MAP D7 Good service, large rooms with kitchenettes and proximity to Central Park are the attractions here. **$339.**

The Upper East Side

WALES > 1295 Madison Ave between E

92nd and E 93rd sts. Subway #6 to 96th St ⓣ1-800/925-3745 or 212/876-6000, ⓦwww.hotelwalesnyc.com. MAP P.137, POCKET MAP D4 Just steps from "Museum Mile", this Carnegie Hill hotel has hosted guests for over a century. Rooms are attractive with antique details, thoughtful in-room amenities and some views of Central Park. There's also a rooftop terrace and free continental breakfast. **$375.**

The Upper West Side

LUCERNE > 201 W 79th St at Amsterdam Ave. Subway B, C to 81 St; #1 to 79th St ⓣ1-800/492-8122 or 212/875-1000, ⓦwww.thelucernehotel.com. MAP P.147, POCKET MAP B5 This beautifully restored 1904 brownstone, with its extravagantly Baroque red terracotta entrance, charming rooms and friendly staff, is just a block from the American Museum of Natural History and close to the liveliest stretch of Columbus Avenue. **$380.**

MILBURN > 242 W 76th St between Broadway and West End. Subway #1 to 79th St ⓣ1-800/833-9622 or 212/362-1006, ⓦwww.milburnhotel.com. MAP P.147, POCKET MAP B5 Once past the classic feel of the lobby, the rooms are less showy but are on the large side, all with kitchenettes. It's a good choice for families, and the hotel offers free use of a swimming pool one block away. **$259.**

ON THE AVE > 222 W 77th St between Amsterdam Ave and Broadway. Subway #1 to 79th St ⓣ1-800/509-7598 or 212/362-1100, ⓦwww.ontheave-nyc.com. MAP P.147, POCKET MAP B5 With its stainless-steel sinks, minimalist baths and dark-wood bed platforms, *On the Ave* feels forward-looking yet out of step. It's clean, comfortable and discounts are available. **$350.**

Hostels

Hostels can offer savings as well as a sociable vibe, but there are, relatively speaking, limited options in the city – at least that fit the bill in terms of quality and prime location. Wherever the case, book ahead: reservations are usually essential. Rates for singles range from $40 to $70 and doubles cost from $80 to $150.

CHELSEA HOSTEL > 251 W 20th St between Seventh and Eighth aves. Subway C, E, #1 to 23rd St ⓣ212/647-0010, ⓦwww.chelseahostel.com. MAP P.93, POCKET MAP C10 In the heart of Chelsea, this is a smart downtown choice. Guests must leave a $10 key deposit. No curfew; passport required and advance reservations near essential. **Shared rooms $68–$78/person, private doubles $165.**

GERSHWIN > 7 E 27th St between Fifth and Madison aves. Subway N, R to 28th St ⓣ212/545-8000, ⓦwww.gershwinhotel.com. MAP P.101, POCKET MAP D10 This funky hostel/hotel is geared toward young travellers, offering Pop Art decor and dormitories with ten, six or two beds per room, and private rooms. There'a also a bar/cocktail lounge. **Dorms from $50/night, private rooms $170–240.**

WHITEHOUSE HOTEL OF NEW YORK > 340 Bowery at Bond St. Subway F, to Second Ave; #6 to Bleecker St ⓣ212/477-5623, ⓦwww.whitehousehotelofny.com. MAP P.70–71, POCKET MAP D18 The only hostel in the city offering single and double rooms at dorm rates; an ideal downtown location adds to the appeal. **Private singles $37, doubles $73.**

ZIP112 HOSTEL > 5/F, 112 N 6th St, Williamsburg, Brooklyn. Subway L to Bedford Ave T 347/403-0577, W www.zip112.com. MAP P.165, POCKET MAP H11 One of New York's hipper neighbourhoods has spawned its hippest hostel, with two spotless female-only dorms (eight bunks), one private room (that will accept men; two single beds), two shared bathrooms, a big kitchen and two computers. Basic breakfast included. **Dorms $65, private room $140.**

B&Bs and apartments

Bed and breakfast accommodation can be a good way of staying right in the centre of Manhattan at an affordable price. But don't expect to socialize with your temporary landlord/lady – chances are you'll have a self-contained room and hardly see them. Reservations are normally arranged through an agency such as those listed below; book well in advance. Try Craigslist (W newyork.craigslist.org) for everything from apartment swaps to short-term rentals; more holiday apartment listings can be found on HomeAway (W homeaway.com), Vacation Rentals by Owner (W www.vrbo.com) and Airbnb (W www.airbnb.com).

B&B agencies

AFFORDABLE NEW YORK CITY > 21 E 10th St T 212/533-4001, W www.affordablenyc.com. Detailed descriptions are provided for this established and customer-oriented network of 120 properties (B&Bs and apartments).Cash or travellers' cheques only; four- and five-night minimums. **B&B accommodation from $95 (shared bathroom) and $135 (private bathroom), unhosted studios $170–250 and one-bedrooms apartments $175–300.**

CITY LIGHTS BED & BREAKFAST > Box 1562 First Ave, NY 10028 T 212/737-7049, W www.citylightsbedandbreakfast.com. More than 400 carefully screened B&Bs (and short-term apartment rentals) on its books, with many of the hosts involved in theatre and the arts. Minimum stay two nights, with some exceptions. Reserve well in advance. **Hosted doubles $80–175, unhosted apartments $135–300 and up.**

CITYSONNET.COM > T 212/614-3034, W www.citysonnet.com. This small, personalized, artist-run B&B/short-term apartment agency offers accommodations all over the city, but specializes in Greenwich Village. **Hosted singles start at $125, doubles are $250, and unhosted studio flats go up to $250 – five night minimum stay.**

COLBY INTERNATIONAL > 21 Park Ave, Eccleston Park, Prescot L34 1QY, England, UK T 0151/292-2910, W www.colbyinternational.com. Excellent B&B accommodations arranged from the UK. Book at least a fortnight ahead in high season. **Singles from $100 (per room); most studios and apartments are more like $200–250 per night.**

B&B and apartment properties

COLONIAL HOUSE INN > 318 W 22nd St, between Eighth and Ninth aves. Subway C, E to 23rd St ⓣ212/243-9669, ⓦwww.colonialhouseinn.com. MAP P.93, POCKET MAP C10 You won't mind that this B&B is a little worn around the edges (though it has recently been updated) – its attractive design and association with Gay Men's Health Crisis make for a feel-good accommodation experience. Only deluxe rooms include en-suite bathrooms, while some rooms even have refrigerators and fireplaces, and sleep four. Continental breakfast included. **Doubles $130, suites up to $300.**

EAST VILLAGE BED AND COFFEE > 110 Ave C, between E 7th and E 8th sts. Subway L to First Ave; F to Second Ave ⓣ917/816-0071, ⓦwww.bedandcoffee.com. MAP P.70–71, POCKET MAP F18 Unusual location in the East Village/Alphabet City, in one of the most cutting-edge neighbourhoods in the city, with cheap, cosy rooms (shared bath), friendly owners, kitchens, free wi-fi and computers, and a tranquil garden. On the downside, it's a long walk to the subway (and there's no breakfast). **$130.**

JONES STREET GUESTHOUSE > 31 Jones St, between Bleecker and W 4th sts. Subway A, B, C, D, E, F, M to W 4th St; #1 to Christopher St contact via email only, ⓦwww.jonesstreetguesthouse.com. MAP P.70–71, POCKET MAP B18 Rare B&B in the heart of the West Village, just off Bleecker; two nicely renovated en-suite rooms, spotlessly clean, with friendly owners in the apartments above (their duplex can also be rented) – closest you'll get to "living like a local". Breakfast is courtesy of a $5 per person voucher at nearby *Doma*. Free wi-fi. **$250.**

ROOM IN SOHO LOFT > 153 Lafayette St at Grand St. Subway N, R, #6 to Canal St ⓣ917/225-3778, listing at ⓦwww.bedandbreakfast.com. MAP P.45, POCKET MAP D20 In a great location at the edge of vibrant Soho, these unique, quirky (and cheap) loft apartments, above a gallery managed by the owners, are a great way to experience the neighbourhood; two en-suite seventh-floor rooms (walk-up only!) and two fifth-floor rooms with shared bathroom. Kitchen included. **$250.**

Favourite places to stay

There's something for every taste in the city, though even if you find the perfect accommodation for you, you'll probably still register some surprise at the (small) size of the room. Here are just a few of our favourites:

Best place for downtown chic: *Blue Moon*, p.177

Best place to blow the expense account: *Waldorf-Astoria*, p.179

Best place for a romantic getaway: *Gramercy Park*, p.178

Best place to be in the heart of it all: *Mansfield*, p.179

Best place for a modest budget: *Cosmopolitan*, p.176

Best place for a room with a view: *Ink48* p.180.

Best place for mixing function with form: *Ace*, p.178

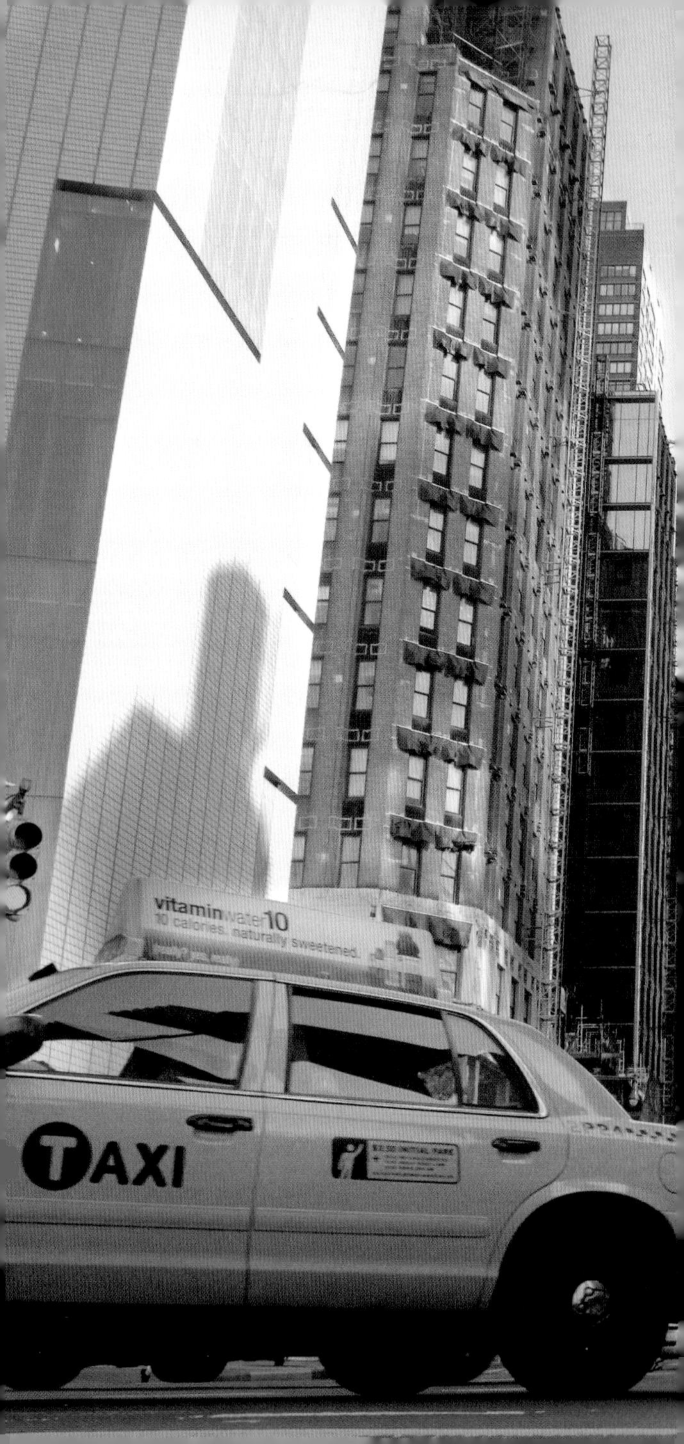
vitaminwater10
10 calories. naturally sweetened.
TAXI

ESSENTIALS

Arrival

By air

New York City is served by three major airports: most international flights use John F. Kennedy, or **JFK** (☎718/244-4444), in Queens, and **Newark Liberty** (☎973/961-6000), in New Jersey, which has easier access to Lower Manhattan. Most domestic arrivals touch down at **LaGuardia** (☎718/533-3400), also in Queens, or at Newark. All three share a website at Ⓦwww.panynj.gov.

Getting into the city

From JFK, the New York Airport Service (☎212/875-8200, Ⓦwww.nyairportservice.com) runs **buses** to Grand Central Terminal, Port Authority Bus Terminal and Penn Station (every 15–20min 6.05am–11pm; 45–60min; $15 one-way, $25 round-trip). The **AirTrain** (24hr daily; ☎1-877/535-2478, Ⓦwww.panynj.gov; $5) runs between JFK and the Jamaica and Howard Beach subway stations in Queens; at Jamaica you can connect to the #E, #J or #Z subway lines, and at Howard Beach, to the #A line, into Manhattan (from both stations: 1hr; $2.25). Alternatively, the **Long Island Railroad** (LIRR) runs faster trains from the Jamaica station to Penn Station (20min; $8.75 peak).

From LaGuardia, New York Airport Service buses (see above) take 45 minutes to get to Grand Central and Port Authority (every 15–30min 7.30am–11pm; $12 one-way, $21 round-trip). Alternatively, for $2.25, take the #M60 bus to 106th Street in Manhattan, where you can transfer to downtown-bound subway lines.

From Newark, **Olympia Newark Airport Express** (☎877/863-9275, Ⓦwww.coachusa.com) runs buses to Grand Central Station, Port Authority Bus Terminal and Penn Station (every 15–30min, 4am–1am; $16 one-way, $28 round-trip). For train services, take the short **AirTrain** (every 3–15min; 24hr) ride to Newark Airport Train Station and connect with frequent NJ Transit or Amtrak trains heading into the city (every 20–30min 4.30am–2.30am; $12.50). The AirTrain costs $5.50, but if you buy a NJ Transit or Amtrak ticket before leaving the system, the AirTrain ticket is included.

Taxis are available at all airports: reckon on paying $25–35 from LaGuardia to Manhattan, a flat rate of $45 from JFK and $50–70 from Newark; you'll also be responsible for the turnpike and tunnel tolls – an extra $8 or so – as well as a fifteen- to twenty-percent tip for the driver. Note that bridges between Brooklyn/Queens and Manhattan are free, but the Queens Midtown Tunnel has a toll of $6.50. You should only use official yellow taxis that wait at designated ranks – just follow the signs out of the terminal.

By bus or train

Greyhound and most other long-distance **bus** lines (with the exception of the Chinatown buses, which arrive in Chinatown, and Mega Bus/Bolt Bus which drop off on the streets of Midtown) terminate at the Port Authority Bus Terminal, W 42nd St and Eighth Avenue.

Amtrak trains come in to Penn Station, at Seventh Avenue and W 33rd St. From either Port Authority or Penn Station, multiple subway lines will take you where you want to go.

Getting around

Buses

Bus and subway information ⓣ718/330-1234 (daily 6am–10pm). New York's **bus system** is clean and usually efficient. It is often extremely slow in peak hours, but it can be your best bet for travelling crosstown. Pay on entry with a **MetroCard** (see opposite; $2.25, express $5.50) or exact fare in coins; you can transfer for free from subway to bus, bus to subway, or from bus to bus, in one direction within two hours of swiping your MetroCard.

City tours

Big Onion Walking Tours ⓣ212/439-1090, ⓦwww.bigonion.com. Excellent walking tours by guides with advanced degrees in American history ($18).
Circle Line Pier 83 at the end of W 42nd St at the West Side Highway, ⓣ212/563-3200, ⓦwww.circleline42.com. Boat cruises around Manhattan ($32 2hr, $36 3hr).
Gray Line ⓣ1-800/669-0051, ⓦwww.newyorksightseeing.com. Double-decker hop-on, hop-off buses touring the main sights (around $39 for 24hr).
Big Apple Jazz Tours ⓣ212/439-1090, ⓦwww.bigapplejazz.com. Fabulous introduction to the Harlem jazz scene, minibus tours take in clubs and jazz history (from $99).
Hush Hip Hop Tours ⓣ212/391-0900, ⓦwww.hushhiphoptours.com. Bus tours of hip-hop haunts, given by legends such as Kurtis Blow and DJ Kool Herc ($29–68).
Liberty Helicopter Tours 12 Ave at W 30th St and Pier 6 on South St, between Broad St and Coenties Slip ⓣ212/967-6464 or ⓣ1-800/542-9933, ⓦwww.libertyhelicopters.com. Helicopter tours ($180 for 12–15min to $245 for 16–20min/person).

Cycling

Bike and Roll Pier 84 (12th Ave and W 43rd St), Central Park (at Columbus Circle), South Street Seaport, Governors Island and Battery Park ⓣ1-866/736-8224, ⓦbikeandroll.com. Open March–Nov daily 9am–7pm. Rates start at $12/hour and $39/day.

The subway

The fastest way to get around New York is the user-friendly **subway**, open 24 hours a day. A number or letter identifies each train and route, and most routes in Manhattan run uptown (north) or downtown (south), rather than crosstown.

Every trip, whether on express or local lines, costs $2.25 if you pay by **MetroCard**, available at station booths or debit/credit card-capable vending machines (you'll pay $2.50 for a single ticket without a MetroCard). MetroCards can be purchased in any amount from $4.50 to $80; a $20 purchase gives you $21.40 on your card. Unlimited-ride cards – almost always the best deal if you intend to be on the go – allow unlimited travel for a certain period of time: a 7-day pass costs $29 and a 30-day pass is $104 (there is no one-day pass).

Taxis

Taxis are reasonably priced – $2.50 upon entry and $0.40 for every 1/5 mile, with a $0.50 surcharge 8pm–6am, and a $1 surcharge Mon–Fri 4–8pm. Most drivers take up to four passengers, refuse bills larger than $20, and ask for the nearest cross street to your destination. It's customary to tip ten to twenty percent. Only use official yellow taxis.

Directory A-Z

Cinema

For first-run movies and blockbusters head to megaplexes such as AMC Empire 25 at 234 W 42nd St, between Seventh and Eighth aves (T 1-888/262-4386) or Regal Union Square at 850 Broadway and 13th St (T 212/253-6266). Good places for indie flicks, old classics and documentaries are IFC Center, 323 6th Ave at W 3rd St (T 212/924-7771, W www.ifccenter.com), Film Forum at 209 W Houston St and 6th Ave (T 212/727-8110, W www.filmforum.org), the Paris Theater at 4 W 58th St (T 212/688-3800, W www.theparistheatre.com) and the Walter Reade Theater at the Lincoln Center, 165 W 65th St at Broadway (T 212/875-5601, W www.filmlinc.com). Tickets at most cinemas are around $12.50 (buy online at W www.movietickets.com).

Consulates

Australia, 34/F, 150 E 42nd St, (T 212/351-6500, W www.australianyc.org).
Canada, 1251 6th Ave, at 50th St (T 212/596-1628, W www.canadainternational.gc.ca/new_york).
Ireland, 17/F, 345 Park Ave, between 51st and 52nd sts (T 212/319-2555, W www.consulateofirelandnewyork.org).
New Zealand, 222 E 41st St, Suite 2510, between Second and Third aves (T 212/832-4038).
South Africa, 333 E 38th St, between First and Second aves (T 212/213-4880, W www.southafrica-newyork.net/consulate).
UK, 845 3rd Ave between 51st and 52nd sts (T 212/745-0200, W www.britainusa.com/ny).

Emergency numbers For Police, Fire or Ambulance dial T 911.

Crime

In two words: don't worry. New York has come a long way in recent years. While the city can sometimes feel dangerous, the reality is somewhat different. New York is America's safest city with a population over one million. Take the normal precautions and you should be fine; carry bags closed and across your body, don't let cameras dangle, keep wallets in front – not back – pockets, and don't flash money around. You should also keep a firm grip on your iPod on the subway (these are occasionally snatched just as the doors close). Mugging can and does happen, but rarely during the day. Avoid wandering empty streets or the subway late at night (especially alone). If you are unlucky enough to be mugged, try to stay calm and hand over the money.

Electricity

110V AC with two-pronged plugs. Unless they're dual voltage (most mobile phones, cameras, MP3 players and laptops are), all Australian, British, European, Irish, New Zealand and South African appliances will need a voltage transformer as well as a plug adaptor (hair-dryers are the most common problem for travellers).

Gay and lesbian New York

There are few places in America where gay culture thrives as it does in New York. Chelsea, Hell's Kitchen, the Villages, the Lower East Side and Park Slope are the biggest hubs of gay life. If you're looking for local resources, check out *Gay City News* (W www.gaycitynews.com), *Next Magazine* (W www.nextmagazine.com), *GO* magazine (W www.gomag.com) or the listings in the weekly *Time Out*.

Health

Drugstores can be found every few blocks – CVS and Duane Reade are the city's major chains, many open 24hr (such as the Duane Reade at 1470 Broadway, near Times Square).

If you do get sick or have an accident, medical costs can be incredibly expensive; organize insurance before your trip, just in case. It costs upwards of $100 to simply see a doctor or dentist, and prescription drugs can be prohibitively expensive – if you don't have US medical insurance, you'll have to cough up the money and make a claim when you get home.

In the unlikely event that you are involved in a serious accident, a medical service will pick you up and charge later. Note that basic emergency care will cost at least $200, ranging to several thousand for serious trauma – that's in addition to fees for drugs, appliances, supplies and the attendant physician, who will charge separately.

Should you find yourself requiring a doctor or dentist, ask if your hotel has links to a local practice, or look in the *Yellow Pages* under "Clinics" or "Physicians and Surgeons".

Doctors in Manhattan often have long waiting lists, however, and will be reluctant to see a new patient at short notice – if you have an accident or need immediate attention head to the 24hr emergency rooms at these and other Manhattan hospitals: New York Presbyterian (Cornell), E 70th St at York Ave (T 212/746-5050); and Mount Sinai, Madison Ave at 100th St (T 212/241-7171).

Internet

Wireless is king in New York. Most hotels offer it for free, it's also available at wi-fi hotspots like Times Square and complimentary at cafés like Starbucks. If you're travelling without your own computer, accessing your email is still possible at internet cafés, though their numbers are dwindling. Try the Cyber Cafe, 250 W 49th St between Broadway and 8th Ave (Mon–Fri 8am–11pm, Sat & Sun 11am–11pm; T 212/333-4109, W www.cyber-cafe.com), which charges around $12/hr.

A great, free alternative is to stop by a branch of the New York City Public Library, where wi-fi and computer internet access and printing are available. You first need to get a guest pass at the Stephen A. Schwarzman Building (the main library building; Mon and Thurs–Sat 10am–6pm, Tues and Wed 10am–9pm, Sun 1–5pm), at 42nd St and Fifth Ave. With the pass, you can reserve time slots at computers in person or via W www.nypl.org.

Left luggage

The best place to leave luggage is your hotel, but you can also use Schwartz Travel Services (daily 8am–11pm; T 212/290-2626, W www.schwartztravel.com; $7–10/item/day) at 355 W 36th St, near Penn Station.

Lost property

If you lose something on a bus or on the subway contact NYC Transit Authority, at the W 34th St/Eighth Ave Station on the lower-level subway mezzanine (Mon, Tues & Fri 8am–3.30pm, Wed & Thurs 11am–6.30pm; T 212/712-4500). For items lost in a taxi call T 311 or file a report online (W www.nyc.gov/taxi); try to get the taxi's medallion number (printed on your receipt).

Money

On a moderate budget, expect to spend at least $200 per night on accommodation in a low to mid-range, centrally located hotel in high season, plus $20–30/person for a moderate sit-down dinner each night and about $15–20 more per person per day for takeout and grocery meals. Getting around will cost $29/person per week for unlimited public transportation, plus $10 each for the occasional taxi ride. Sightseeing, drinking, clubbing, eating haute cuisine and going to the theatre will add exponentially to these costs.

With an ATM card you'll have access to cash from machines all over New York, though as anywhere, you will usually be charged a fee for using a different bank's ATM network (usually $3). Most banks are open Monday–Friday 8.30am–5pm, and a few have limited Saturday hours (major Citibank branches tend to open Sat 9am–3pm). Major banks – such as Citibank and Chase – will exchange travellers' cheques and currency at a standard rate. For banking services – particularly currency exchange – outside normal business hours and on weekends, try major hotels, though the rate won't be as good.

Opening hours

The opening hours of specific attractions are given throughout the Guide. As a general rule, most museums are open Tuesday through Sunday, 10am–5 or 6pm, though most have one night per week where they stay open at least a few hours later. Government offices, including post offices, are open during regular business hours, usually 9am–5pm. Store hours vary widely, though you can generally count on them being open Monday–Saturday from around 10am–6pm, with limited Sunday hours. Many of the larger chain or department stores will stay open to 9pm or later, and you generally don't have to walk more than a few blocks anywhere to find a 24-hour deli. On national public holidays, banks and offices are likely to be closed all day, and some shops have reduced hours.

Phones

In the US, AT&T and T-Mobile use the GSM standard for mobile phones, and most foreign companies partner with them to provide service to travelling customers. Note that unless you have a tri-band phone, it is unlikely that a mobile bought for use outside the US or Canada will work inside the States. If you have a Blackberry or smartphone these should work in the US, but roaming charges, especially for data, can be extortionate; even checking voicemail can result in hefty charges. Check with your phone company before you travel.

The cost of a local call on a public payphone is 25–50¢ for three or four minutes, depending on the carrier (each phone company runs their own booths). Calls elsewhere within the US are usually 25–50¢ for one minute; overseas rates are much pricier, so buy a prepaid calling card ($5, $10 or $20), from a grocery store or newsstand.

To call home internationally: dial 011 + country code + number, minus the initial 0 (to call Canada, just start with the area code). Country codes are as follows: Australia (61), New Zealand (64), UK & Northern Ireland (44), and Ireland (353).

Post

International letters and postcards usually take about a week to reach their destination; rates are currently

85¢ for letters and postcards to Canada, and $1.05 to all other countries. To find a post office or check up-to-date rates, see Ⓦ www.usps.com or call Ⓣ 1-800/275-8777.

Smoking

Since 2003 smoking has been banned in virtually all indoor public areas (including malls, bars, restaurants and most work places) in New York – fines start at around $100 for breaking this law.

Time

New York City is on Eastern Standard Time (EST), which is five hours behind Greenwich Mean Time (GMT), three hours ahead of Pacific Standard Time, fourteen to sixteen hours behind East Coast Australia (variations for Daylight Savings) and sixteen to eighteen hours behind New Zealand (variations for Daylight Savings).

Tipping

Tipping in a restaurant, bar, taxi, or hotel lobby, on a guided tour, and even in some posh washrooms, is a part of life in New York. In restaurants in particular, it's unthinkable not to leave the minimum (fifteen percent of the bill or double the tax) – even if you disliked the service.

Tourist information

For general enquiries, call Ⓣ 311. The best place for information is NYC & Company (the official visitors bureau), 810 Seventh Ave at 53rd St (Mon–Fri 8.30am–6pm, Sat & Sun 9am–5pm; Ⓣ 212/484-1222, Ⓦ www.nycgo.com). They have bus and subway maps, information on hotels and accommodations (including discounts), touch-screen databases and up-to-date leaflets on what's going on in the arts and elsewhere. You'll find other small tourist information centres and kiosks all over the city; Times Square, 1560 Broadway, between W 46th and W 47th sts (daily 8am–8pm); inside Federal Hall at 26 Wall St (Mon–Fri 9am–5pm); City Hall Park on Broadway opposite the Woolworth Building (Mon–Fri 9am–6pm; Sat & Sun 9am–5pm); and Chinatown, at Canal/Walker/Baxter sts (daily 10am–6pm).

For information about what's on, the *Village Voice* (free in Manhattan, Ⓦ www.villagevoice.com) is the most widely read free weekly, mainly for its comprehensive arts coverage and investigative features. Its main competitor, the weekly *New York Press* (Ⓦ www.nypress.com), is an edgier alternative and has excellent listings. Other leading weeklies include glossy *New York magazine* ($4.99), which has reasonably comprehensive listings, the venerable *New Yorker* magazine (Ⓦ www.newyorker.com; $5.99) and *Time Out New York* (Ⓦ newyork.timeout.com; $4.99) – a clone of its London original, combining the city's most comprehensive what's-on listings with New York-slanted news stories and entertainment features.

The *New York Times* ($2; Ⓦ www.nytimes.com) is an American institution and prides itself on being the "paper of record". It has solid, sometimes stolid, international coverage, and places much emphasis on its news analysis.

Travelling with children

Perhaps contrary to belief, New York is a child-friendly city: there's tons to keep their attention, including many sights specifically geared towards kids, and lots of public spaces in which to blow off steam.

Though some parents might have fears of taking small children on the subway, it's perfectly safe; indeed, the kids will probably get a kick out of it, crowds, noise and all. Your main problem will be getting your stroller (if you're using one) up and down the stairs – though you'll often find people willing to lend a hand. Most restaurants, save perhaps the fanciest and trendiest, easily accommodate children.

If you're in need of a babysitter, consider contacting the Babysitters' Guild (T212/682-0227, Wwww.babysittersguild.com), a fully licensed organization with a carefully selected and experienced staff.

For listings of what's going on when you're in town, check out NYCkidsarts Cultural Calendar (Wwww.nyckidsarts.org), GoCityKids (Wgocitykids.com) or magazines like *Time Out* and its specialized edition for kids (Wnewyorkkids.timeout.com), *TONY Kids*.

Travellers with disabilities

New York City has had disabled access regulations imposed on an aggressively disabled-unfriendly system. There are wide variations in accessibility, making navigation a tricky business.

At the same time, you'll find New Yorkers surprisingly willing to go out of their way to help you. For wheelchair users, getting around on the subway is next to impossible without someone to help you, and even then is extremely difficult at most stations. Several, but not all, lines are equipped with elevators, but this doesn't make much of a difference. The Transit Authority is working to make stations accessible, but at the rate they're going it won't happen soon.

Buses are another story, and are the first choice of many disabled New Yorkers. All MTA buses are equipped with wheelchair lifts and locks. To get on a bus, wait at the bus stop to signal the driver you need to board; when he or she has seen you, move to the back door, where he or she will assist you. For travellers with other mobility difficulties, the driver will "kneel" the bus to allow you easier access. For more travel information for people with disabilities call T718/596-8585 (daily 6am–10pm).

Taxis are a viable option for visitors with visual and hearing impairments and minor mobility difficulties. For wheelchair users, taxis are less of a possibility unless you have a collapsible chair, in which case drivers are required to store it and assist you; the unfortunate reality is that most drivers won't stop if they see you waiting. If you're refused, try to get the taxi's medallion number and report the driver at T311. Most of the major hotels in New York have wheelchair-accessible rooms, including roll-in showers.

Traveler's Aid, a nonprofit organization, has professional and volunteer staff who provide emergency assistance to disabled or elderly travellers at JFK Airport: you can find volunteers at the Ground Transportation Counters in each terminal or via their main office in the arrivals area of Terminal 6 (daily 10am–6pm). They also operate at Newark Airport. The Mayor's Office for People with Disabilities, 100 Gold St, 2nd fl (T212/788-2830, Wwww.nyc.gov/html/mopd), offers vaulable general information and resources for travellers with disabilities.

Festivals and events

CHINESE NEW YEAR

The first full moon between Jan 21 and Feb 19

Chinatown bursts open to watch a giant red, green and gold dragon made of wood, cloth and papier-mâché run down Mott Street.

ST PATRICK'S DAY PARADE

March 17

Irish bands and organizations celebrate an impromptu 1762 march by Irish militiamen on St Patrick's Day. A parade heads up Fifth Avenue between 44th and 86th streets.

CELEBRATE BROOKLYN/RIVER TO RIVER/SUMMERSTAGE

June–Aug

These three summer-long music festivals, featuring many free events, take place in Prospect Park's Bandshell, Battery Park and Rumsey Playfied in Central Park.

GAY PRIDE

Third or fourth week of June

www.nycpride.org

The world's biggest Pride event kicks off with a rally and ends with a parade, street fair and dance. Activities centre on the West Village.

Public holidays

January 1: New Year's Day; **3rd Monday:** Dr Martin Luther King Jr's Birthday; **February 3rd Monday:** Presidents' Day; **May Last Monday:** Memorial Day; **July 4:** Independence Day; **September 1st Monday:** Labor Day; **October 2nd Monday:** Columbus Day; **November 11:** Veterans' Day; **4th Thursday:** Thanksgiving Day; **December 25:** Christmas Day

US OPEN

First two weeks of September

www.usopen.org

Try to catch a day session for this Grand Slam tennis tournament, held in Flushing, Queens.

WEST INDIAN DAY PARADE AND CARNIVAL

Labor Day www.wiadca.com

Held on Eastern Parkway, Brooklyn's largest parade is modelled after the carnivals of Trinidad and Tobago and features music, food, dance and colourful floats with sound systems.

VILLAGE HALLOWEEN PARADE

Oct 31 www.halloween-nyc.com

New Yorkers get their freak on at America's largest Halloween celebration. Spectacular puppets, sexy cross-dressers and scary monsters parade up Sixth Avenue from Spring to W 23rd sts.

NEW YORK CITY MARATHON

First Sunday in November

www.ingnycmarathon.org

Some 35,000 international runners assemble for this 26.2-mile run through the five boroughs. One of the best places to watch is Central Park South, near the finish line.

MACY'S THANKSGIVING DAY PARADE

Thanksgiving Day

www.macysparade.com

New York's most televised parade, with big corporate floats, marching bands from around the country and Santa Claus's first appearance of the season. It winds its way from W 77th Street down Central Park West to Columbus Circle, then down Broadway to Herald Square.

Chronology

Early days > New York and the surrounding area is occupied by Native Americans, most notably the Lenape tribe.

1609 > English explorer Henry Hudson, working for the Dutch, sails past Manhattan upriver as far as Albany.

1624 > Dutch colony established on Governors Island.

1626 > Peter Minuit arrives as governor. He moves the Dutch settlement to Manhattan, which is named New Amsterdam, and numbers some 300 inhabitants.

1647 > New Amsterdam's most famous governor, Peter Stuyvesant, is appointed.

1664 > Revolt against Stuyvesant's dictatorial rule coincides with surrender to British naval troops, who rename the colony New York.

1754 > Ivy League Columbia University begins life as King's College.

1776 > British naval vessels arrive to capture New York after the Declaration of Independence; fire destroys much of the city, which is occupied by British troops until 1783.

1789 > George Washington takes the oath as America's first president on Wall Street. New York is capital of the new nation for one year.

1792 > Buttonwood Agreement, signed by 24 stockbrokers on Wall Street, signals beginning of New York Stock Exchange. It is formally organized in 1817.

1812 > British blockade of Manhattan during the War of 1812.

1825 > Opening of the Erie Canal makes New York a major shipping port. Fulton Street dock and market area built.

1830–50 > First wave of mass immigration, principally German and Irish. The Lower East Side developed.

1831 > Founding of New York University (NYU).

1835 > Great Fire of New York destroys most of the buildings on the southern tip of Manhattan around Wall Street.

1856–71 > The city is ruled by a corrupt group of politicians known as Tammany Hall. Their leader is deputy commissioner William "Boss" Tweed, who is finally indicted for corruption in 1873.

1858 > The first Chinese immigrants arrive in what would become Manhattan's Chinatown; 12,000 live here by 1890.

1861–65 > Though not a theatre of the Civil War, class and racial tensions lead to the Draft Riots of 1863, in which 1000 people are killed.

1876 > Central Park opens to a design by Fredrick Law Olmsted and Calvert Vaux.

1880s > More immigrants (southern Italians and eastern European Jews) settle in the Lower East Side.

1883 > The Brooklyn Bridge links Manhattan with Brooklyn.

1885 > Emergence of Tin Pan Alley on 28th St in Manhattan, where music publishers and popular songwriters like George Gershwin ply their trade.

1886 > The Statue of Liberty, a gift from the French people to America, is unveiled.

1891 > Carnegie Hall completed, funded by Scottish-born steel magnate and philanthropist Andrew Carnegie.

1898 > The outer boroughs of Brooklyn, Queens, the Bronx and Staten Island are formally incorporated into New York City. The population swells to three million.

Early 20th century > The first skyscrapers are built, most notably the Flatiron Building (1902) and the Woolworth Building (1913).

1902 > Macy's opens at Herald Square.

1913 > The New York Highlanders baseball team (established here in 1903) becomes known as the New York Yankees.

1915 > The Equitable Building fills every square inch of its site on Broadway, propelling zoning ordinances in 1916 that demand a degree of setback to allow light to reach the streets.

1920 > Prohibition forbids the sale of alcohol. Economic confidence of the 1920s brings the Jazz Age and Harlem Renaissance.

1925 > Jimmy Walker is elected mayor. New York Giants football team established.

1927 > Duke Ellington's band begins famous residency at the Cotton Club in Harlem.

1929 > Wall Street Crash. America enters the Great Depression. Many of the lavish buildings commissioned and begun in the 1920s reach completion. Skyscrapers combine the monumental with the decorative in a new and distinctive Art Deco style: Chrysler Building (1930) and Empire State Building (1931). Rockefeller Center, the first exponent of the idea of a city-within-a-city, is built throughout the decade.

1932 > Lucky Luciano takes control of the Five Families of the New York mafia; he is imprisoned in 1936.

1934 > Fiorello LaGuardia elected Mayor (which he would remain until 1945). To rebuild New York after the Depression, he increases taxation, curbs corruption and improves the city's infrastructure with new bridges, roads, and parks (with much federal funding).

1939 > Blue Note Records founded. Jazz legend Charlie Parker moves to New York, where he helps create bebop; he dies in the city in 1955.

1949–1950 > Miles Davis records his seminal album *Birth of the Cool* in New York for Capitol Records, heralding a new era in jazz.

Late 1940s to 1950s > The East Village becomes home to the Beat poets – Jack Kerouac, Allen Ginsberg and William Burroughs.

1950 > United Nations established in New York. The UN secretariat building introduces the glass curtain wall to Manhattan.

1958 > The plaza of the newly built Seagram Building causes zoning regulations to be changed again – this time to encourage similar public spaces.

1959 > Frank Lloyd Wright's Guggenheim Museum opens.

1961 > Bob Dylan moves to Greenwich Village and becomes a leading figure in the folk music movement.

1964 > Race riots in Harlem and Brooklyn. Jimmy Hendrix moves to Harlem and becomes a regular performer at *Cafe Wha*? in Greenwich Village. The minimalist Verrazano Narrows Bridge links Brooklyn to Staten Island.

1965 > Malcolm X is assassinated at Washington Height's Audubon Ballroom.

1968 > New Madison Square Garden is built on the site of the old Penn Station.

1969 > The Stonewall riots in Greenwich Village inaugurate the gay-rights movement.

Early 1970s > A low point for New York as the city struggles to attract investment; Harlem drug lords Frank Lucas and Nicky Barnes flood the city with heroin. However, The World Trade Center Towers are built in 1972, dramatically altering the New York skyline; hip-hop emerges on the streets of the South Bronx.

1973 > CBGB opens on the Lower East Side; becomes epicentre of Punk music; Blondie and the Ramones perform in 1974.

1975 > Mayor Abraham Beame presides over New York's decline as city financing reaches crisis point and businesses leave Manhattan. New York comes close to financial collapse, as its lack of essential services and collapsing infrastructure drive people away.

1977 > New York City Blackout (25hr): city suffers looting and civil unrest. *Discothèque Studio 54* opens – remains home of cool until 1986.

Late 1970s > Vociferous Ed Koch elected mayor (1978). Virtually no new corporate development until the Citicorp Center (1977) adds a new profile to the city's skyline; its popular atrium is adopted by later buildings.

1979 > The first hip-hop record, *Rapper's Delight*, released by The Sugarhill Gang (actually from New Jersey).

1980 > John Lennon is murdered outside his apartment on the Upper West Side.

1980s > Corporate wealth returns to Manhattan. The mixed-use Battery Park City opens to wide acclaim. Donald Trump emerges as a major real-estate developer.

1984 > Rick Rubin and Russell Simmons create Def Jam Records. Beastie Boys become their first major success.

1987 > Black Monday: the stock exchange crashes and the Dow Jones index plunges 508 points in one day.

1988 > The Tompkins Square Park Police Riot, which inspires a scene in the musical *Rent*.

1989 > David Dinkins becomes first black mayor of New York City, defeating Ed Koch and Rudolph Giuliani.

Early 1990s > NYC's budget deficit again reaches record proportions. East Coast hip-hop renaissance led by Nas, Notorious B.I.G. and later Mos Def and Jay-Z.

1993 > Puerto Rican salsa superstar Héctor Lavoe, "El Cantante", dies in New York.

1994 > Rudolph Giuliani is elected mayor – the city's first Republican mayor in 28 years, signalling a desire for change.

1996 > Prosperity returns to New York. Times Square is redeveloped, and the city becomes one of the safest and statistically most crime-free cities in the country.

2001 > World Trade Center's Twin Towers are destroyed in September 11 terrorist attacks. Entrepreneur Michael Bloomberg succeeds Giuliani as mayor. He pledges to continue Giuliani's tough line on crime and quality of life in the city. One of his first acts is to ban smoking in all public places, including bars, in 2003.

2002 > Tribeca Film Festival established with the backing of Robert DeNiro.

2003 > Daniel Libeskind is selected to design the new World Trade Center. His initial design goes through many revisions under pressure from the city and victims' relatives.

2005 > Michael Bloomberg is re-elected mayor.

2006 > Legendary punk club CBGB closes.

2007 > New York Giants win Superbowl XLII.

2008 > US mortgage crisis finally hits Wall Street in a big way: the Dow Jones slumps 500 points and, after more than 150 years, Lehman Brothers goes bankrupt; several other merchant banks are sold.

2009 > Michael Bloomberg is re-elected mayor for a third time, after backing a controversial extension of term limits. Yankees win World Series for 27th time. Miracle on the Hudson: Captain "Sully" Sullenberger lands his Airbus on the Hudson River after a bird strike takes out the engines at La Guardia airport.

2011 > National September 11 Memorial opens on 10th anniversary of 9/11.

2012 > NY Giants and Eli Manning win Superbowl XLVI – beating Boston's New England Patriots in the final for a second time.

SMALL PRINT

PUBLISHING INFORMATION

This second edition published February 2013 by **Rough Guides Ltd**.
80 Strand, London WC2R 0RL
11, Community Centre, Panchsheel Park, New Delhi 110017, India
Distributed by the Penguin Group
Penguin Books Ltd, 80 Strand, London WC2R 0RL
Penguin Group (USA) 375 Hudson Street, NY 10014, USA
Penguin Group (Australia) 250 Camberwell Road, Camberwell, Victoria 3124, Australia
Penguin Group (NZ) 67 Apollo Drive, Mairangi Bay, Auckland 1310, New Zealand
Rough Guides is represented in Canada by Tourmaline Editions Inc., 662 King Street West, Suite 304, Toronto, Ontario, M5V 1M7
Typeset in Minion and Din to an original design by Henry Iles and Dan May.
Printed and bound in China

208pp includes index
A catalogue record for this book is available from the British Library
ISBN 978-1-40936-020-9

1 3 5 7 9 8 6 4 2

MIX
Paper from responsible sources
FSC™ C018179
FSC www.fsc.org

ROUGH GUIDES CREDITS

Text editors: Lucy Cowie, Alison Roberts
Layout: Umesh Aggarwal, Ankur Guha
Photography: Greg Roden, Curtis Hamilton, Nelson Hancock, Angus Oborn, Susannah Sayler
Cartography: Ed Wright, Katie Bennett
Picture editors: Sarah Cummins, Mark Thomas
Proofreader: Jan McCann
Production: Rebecca Short, Linda Dare
Cover design: Nicole Newman, Dan May, Sarah Cummins and Chloë Roberts

THE AUTHORS

Martin Dunford is the author of Rough Guides to New York, Rome, Italy and Amsterdam, among others, and is consultant publisher for the series and a freelance writer, editor and publishing consultant. He lives in London and Norfolk, with his wife Caroline and two daughters, and is currently working on a new guide to Norfolk and Suffolk. When not involved with Rough Guides, he watches his local football team, Charlton Athletic, and rehearses for increasingly rare appearances of the Rough Guides house band, the New Cross Dolls. He likes sailing, would love to spend more time travelling, especially in India, and his favourite type of holiday is camping, preferably in Belgium.

For many years, **Andrew Rosenberg** headed up the Rough Guides editorial office in New York City. He is now a freelance editor, writer and copy editor and lives in Brooklyn with his wife Melanie, son Jules and cats Caesar and Louise.

Stephen Keeling has been calling New York City home since 2006. He worked as a financial journalist for seven years before writing his first travel guide and has written several titles for Rough Guides, including books on Puerto Rico, New England, Florida and Canada.

ACKNOWLEDGEMENTS

Stephen Keeling would like to thank Anna Catchpole, Yuien Chin, Debra Harris, Andrew Luan, Victor Ozols, Gordon Polatnick, Neal Shoemaker, Kate Stober, Thatiana Wilkinson, fellow author Andrew Rosenberg for his hard work, advice and support, Lucy Cowie for her enthusiasm and fine editing, and Tiffany Wu, whose love and support made this book possible.

Andrew Rosenberg would like to thank Alison Roberts for all her hard editorial work; Mani Ramaswamy and Natasha Foges for getting the edition kicked off; co-author Stephen Keeling; Peter Mullan, from Friends of the High Line; and, for the love, company, support and ideas, Melanie and Jules.

SMALL PRINT

HELP US UPDATE

We've gone to a lot of effort to ensure that the second edition of **The Pocket Rough Guide to New York City** is accurate and up-to-date. However, things change – places get "discovered", opening hours are notoriously fickle, restaurants and rooms raise prices or lower standards. If you feel we've got it wrong or left something out, we'd like to know, and if you can remember the address, the price, the hours, the phone number, so much the better.

Please send your comments with the subject line "**Pocket Rough Guide New York City Update**" to ⓔ mail@roughguides.com. We'll credit all contributions and send a copy of the next edition (or any other Rough Guide if you prefer) for the very best emails.

Find more travel information, connect with fellow travellers and book your trip on ⓦ www.roughguides.com

PHOTO CREDITS

Index

Maps are marked in **bold**.

D

E

F